DECONSTRUCTING
MEN & MASCULINITIES

D1737264

DECONSTRUCTING MEN & MASCULINITIES

MICHAEL ATKINSON

OXFORD
UNIVERSITY PRESS

OXFORD

UNIVERSITY PRESS

8 Sampson Mews, Suite 204, Don Mills, Ontario M3C 0H5
www.oupcanada.com

Oxford University Press is a department of the University of Oxford.
It furthers the University's objective of excellence in research, scholarship,
and education by publishing worldwide in

Oxford New York

Auckland Cape Town Dar es Salaam Hong Kong Karachi
Kuala Lumpur Madrid Melbourne Mexico City Nairobi
New Delhi Shanghai Taipei Toronto

With offices in

Argentina Austria Brazil Chile Czech Republic France Greece
Guatemala Hungary Italy Japan Poland Portugal Singapore
South Korea Switzerland Thailand Turkey Ukraine Vietnam

Oxford is a trade mark of Oxford University Press
in the UK and in certain other countries

Published in Canada
by Oxford University Press

Copyright © Oxford University Press Canada 2011

The moral rights of the author have been asserted

Database right Oxford University Press (maker)

First Published 2011

Library and Archives Canada Cataloguing in Publication

Atkinson, Michael, 1971–
Deconstructing men and masculinities / Michael Atkinson.
(Themes in Canadian sociology)

Includes bibliographical references and index.

ISBN 978-0-19-543076-9

Masculinity—Social aspects—Canada. 2. Masculinity—
Canada. 3. Sex role—Canada. 4. Men—Canada—Social conditions—
21st century. I. Title. II. Series: Themes in Canadian sociology

HQ1090.7.C2A85 2010   305.310971   C2010-902171-1

Cover image: © iStockPhoto.com/browndogstudios

Oxford University Press is committed to our environment. This book is printed on Forest Stewardship
Council certified paper, harvested from a responsibly managed forest.

Printed and bound in Canada
1 2 3 4 – 14 13 12 11

Contents

Preface

This is a book about life beyond and outside of the much-hyped North American *masculinity crisis*. Sociologists and cultural critics have studied, for nearly three decades, whether a huge swathe of men (normally, white guys, between ages 25 and 45, and from the middle-classes) have unduly suffered from gender discrimination, rejection, anxiety, and negation within families, schools, churches, workplaces, media, and governments. Proponents of the masculinity crisis thesis bemoan how Generations X and Y men find themselves labelled culturally evil simply because they are men, and unfairly treated at times because of a general wave of *misandry* (i.e., a hatred of men and masculinity) in popular culture. Statistics regarding the growing failure of boys in schools, rising crime rates amongst disadvantaged youth, unemployment rates among men, family court rulings in divorce cases against fathers, and plummeting levels of self-esteem among boys and men arguably reveal how something is culturally amiss. The subject of the masculinity crisis is a politically loaded one, sparking heated debate about whether crisis advocates have brought to social attention a critical generational shift in cultural ideologies about masculinities, or if the crisis discourse is easily decoded as a collective backlash against women, ethnic minorities, and Others in Canada. Oh yes, a touchy subject is always fascinating.

A significant component of my academic interest in the notion of a masculinity crisis is quite personal, as a man who, according to certain streams of masculinity theory, should be in deep crisis. I am 38 years old, English-Canadian, middle-class, straight, urban-dwelling, and White. Mine is a social position rife with historical privilege and authority. This is a book about whether millions of men demographically and biographically like me (and others not like me) feel, perceive, embody, resist, and subvert crisis trends. The book examines whether men have a legitimate cultural right to claim gender crisis or to challenge contemporary gendering processes in Canada. Throughout the book I argue that the discourse of crisis is indeed a clever power play waged among clusters of men in an effort to exercise a very traditional kind of social power. In many ways, it is a quintessential example of what Jean Baudrillard (1990) refers to as a *non-event*. A non-event is something that is much hyped, debated, and collectively anticipated with fear or excitement, but does not materialize as anything socially important or culturally relevant in the end. With that said, I hope to show how crisis is lived and embodied by many men in Canada, and how misandry is starkly evident in pockets of Canadian society. The case studies in/of masculinity I present in the book reveal how masculinities for many Canadian men can be crisis-filled; at the same time, crisis masculinities offer an opportunity for men to rework the social performance of 'new masculinities' in incredibly power-producing ways; such is the paradoxical basis of the masculinity crisis as a non-event.

For many more reasons than I would care to outline, this book represents my own coming to terms with the masculinity crisis discourse as a physical cultural studies researcher, and with my post-structuralist (and neo-existentialist) theoretical leanings. For many students who encounter cultural studies and post-structural theories for the first time, each can be daunting, disintegrative, and dissonant. This is especially true as, apart from their neo-Marxist leanings, cultural studies, post-structural and existentialist theories often congeal as a confusing and frustrating jumble. Readers of this book might seek a neatly conceptual whole or a tidy meta-narrative theoretical point structuring every chapter. Such a structure is not to be found, I am sorry to say. My tour across and within the theories employed in the book is designed to illustrate how the struggle for socio-cultural power and control continues to be one of the most compelling sociological problematics. Cultural studies and post-structural theories tend to be about identity and power, while existentialist theories revolve around questions of experience, reality, and Being. When stitched together in totality across the book, I hope my excursions with theories of power and those of experience illustrate a nuanced and at times chilling portrait of power dynamics in a range of social settings for the men with whom I have interacted in one manner or another over the past decade and a half as a researcher. *Therefore, this is a book about power, control, and lived experience. Each chapter presents a case study in power and its relationship to masculinities at an historical time when gendered identities are believed to be fragmented, challengeable, and plastic. It questions, in a range of theoretical ways, whether or not much of the recent hype regarding the crisis of masculinity bears any real-world relevance or whether it is indeed a non-event.*

When colleagues, students, or family members discover my interest in crisis masculinities, they inevitably ask me if I believe the crisis to be real. Reality and truth are troubling concepts. My examination of the masculinity crisis sought situated and experiential constructions of its truth in a range of places: from media representations of men, to official statistics about men's roles and statuses within social institutions, to how men embody crisis and the complex manners by which struggles for placement in socio-cultural hierarchies are gendered. The masculinity crisis is only a way to classify or label the representation of the truth-claiming activities of a host of men and women; there is no black and white about its presence or lack thereof. The crisis is part of and a composite of struggles, discourses, sets of behaviours, nature of relationships, and ongoing contests between people for power. A fundamental premise underwritten in this book is ultimately that I cannot offer truths or 'the' truth about the masculinity crisis, only my reading of its social performance in varying social contexts in Canada.

The book is intentionally authored as one with academic tones and proto-typical jargonism, but I have also tried to speak in emotional, direct, and interpersonal ways across the pages. My goal in writing the book is to write a narrative about masculinity that speaks to and connects with audiences in intel-lectual, emotional, and existential ways. The kind of sociology I was taught— one without interpersonal connection, any attempts by an author to share a personal presence with readers, or evaluative claims—has perhaps run its historical course. So, I wrote this book in a manner that far too few sociologists, I think, accept as sound or appropriate analytic practice. My students often tell me that while they love sociological ideas, they hate sociological texts because they cannot identify with detached accounts and theoretically distant render-ings of reality. This book is in places raw and unapologetic, value-laden, and critical. The lack of traditional value-freedom and complete detachment in the book will undoubtedly raise eyebrows and concerns among some readers. After reading Thiele (2005), I decided to become far less afraid of placing emotion, values, morality, and subjectivity alongside data I have spent the better portion of the last two decades collecting. Indeed, it evolved into a book that deliber-ately invites sociological/personal commentary, reflection, and, I hope, critique of what a range of groups inside and outside of the academy think we know about masculinity and its relationship to power. The book does not strive to preach or proselytize, but rather to prod and provoke.

Ian Curtis, the front man and haunted figure of the Manchester-based band Joy Division, once wrote in a poem, 'What once was innocence is now turned on its side'. His words referred partially to his own failed masculine role perfor-mances as a father, husband, and bandmate. I have listened to Joy Division for over 20 years, and Curtis's ability to self-reflect on the fragile nature of masculinity in society is as aesthetically brilliant as it is sociologically savvy. I will never claim to be an Ian Curtis, but the pages of this book are written to evoke a sense of how masculinity is not an unproblematic, stoic, and irreverent identity as is often claimed by social commentators. I strive to turn debates about the crisis, and of masculinity in Canada itself, on their side.

Finally, I would like to thank everyone who has helped with this writing project along the way. I owe the greatest debt of gratitude to everyone who has participated in my research over the past few years. Your voices and stories are the backbone of this book. I also wish to thank the anonymous reviewers for their thoughtful comments on the earliest phases of the manuscript, and everyone at Oxford University Press (especially my editors Dana Hopkins, Jodi Lewchuk, and Nancy Reilly) for their incredible support and enthusiasm. Finally, this book is dedicated to my sons Eoghan and Finnegan, who inspire me each day to write about the incredible wonders of life as a boy.

Introduction: Masculinity in Crisis?

The word 'crisis' is a loaded one. As I read through newspapers each morning, the idea of *crisis* is peppered across their pages. I read about the Canadian energy crisis, the food shortage crisis (and yet the obesity crisis too), the housing crisis, a full spate of human rights crises, drug and alcohol crises, health care and hospital crises, environmental crises, employment crises, gang and youth violence crises, and dozens of others. Public optimism runs out in Canadian society from time to time in the face all of these crises. I pause to consider my two sons, Eoghan and Finnegan, and wonder what kind of crisis-filled world they will encounter as adolescents or adults. At the point of contemplation, I force myself to remember that not all crises are created equally. Some crises are tangible, material, pressing, and life-threatening. Others materialize in public discourse as frightening but illusory constructions, a crafty trick of architecture and mass representation.

When examining the historical foundations of masculinity (which countless scholars have done rather well—see Atkinson, 2008a; Newkirk, 2003; Clare, 2000; Hearn, 1999), and to what social goals and ends it has been constructed and applied for millennia across Western cultures, we recognize how the idea itself is practically synonymous with crisis. Masculinity is not only the social product of, but a key *interpretive resource* (Gubrium and Holstein, 1997) used to rationalize war and interpersonal violence; sexual conquest; material acquisition; imperial expansion and colonialism; the domestication of animals; the exploitation of earth's natural resources; the creation of social power imbalances between men and women; the rise of market capitalism; and a host of other social processes. Men and constructions of masculinity are far more complex than such a reductionist proposition, but few may argue against the assertion that the linking of destructive collective behaviour to the affirmation of dominant masculine statuses and identities has historically victimized millions, if not billions. Stated differently, masculinity is almost universally associated with the social production of crisis situations. Societies driven by stoic and essentialized notions of masculinity rarely produce pacified social environments (DeKeseredy et al. 2005; Kimmel, 2000; Pinar, 2001). Research among feminist and profeminist sociologists of the 1970s and 1980s broke new ground by engaging arguments relating to how men themselves, and not only women, are deeply scarred and alienated by stereotypical or 'ideal-typical'

(Weber, 1958) notions of maleness. Among the many questions raised about dominant, patriarchal, or *hegemonic masculinity* (Connell, 2005; Donaldson, 1993) in this period pertained to which men, precisely, are actually privileged by impossible or untenable expectations, standards, and norms of manliness extolled in Western nations like Canada.

Sociologists are fascinated by social crises. Consider some of the major socio-logical sub-disciplines and their substantive foci: the transition from pre- to modern to postmodern societies; structural inequality; crime and deviance; social conflict; globalization and politics; self-definition and collective identity; the technologization of society; health and illness; and the list goes on. Given what sociologists research and teach, students routinely ask me if sociolo-gists are by nature pessimistic and crisis-preoccupied. Such doom and gloom often fills a sociological lecture theatre on any given day during the academic semester. Maybe sociologists are a group of academic naysayers, desperate to tell others in the proverbial academic barnyard that the sky is falling. Or, maybe one of the fundamental public sociological roles is to deconstruct how crises socially emerge, and how they are defined and managed by people. Sociolo-gists are not merely the manufacturers of public crises, but rather watchdogs and interventionists striving to challenge anyone who stands up and claims, 'Crisis is here'!

About ten years ago, I ethnographically stumbled onto one of the crises creeping into both popular cultural and sociological discourses: the masculinity crisis. While in the first ethnographic throes of a project on the shifting uses and constructions of tattooing in Canada (Atkinson, 2003a), I met and interviewed a number of young men who marked their bodies with tattoos as gestures and representations of perceived loss. The men (each of them White, middle-class urbanites in their late thirties) told me that while their tattoos were filled with multiple meanings and subject to situated definition, their tattooing projects were at least partially undertaken as a technique for looking more masculine in an increasingly feminized (read *emasculated*) social world. Through their narratives (which I suspect are carefully rehearsed) they articulate how tattoos encapsulate feelings of doubt, anxiety, and confusion about what it means to be a 'lost man' in contemporary Canada. Two of the men barraged me with stories about a contemporary war on masculinities in Canada. The exploration of historically masculine body work like tattooing is to them a magical crisis resolution as a technique for affirming and brashly asserting a physical mascu-linity in a cultural milieu which they perceived to be saturated by feminizing trends, policies, and systems of representation.

I remember thinking to myself, 'Crisis . . . what the hell are these guys talking about? What crisis?' Nothing I knew theoretically as an academic, or culturally as a Canadian, resonated with their stories. How can a crisis of masculinity exist in a neo-patriarchal society still so deeply cleaved along gender lines? Neither men nor masculinity have, to borrow from Canadian music legend Neil

Young, 'burned out or faded away'. So I ignored the contents of their respective stories as strangely interesting 'negative cases' of tattoos and their meanings, and moved on to other conceptual lines of inquiry in the study.

Here's where the story becomes more interesting. Shortly after the tattoo study, I delved into ethnographic projects on Straightedge youth in eastern Canada, violence in Canadian ice hockey, cultures of nutrition and dieting in Ontario gym cultures, endurance and multi-sport (triathlon and duathlon) figurations in Ontario, 'free running' (Parkour) movements in central and eastern Canada, and cosmetic surgery among men in central Canada. In narrating their life histories, the boys and men within the separate studies routinely used words, phrases, and illustrative descriptors that alluded to this mysterious masculinity crisis. I could not ignore the regularity of crisis discourses in their interview transcripts, and I found myself envisioning my separate projects as connected conceptually: 'concatenated' (Stebbins, 1992) research efforts on the masculinity crisis. I remember reading Nathanson and Young's (2001) book, *Spreading Misandry*, in the summer of 2004, and thinking I might mine my arsenal of qualitative data on men's lives in Canada to explore whether men felt at risk of, or targeted for, being male in Canada as the authors suggest. I pored through a massive amount of my data, spanning a decade, to analyze any crisis constructions of masculinity and its representations. I sifted through hundreds and hundreds of pages of field notes covering several thousand hours of fieldwork with men and boys in a variety of social contexts; over 700 life history interviews with men about their backgrounds, physical habits, and social attitudes; reams of archival documents about masculinity and its construction in particular cultural settings; and, over 3,000 media documents pertaining to my separate research projects. Each contained narrative clues about masculinity and contemporary discourses and sentiments about an emerging crisis.

I decided to conduct more focussed sociological research on the crisis. Many sociologists and cultural critics had already weighed in on the subject. Impassioned crisis and anti-crisis perspectives abound in the literature (Edwards, 2006; Robinson, 2000; Whitehead, 2006). In what follows, I briefly review and conceptually package what the bulk of the 'crisis' literature teaches.

What? . . . A Masculinity Crisis? . . . Really?

Thinking about a social crisis means considering *presences* and *absences* in a society. We might argue that the global oil crisis is one of empirical measurability because of a dire absence of accessible oil and a global demand for its presence. Gun violence among youth is often constructed as a crisis because it signals a socio-cultural failure to protect the lives of innocents; perhaps it also speaks to an absence of institutional means to encourage restraint and civilized behaviour from an Eliasian perspective (Elias, 2004), an absence of disciplinarity from a Foucauldian standpoint (Foucault, 1977), or a presence of fatalistic youth cultures plagued by problems of economic and cultural marginality (Tanner, 2001). A crisis is also a social situation of physical, cultural, and ideological extremes and uncertain structural outcomes. A crisis is an in-between space for an entire society, wherein resolving the crisis may reconfigure, in Deleuze and Parnet's (1987) terms, both the tiny (molecular) and the large, institutional (molar) features of society. Social crises are broad and sweeping, affecting the operation of social institutions; ideological principles and tenets underpinning collective cultures; the formation and representation of identities across a range of groups; physical and cultural practice; and the distribution of resources between people. Sociologically speaking, crises are no laughing matter.

Given the above construction, can masculinity actually be in crisis in Canada? Is this just a myth? Does the crisis amount to nothing more than the whiny, sour grapes of a few angry men who believe that their divine right as male citizens has been challenged? Or, is it an academic or media fabrication and moral panic that has been extracted and elaborated as a newsworthy trend? Can a masculinity crisis be empirically grasped, witnessed, felt, experienced, or understood?

Susan Faludi's book, *Stiffed: The Betrayal of the American Man* (1999), brought the masculinity crisis to public consciousness. Scholars including Goldberg (1977) and Bednarik (1981) warned about an impending crisis of masculinity in the 1970s and early 1980s, but Faludi's reputation as an author who convincingly blew the lid off contemporary gender politics with her 1992 book, *Backlash,* really captured people's attention. Faludi's *Stiffed*, and other noteworthy texts including *Masculinity in Crisis* (Horrocks, 1994), *Unmasking the Masculine* (Peterson, 1998), *Men's Lives* (Kimmel and Messner, 1999), and *The Scapegoat Generation* (Males, 1996), tabled serious and emotionally penetrating analyses of how many men in contemporary North American life struggle with normative expectations about masculinity, confused gender identities and roles, and feelings of guilt over being complicitly patriarchal in modern North America. By the time Tiger (2000) published the controversial book *The Decline of Males,* and Farrell (2001) wrote the equally provocative and inflammatory *The Myth of Male Power*, fervent masculinity crisis discourses were popping up in academic and popular cultures. Although one definition of the crisis will never suffice, let me give it a preliminary shot.

The *masculinity crisis* stems from a fundamental ideological resistance to the historical/traditional Western associations between sexed/biological identity (boy/girl, man/woman with particular reproductive organs and genetic markers) and particular corporeal, cognitive, emotional, and social capabilities. These include strength, reason, rationality, intelligence, drive, resolve, restraint, creativity, assertiveness, and leadership. A neophyte student of the sociology of gender knows that men have been associated with these capabilities, and thus masculinity becomes the cultural catch term for the quality of being, living, acting, functioning, and representing as an ideal-type man (Connell, 2005). The gendering of social roles and responsibilities along biological, or what have been also called *essentialist,* lines is a primary basis of patriarchy and the sexed ordering of societies across the planet. Over the course of the twentieth century, the biological–social connections between sex, gender, and social power were progressively debated and resisted by both women and men. A result, to crisis advocates, is that men have been evicted from, or forcibly prevented from accessing, white-collar jobs, higher educational streams, and other sites of social power as a form of social punishment for thousands of years of patriarchy. On an ideological level, attacks on the very social construction of masculinity (and men's exclusive ownership over so-called masculine attributes) have created cultural chaos as men no longer know how to act in gender-appropriate ways.

Now let's get a touch more theoretically complicated. Whitehead (2002) contends that with the rearrangement of family, economic, political, educational, sport–leisure, technological–scientific, and media power bases in the second half of the twentieth century, dominant masculinity identities and codes have been challenged within most social settings. Men no longer possess exclusive ownership over the social roles once held as bastions for establishing and performing patriarchal masculine hegemony; bad news for hegemonic men, good news for many, many marginal others. Hise (2004) and Tiger (2000) suggest that with an increased presence of femininities in (especially middle-class) social institutions, a resulting masculine anxiety follows. When such masculine anxiety is coupled with the proliferation of gender equity movements, ideologies of political correctness, and the spread of *misandry* (the hatred or denigration of males) in popular media (Nathanson and Young, 2001), some men perceive a cultural war against men/masculinity in countries like Canada. In the midst of the perceived crisis, certain men refuse to acknowledge or embrace new masculinities in any way, and retrench into very traditional, self-essentializing, and hegemonic masculine images and embodied performances. Yet, others discover innovative ways to reframe their bodies/ selves as socially powerful in newly masculine manners (later in this book, I call this the practice of doing *pastiche hegemony*).

The emerging literatures on contemporary masculine politics in Western nations like Canada do generally suggest that the institutional sources of men's social control have been fractured materially by ongoing structural and cultural change (see also Mosse, 1996). Collier (1998) outlines how movements toward gender equality in families, educational sites, workplaces, religious institutions, and a host of other institutional sites calls into question the very basis of masculine hegemony, and have created measurable changes in the workplace. As an extension of what Elias (2002) refers to as the 'parliamentarisation of conflict', gender stratification and related power imbalances have been systematically disputed through highly institutionalized, formal, and rationalized rule systems, and via complex forms of gender representation in the media. The splintering and redistribution of masculine control across institutional land-scapes is generally believed to be the cause of the masculinity crisis (White-head, 2002). In Faludi's (1999) terms, men have simply 'lost their compass' for navigating the social world.

Anti-crisis advocates quickly note how most men's relative positions of authority, access to resources, ability to shape institutional discourses and forms of cultural representation, and use of physical forms of power over women have only moderately shifted (see Heartfield [2002], Gill [2005], and Gill, Henwood, and McLean [2005]). There is no, and can be no, uniform crisis of masculinity since there are neither dire nor spectacular social pres-ences/absences for most men in countries like Canada. Discourses about the masculinity crisis—which almost always focus on White men—tend to obfus-cate the empirically measurable and statistically consistent trends that indi-cate contemporary men are collectively as powerful as men in any previous generation. Within a larger system of White, European, Christian, heterosexist dominant masculine hegemony, men in marginal socio-economic, race, ethnic, and sexual groups do continue to be 'in crisis' (i.e., they are more likely to be under-employed, physically abused, imprisoned, and at risk for certain illnesses or medical conditions). Even so, their relative positions of power and authority *within their local communities* are better than women's (Dipiero, 2001; Pease and Pringle, 2002).

Faludi (1999), Schenk (1996), and Young (1997) might respond by arguing that the baseline problem of the crisis is real, and it palpably affects the lives of millions of North American men. Post–Second World War North America evolved as a social landscape wherein the seemingly inexorable link between men, masculinity, and mastery of the social and physical world withered and died. For Faludi , Western civilization was founded on the need and desire for men to master the world along every conceivable line. The myth of mas-culine mastery (in this instance the ability of men to exert and hold power) is replete in historical art, literature, painting, and is now lamented nostalgi-cally in popular culture. One of my favourite lines from Wolfgang Peterson's 2004 movie *Troy* is delivered by Achilles (played by the bronzed, muscled, and insanely handsome Brad Pitt), just as his Myrmidon platoon are poised to attack the Trojan beach several minutes ahead of their Greek compatriots. Perched majestically at the bow of the boat, addressing his crewmen, he pro-claims: 'Myrmidons, my brothers of the sword. I'd rather fight beside you than any other army of thousands. Let no man forget how menacing we are . . . we are lions. You know what's there, waiting beyond that beach. Immortality . . . take it, it's yours!' His 50 Myrmidons (a term historically used to describe the loyal, obedient, aggressive, ant-like followers of strong male leaders) reck-lessly attack a force of several hundred Spartans, and tear through their ranks in several bloody minutes. Achilles leads the spectacular campaign of violent conquest up the beach. Meanwhile thousands of Greek soldiers in boats raise their spears and chant Achilles' name as they wait to reach the shore. At the apex of the battle, when the victory is achieved and the Spartan temple of Apollo is sacked and desecrated, Achilles raises his sword and Greek soldiers howl in celebration. This is the quintessential, erotic allusion of masculine power and control; and it resonates, if box office receipts tell us anything, with legions of Myrmidons in North America.

Identity and civil rights movements of the second half of the twentieth century fractured the ancient Greek fairy-tale of power, honour, and immortality. Men are no longer always viewed as masters of the universe, unchallenged charters of social life, protectors of the domestic realm, or the sole proprietors of cultural power industries. Not only has the mastery myth been dislodged and destabilized in countries like Canada, the argument follows, but even the idea of humans' collective ability mastering anything has been drawn into considerable doubt. Such is one of the hallmarks of what Giddens (1991) calls *late modern* society. If our belief in mastery (and its close conceptual cousin, the teleological, or progression, toward a better society) died, how can traditional masculinity continue to exist? What happens to generations of boys, adolescents, and men who once believed that males become men by controlling, mastering, and protecting? Where is the heroic Achilles or Hector to lead the Myrmidon hordes into the future of our illusion? How could they live in a world that increasingly calls hegemonic masculinities socially toxic.

A generation of boys born in the late 1960s and early 1970s felt pressure both to be masculine in traditional terms, yet also to loathe what masculinity and patriarchy does to women; to be, in the same instance, a person who venerates but is ashamed about one's ascribed and achieved masculinity. In other terms, these males were put in a position where they felt they had to strive to be in control of yourself and a leader/master among others, but to realize that masculine control is both an oppressive myth and a marginalizing practice. Again, I think Faludi (1999) captures the dilemma eloquently by suggesting that the ultimate deathblow to traditional hegemonic masculinity was struck when a growing number of young boys viewed masculinity and the myth of masculine mastery not as an enabling force, but rather a constraining, controlling force. I think I am one of those boys. Douglas Coupland refers to these boys in his 1991 book *Generation X*—an undefined, undetermined generation of young men. When I first read Coupland, long before Faludi rocked my sociological world, I reflexively thought about my own childhood and wondered if my masculinity was in crisis.

I was born in Kingston, Ontario, in 1971. I have two parents who live in a small, rural town in Ontario in their dream home. My father is a university professor and accountant, and my mum, a life-long homemaker. I have an older brother and an older sister. My father has worked extended days for as long as I can remember. He is a quiet, emotionally contained man like his father,

Frederick Temple Atkinson. Grandfather Atkinson was a tall, impressive, and sharply contoured figure exuding control. He was the ideal-type masculine persona of the first half of the twentieth century: an educated man, a providing husband and father, and an economic player in the forestry industry in Canada. But he also painted, carved and sculpted, boxed, dabbled in gourmet cooking, and served his country in battle. He fought with the Royal Rifles of Canada in World War II, and for four years struggled to survive while interned in a prisoner of war camp outside of Hong Kong. When he returned to Canada after the war, my grandfather reintegrated into the Quebec paper mill processing industry and upper–middle class society. Scarred, drained, and diseased from battle, he withdrew into himself, particularly after the death of my Uncle Michael (my namesake), who committed suicide with a rifle at 14. My grandfather died when I was a very young boy. I have only murky memories of his big hands, deep voice, and greyed hair, his basset hound, his pipe, his war memorabilia, and the aura of manliness surrounding him. My father has, on probably four occasions in my life, spoken to me about him. My grandfather's memory still casts a long shadow over both of us.

My everyday masculine role model growing up was my brother Spartacus (no, not a pseudonym, but it fits the imagery well) who is nearly ten years older than me. Life in the suburban, Canadian middle class was pretty easy for both of us. We always had things, and my only defined duties in life were to be kind to others, behave in public, do well in school, and 'make something' of myself. No massive detail of chores every day, no summer days spent breaking my back to help pay family bills, just good behaviour demanded inside and outside of the house. 'Occupy yourself with something, son'. A book, a video game, sports. My brother did all of this with me, and I loved him for it. Many of my friends looked up to him. He stood, even when he was a young guy, over six feet tall and had an Achilles-like presence. Deep voice, dark hair, and all of the women in our neighbourhood (let alone girls his age) loved him. My brother was always in control, it seemed, always confident, always a master of his and others' fates. Stitched into my childhood was a quintessential male grandfather, a hard-working, emotionally detached but devoted and providing father, and a suave carefree, care-giving brother to help mould my image of masculinity. None of the male role models in my life, like many of my friends', exhibited anything other than control. I, by contrast, have never felt in control of much as a boy and then as a man of the X generation. Or maybe I have always been in control and never knew it. Conscious or not, I've never viewed my apparent lack of masculine control as a crisis. We'll come back to this later.

Faludi (1999) describes boys and young men of my generation as part of an 'ornamental' culture. In sociological-speak, she refers to the emergence of late-modern/postmodern societies in which life is increasingly representational, commodity-fetishized, and image-oriented rather than tangible, material, and real in a modernist sense. For example, as the much used saying goes, 'it's the clothes that make the man'—meaning that what you wear (i.e., its brand) is far more of a representation of 'you' than your character, biography, or body itself. Such is the simulated virtual world of representation Baudrillard (1983) theorizes in *Simulations*, and the exchange value–preoccupied culture Virilio (1986) describes in *Speed and Politics*. Men in the ornamental culture are not masters of the teleological unfolding of society toward cultural perfection and control; such is only one image and one potential reality of masculinity. Control and mastery—very much Enlightenment doctrines of rationality and hope— are no longer tenable meta-narratives in an ornamental culture fascinated by and fixated on multiple and shifting realities about masculinity (or anything else) and how it can be represented in unique ways in the process of selling consumer goods and services.

Adam Brooks's 2008 movie *Definitely Maybe* reminds me of ornamental masculine life. The movie's main character, Will Hayes (played by Ryan Reynolds), is portrayed as a stereotypical middle-class White male of the 1990s, who confronts his ornamental masculinity in a post-college, Bill Clinton Democrat, death of the cinematic action hero, New York world. Hayes defines and redefines his masculinity through the processes of moving from small town to urban life, frequently entering and exiting emotionally challenging relationships, switching careers, having a child, and shifting his social ideologies as the world around him constantly and unpredictably changes. Hayes is, for all intents and purposes, the typical ornamental man whose chameleon self must adapt in his late modern world of impermanence and doubt. Hayes's masculine ideologies are constantly called into question and reduced through the film. He is not a controller, not a fixed or stable figure, not a master of his masculine fate. He is flexible, reflexive, self-deprecating, and eventually hopeful in his own male multiplicity. Ornamental culture is, by definition, a culture of these types of ontological boundary crossings where interpreting and enacting multiple masculine realities is the daily task.

Hardt and Negri (2004) argue that with the transition from modern industrialism to late modern industrialism—or, what they dub as the 'informatization of production'—most cultural practices and systems of identity representation (such as those pertaining to masculinity) in the West have been reconfigured in ornamental ways. Many post-structuralists draw attention to how the fragmentation of work (into service economies, education, religion, health and medicine, the arts, the media, and other institutional spheres that are part of living in an ornamental culture) produces generational feelings of distrust toward any culturally overarching truth claim, such as those pertaining to masculinity, masculine control, and patriarchy (see Jameson [1991], Lyotard [1979], and Borgmann [1993]). The splintering of cultural truths and social identities into a billion pieces leads to what Lull (2001) refers to as the contemporary 'looseness of [cultural] meaning' in ornamental cultures. In an ornamental culture, logics of multiculturalism, (mass) market consumption, and reflexive representation all destabilize notions of dominant or authentic masculinity in any space (Andrews, 2006; Hannerz, 1996). Gayatri Spivak (1994) argues that the decentring of dominant cultural identities (like masculine identities) and the exploration of polymorphous or subaltern cultures, in popular culture and elsewhere, allows for a vast array of representational practices to be deployed within institutional landscapes. The so-called crisis of masculinity in Canada and elsewhere is a logical but unanticipated outcome in cultures beset with ideologies and practices of cultural boundary crossings.

Defining the Crisis

With all of the above said, let's try to simplify once more. From the lines of argument presented above, and by extracting from literally dozens of books, chapters, and journal articles offered by sociologists and social psychologists, the masculinity crisis is typically defined by **five important features**. The perceived existence and implications of each feature will be explored in detail across the chapters of this book.

First, the masculinity crisis, as the popular doctrine goes, refers to a composite state of anxiety, fear, ennui, frustration, and anger certain men feel regarding the perceived loss of male power and status within key social institutions such as family, economy, and government. Discourses about the crisis frequently underline the apparent redistribution of power between men and women in Canada and elsewhere, and its cognitive–emotional impact on men. Still, critical debate continues as to whether men's collective access to power and authority in such institutions has actually been affected. In this book, I argue that defining the crisis as either real or imagined is indeed a slippery, and wholly unproductive (let alone empirically irresponsible) sociological line of inquiry. What is important to me (and, I suspect, others who know men who view themselves as in the midst of a crisis) is understanding the localized, contextual, and group-specific constructions of the crisis and how they manifest into physical cultural practices in everyday life. What drives me as a sociologist is the task of understanding why, at this particular historical juncture, more men (many of whom have tremendous social privilege and status) feel in crisis. Didn't W.I. Thomas once write something about the importance of defining a situation as real? Yes, I seem to remember that legendary passage on my 'Introduction to Sociology' course notes somewhere.

Second, the masculinity crisis finds social expression and complex representation through the collective action of clusters of men who organize political groups to fight back, struggle, negotiate, manage, or resist in one capacity or another. Despite Faludi's (1999) and Clare's (2000) assertions that men have not organized politically to solve their crises, a considerable number of men's groups have indeed crystallized as contextual reaction–formation subcultures. Emergent men's groups in the crisis are far more heterogeneous and socially progressive than those stereotypically identified as backlash or anti-women/ feminist movements (Seidler, 1991; Flood, 1998; Schwalbe, 1996).

Third, the perceived masculinity crisis is empirically observable through physical cultural practices and modes of male (and female) representation. Over the past two decades, the social performance of masculinity in public life has been deeply contoured by widespread public ideologies and doctrines, which suggest that men have a moral and ethical responsibility to be more consciously aware of, and responsible for, their public images as 'new men' (Atkinson, 2008a). A full spate of rather innovative physical cultural practices have been inserted into the common body projects of men, and have been reconciled as newly masculine habits. Body projects and practices such as cosmetic surgery, yoga, wearing makeup, and even crying openly in public have been derided by and among men historically in North America; their increased prevalence in Canada, however, must be contextualized within an ornamental cultural milieu that seasonally redefines normative masculinity. At the same time, hyperbolic expressions of masculinity have cropped up across popular cultural landscapes and have been given new significance in an era when softer embodiments of masculinity are increasingly permitted.

Fourth, the crisis of masculinity is reflective of a general ontological instability created by late-modernization, the emergence of ornamental cultures, and the death of many Western meta-narratives and historical truth-claims. Late modernity is a time, notes Lash (2007), where modernist ontologies are breaking down, and in which multiple definitions of reality compete in everyday life. He argues that power and status is most frequently attained by a social group in late modern societies as an outcome of battles to define the ontological order (i.e., what is real, or truthful, or permanent in social life). In a late modern, ornamental society categorized by a continued questioning of the nature of reality, few enduring 'maps of meaning' (Williams, 1977) exist to provide its members with compasses for definitively navigating the social world. Statuses, identities, and social roles which were historically believed to be essential, fixed, and inherent (such as those related to sex and gender) have lost their fixity. An identity like masculinity, then, is no longer culturally taken-for-granted as a single thing but rather a status that is subject to contextual negotiation and construction. Viewed from this perspective, the 'crisis' pertains to men who struggle with how to define and then be appropriately (read *flexibly*) gendered as male across many social situations. Beginning in chapter 1 of this book, I refer to the practice of tactically wearing different guises of masculinity as the corporeal, or physical, act of performing *pastiche hegemony*; an incredibly powerful social technique in ornamental culture.

Fifth, a crisis of masculinity has been perceived by people who see men (and in particular, young men and boys) targeted as problems and worthy of heightened surveillance and institutional regulation. Discourses about violent crime, risk-taking in the form of narcotic and alcohol consumption, poor performance within and alienation from school, ill health and obesity, and increased unemployment rates among working-class men highlight problems with how masculinity manifests in the current era. Theorists of masculinity have equally documented how swathes of North American men do not live as quintessentially hegemonic figures, but rather exist on the periphery of masculine power and authority circles. To these men, codes of dominant White, Christian, and middle-class masculinity have always been a source of cultural alienation and disenfranchisement. At the same time, men are encouraged by transnational late modern corporations and technological/science industries to see their bodies and selves as deficient and in need of correction via market commodities and services. In the ornamental culture of late modern society, masculinity is never achieved; it is only an image, an outer facade of embodied public performance requiring constant self-monitoring, investment, and affirmation from others. To this end, the widely publicized and mass-mediated crisis of masculinity is potentially an innovative mode of social control deployed within and across social institutions in order to mould generation after generation of Myrmidons.

Perceiving the Crisis

One of the main analytical points I repeat throughout this book is that the crisis of masculinity (or what we should probably call the crisis of multiple masculinities) is one of perception, and not of an objective, unchanging reality that has altered the life histories and experiences of all Canadian men. Men who perceive and react to changes in the normative masculine order do so in different degrees and within a range of sensibilities. At the same time, I find it difficult to accept, as a sociologist interested in and devoted to the study of historic and contemporary masculinities, that the gender category is no more or no less in crisis (in a sustained sense) than any previous era. Masculinities have always been closely linked with crisis in physical, emotional, and social ways. Yet discourses about and reactions to the masculinity crisis are unique at this point in Canadian history. Of particular interest to me is not how quantifiable masculinity crises are in the current era, but how the perception of crisis is tactically employed, resisted, or rejected as a technique for doing collective identity (among men and women) in a late modern, ornamental world. In a crisis- and moral-panic-preoccupied Canada, it is the battle over *defining* crisis and proposing forms of intervention that fascinates me.

Figure 1 represents the ways men I have engaged with in the 'empirical' world tend to construct and attribute a certain degree of blame to their gender crisis. Over the past ten years, men in a variety of social and cultural fields have described feeling at risk from at least one, but usually several, of the social causes identified in Figure 1.

Almost uniformly, men who believe that masculinities are under attack within Canadian social institutions also argue that anti-male cultural ideologies and

FIGURE 1 Perceiving the Crisis

political practices of equality have unfairly dislocated them from structural positions of power and authority. Chapters 1, 2, and 3 in this book describe how particular men wrestle with feelings of *structural dislocation* in both pro- and anti-social ways as part of doing a crisis masculine identity. Related to the above, men in crisis frequently lament how acting like a traditional man is relatively intolerable in a majority of social settings and *in situ* contexts. Further still, men feel pressure to adjust their social roles in status sets to reflect membership in contemporary terms. Men are still expected to engage the roles of husband or partner, father or caregiver, employee, and others, but with differently gendered performance expectations in mind. Given the diffuse social expectations for these men to behave in newly (and differently) masculine manners, they express frustration and confusion about how they should act normatively. Chapters 4 and 5 particularly address how gendered social roles within Canada may be in flux during the current crisis.

Many of the men whom I have encountered have articulated how they feel both objectified and essentialized ethnographically in commercial, scientific, and relational zones. Several things have played a role in the fabrication of a culture in which men are appreciated as little more than genes and muscles: the mass marketing of products to ornamental men; the medicalization of men's body problems; and, these men feel, women's ability, now more than ever, to openly sexualize men's bodies. They argue that discourses about diffuse social problems such as crime and violence, economic crisis, educational disruption, and obesity also unfairly depict both men and masculinities along essentialist lines (i.e., the simple biology of men is a root cause of a full host of social problems). Chapters 2, 3, 4, and 6 respectively provide case studies of how and why particular Canadian men feel both scientifically essentialized and culturally denigrated in the crisis.

Clusters of Canadian men report feeling as if masculinity has been placed on public trial within the mass media since the late 1970s. These men take issue with a pervasively tolerated misandry in popular culture, viewing it as a backlash against traditional expressions of masculine identity and residual patriarchy. Television programs such as *Home Improvement, Married with Children,* and *Sex and the City,* films including *9 to 5, Sling Blade,* and *Thelma and Louise,* and a selection of music from pop stars including Beyoncé ('If I Were a Boy'), Alanis Morissette (with songs like 'You Oughta Know'), and the Dixie Chicks (their song 'Goodbye Earl') did little to portray masculinity as anything other than loutish, primitively essential, victimizing to women, and culturally passé. In this case, men learn to feel ashamed and embarrassed of themselves through the widespread representational indictment of masculinities across popular cultural landscapes. Chapter 6 focuses on the enduring presence of misandry in Canadian popular culture.

Finally, and analytically connected to each of the above causes in a latticework of everyday experience, men I have interviewed in research efforts speak of a brand of Foucauldian *governmentality* (1977) in Canadian society, which targets and polices particularly 'dangerous' masculinities. The men express feelings of being surveilled, or in other words of being ideologically and biologically controlled in their social lives via the exercise of laws, social policies, and practices geared toward, in their opinion, the silencing, decentring, and ostracizing of men. Chapters 1, 2, and 3 especially home in on new governmental modes of managing boys, men, and masculinities in late modern Canada.

Throughout the seven substantive chapters of the book I explore how men who share ideal-typical constructions of the masculinity crisis seek to alleviate their crises via a range of physical cultural practices. Figure 2 provides a preliminary analysis of the range of responses.

Figure 2 presents an overview of the multiple lines of intersection and connection between perceived causes of the masculinity crisis in Canada and men's typical physical cultural responses. In the centre of the diagram is the crisis subject, masculinity. Branching away from the subject are the perceived causes of crisis as articulated by men. Branching out even further, the colour-coded spheres contain typical responses to the crisis, related to each attributed cause. Since many of the behavioural outcomes are associated with several perceived cultural conditions, they are multiply colour-coded. Each of the main colour codes describes a quasi-unique conceptual technique for managing the men's perceived crisis states, ranging from the hyper-sexualization of one's masculinity and *mimboism* (or, male bimboism—a term, I must confess that I poached from the television show *Seinfeld*), to subcultural excesses in

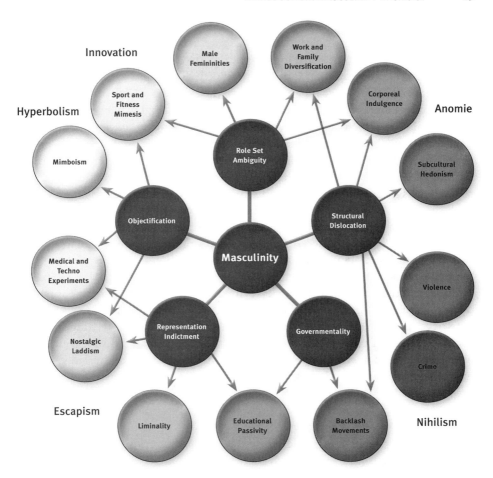

FIGURE 2 Responses to the Crisis

nostalgically male pastimes, to one's self-feminization, and to the use of medical apparatuses to shore up one's outwardly male image.

Several of the dimensions and significance of this diagram will be explained over the course of the seven substantive chapters of this book. However, as a brief introduction to what it portrays, the boxed dimensions outside of the maze of causes and responses categorize five main thematic mindsets shared by men who perceive masculinity to be in crisis. Men who feel *anomie* generally tend to view their worlds as structurally dislocated, role-ambiguous, and can respond to feeling adrift as a man in a range of ways, depending on their complex biographies, connecting identities (i.e., race, ethnicity, religion, sexuality, class, and so forth), and social environmental landscapes. Men who are *nihilistic* overwhelmingly feel structurally dislocated and targeted as men in a social world they believe is progressively hostile toward them. They are quint-essential examples of 'social dynamite', as populations on the brink of losing it. Men who *seek to escape* feel at once objectified and essentialized as men within a popular culture that labels masculinity as primordial or uncivilized. They generally act out in one of two ways. They either distance themselves from problematic forms of masculinity, or they fully embrace new and innova-tive techniques, which are culturally accepted, for proving one's masculinity. Other men engage in hyperbolically, and deeply essentializing, behaviours and expressions to symbolically act like an 'Achilles-lite'. Such men immerse them-selves in the world of fake war, promiscuity, and physical consumption in order to appear as recreationally hegemonic men. Finally, there are the many Will Hayeses of the contemporary masculine order, who find considerable social power in being flexibly male in a Canadian society still buttressed by residual patriarchy. They are late modern masculine thespians who adorn themselves with, and just as easily remove, a range of masculinity masks in everyday life. They are extraordinary dramaturgists (see Goffman, 1959, 1963), whose seem-ingly fragmented and dissonant performances of masculinity make up the parts of an interesting mosaic of identity. They are males who feel in crisis but who never appear in crisis. I know hundreds of these men. You have probably spoken to or seen one today . . . maybe he works beside you, maybe you pass him every morning while he walks his dog, maybe you see him on television, maybe you lie down beside him every night, maybe he is you.

Summary

A few pages earlier in this Introduction, I cut short a narrative about my own masculinity. It's time to pick up those autobiographic strands once more. I mentioned that I am not sure if I am in crisis, have ever been in crisis, or ever will be in crisis. But thinking reflexively about the shapes and dimensions of the idea of masculinity in crisis, I must confess a certain sense of experiential affinity with, and intersubjective understanding of, men's crisis narratives.

I am a bit of a masculine dilettante. Growing up with a range of male role models, it is difficult to think I would turn out otherwise. At times, the hard and domineering (yet underwritten as frail and ultimately victimized) mas-culine image of grandfather has steered my social performances and expecta-tions; every time I stepped into a particularly intense sporting battle I thought of and tried to emulate his persona. At other times, his early exit from my life reminded me of that which is lost in the blind adherence to traditional male 'being' and 'doing'. My father's quiet, hard-working, emotionally reserved nature pushed me to excel academically, and to believe that men should pro-vide for or be economically foundational in a family. Yet his sensitivity, ability to be calm, and his generosity made me question the rough edges of stereotypical masculinity. My brother's spectacular displays of confidence and abilities to command a gaze lead me to act on stage in my youth, have confidence to speak my mind in front of others, and embrace women (literally and figuratively). His hedonistic and Peter Panesque inability to grow up has, however, reminded me of the emptiness of traditional male quests for control and desire for lauded physical presences. His five divorces underline the point.

Each of these men was, and some still are, affected by spectacular presences and absences of masculinity. The role sets that comprise my life each ring with the crisis of traditional masculinity; I am a performing embodiment of male stereotype in many, many respects. I just now glance down at the hyper-masculine tattoos covering both of my arms and remember such a stark reality.

Here is, as they say in England, where the proverbial penny drops. The often unwritten characters in this boy's emerging masculine identity are two relentlessly strong, intelligent, and opinionated women; my mother Anne (who came from a large family, grew up in semi-rural Nova Scotia without a father, survived a first marriage which saw her brutally beaten and sexually assaulted regularly, fought depression through most of my young life, battled and survived cancer, and yet managed to raise three incredibly strong-willed children while deploying the flair of a mother unfettered by personal trauma) and my sister, Bronwyn. Bronwyn was the first feminist I knew, before I even knew the textual description of feminism. With only eleven months separating our births, she, the elder, counteracted practically every image and stereotype about men/women I learned on the playground, in the classroom, in the home, and while watching television. She feminized me in many ways as we shared conversations about fashion, music, school, friends, religion, politics, and prac-tically everything else. My style, language, attitudes, and future horizons were shaped deeply by her irreverence to traditional masculinities. My mum and Bronwyn forced what I considered to be proto-typical masculinity into crisis at an early age. They would at times be reluctant supporting cast members in the dramaturgical replication of traditional masculinity roles and statuses in our household. But for the most part, my appreciation for multiple masculini-ties stems from their unwillingness to be subservient, and their intolerance of the tight parameters of ascribed gender roles.

Still, sometimes consciously or unconsciously, I interpret, rationalize, befriend, enact, expect, alienate, command, speak, and represent as a male amalgam of role models of my life. There is indeed *residual patriarchy* in my life and the lives of many other men my age, which is both buried deep in our habituses (Elias, 2004 [1939])—in other terms, our socially learned second natures—and reared through daily social interaction. We will pick up the concept of the habitus in greater detail in chapter 2.

Though I have come to understand and resist masculine hegemony in my life, as a man/male subject in Canada, I still benefit greatly from dominant social structures, cultures, ideologies, and systems of representation that privilege my gender. Such is the first paradoxical essence of the masculinity crisis for scores of men in my generation; I am/do traditional masculinity at times even though I know better; giving up that which is ostensibly so privileging is a tall sociological order. This, to me, is the diffuse crisis of masculinity so many Canadian men narrate. It is the crisis Stoltenberg (1993) poignantly outlines in *The End of Manhood*. The crisis for many men is about wanting but not wanting to change one's male identity, and of figuring out how to fashion a new patriarchal society and pastiche hegemony that seems harmless and accommodating to everyone. At times, the crisis is narrated by men through tales of frustration, self-doubt, distress, promise, happiness, and even stories of indifference. Men who are immersed in such crisis are pushed and pulled by multiple *masculine realities* and expectations. These men face masculine realities that are paradoxical, contradictory, rewarding, disempowering, and confusing all at the same time. The masculinity crisis refers to, in this summary way, a 'liminal' (Turner, 1969) cultural no man's land. Such a dense and often misunderstood (or at least under-theorized) connection and tension between residual patriarchy, hegemony, and crisis masculinities weaves itself throughout the pages of this book.

Across each of the chapters, we explore various epistemologies of crisis standpoints and their related ornamental ontologies. Statistical data, stories from and narratives about men 'in [and out of] crisis', media reports, and academic references are used liberally to highlight my arguments. Writing in portions of the book will be layered with typical academic-speak (I cannot avoid doing this!), while at other points I want people to read how men tell their own narratives about what it is like to be in crisis, and beyond crisis. On these analytical grounds and others, let's encounter the men: those plagued with doubt, knee-deep within a murky field of shifting perceived gender codes, and each driven to apologize as, but yet be unapologetically, male.

Discussion Questions

1. Without thinking too sociologically about the issue, use your own personal experience to address whether or not you believe a masculinity crisis exists.
2. My argument is that crisis does not have to be structurally or materially real to have a social effect; it only has to exist as a state of mind. What is your reaction to this?
3. Can you think of other ways in which men may react to crisis than what has already been discussed?
4. If crisis does exist, which social groups of men do you think are most at risk of being in crisis?
5. What groups of men are not in crisis? How? Why?

Key Readings

Farrell, W. (2001). *The Myth of Male Power: Why Men are the Disposable Sex*. London: Finch. In this highly controversial book, Farrell argues that a full spate of gender statistics and common-sense beliefs simply mask how North American men are not nearly as hegemonic as we are led to believe. For instance, Farrell argues that men are actually far more likely to be victims of violence in the home than women, and are far less likely to have substantial access to higher education.

Faludi, S. (1999). *Stiffed: The Betrayal of the American Man*. New York: Chattus and Windus. As indicated throughout the Introduction above, this is the gold standard for anyone seriously interested in masculinity crisis reading. Through a series of well-explained and historically referenced case examples, Faludi paints an important socio-cultural picture of how gender hegemony has changed in the past 50 years.

Garcia, G. (2008). *The Decline of Men: How the American Male is Turning Out, Flipping off, and Giving Up His Future*. New York: Harper. In an eye-opening exploration of contemporary American manhood, *The Decline of Men* shows how men are struggling to redefine what being a man means at a time when globalizing processes have restructured world cultures. Their confusion has led to rampant male malaise, which has left many men feeling alienated and disconnected. Unable to communicate effectively their frustrated thoughts or emotions, Garcia argues that hoards of men are opting out of their 'male obligations' entirely, producing an entire generation of men who are abandoning their own potential and failing the mothers, wives, and girlfriends who love them.

Tiger, L. (2000). *The Decline of Males: The First Look at an Unexpected New World for Men and Women*. Los Angeles: Golden Books Publishing. Biological anthropologist Lionel Tiger, best known for developing the concept of male bonding in his *Men in Groups*, juxtaposes the rise of feminisms with the decline in social life satisfaction of men. If there were a male counterpart to feminism, this is where it would be found. Quite controversially, Tiger attributes the decline of family values, increased crime rates, and burgeoning social problems to the war against masculinity.

Whitehead, S. (2002). *Men and Masculinities: Key Themes and New Directions*. Oxford: Polity. Whitehead suggests that his book is part of a third wave in the sociology of men and masculinity, analogous to the third wave of feminism. Where previous profeminist masculinities scholarship draws on Marxism, functionalism, social constructionism, and psychoanalysis, this third wave is characterized by its grounding in poststructuralist, postmodern, and recent feminist perspectives. Thematically, the book covers useful introductory terrain, including discussion of masculinities, male power, men and feminism, men at work and play, and male bodies.

Key Terms

Essentialism: A belief that gender attributes have a direct correlation with biological capabilities and differences between the sexes. A belief, then, that gender practices simply reflect biologically given tendencies in men and women.

Hegemonic masculinity: The normative or culturally dominant ideal of masculinity to which men in a society are supposed to strive for and emulate. It is not necessarily the most prevalent masculinity, but rather the most socially revered. Characteristics associated with traditional hegemonic masculinity include aggressiveness, physical strength, drive, ambition, lack of emotion, and self-reliance.

Late modernity: The current social period in which the hallmarks of modern social life have all been accelerated. These hallmarks include the rise of the nation state, industrialization, spread of capitalism, globalization, rise of representative democracies, privatization and secularization of life, increasing presence of science and technology in society, urbanization, and proliferation of mass media.

Masculinity crisis: A term of classification referring to a perception among groups of men that their structural positions in society and their cultural worth within social networks have been hindered or challenged simply because they are traditionally male. Men in crisis feel as is they are discriminated against in contemporary culture as a form of reverse sexism, suggest that media tend to construct men negatively, and point to how a rash of new social problems among boys can be attributed to a general disliking of all things traditionally male in Canadian society.

Misandry: A term referring to a general hatred of men and masculinity, or the patterned derision of behaviours and attitudes associated with males.

Ornamental culture: Susan Faludi's (1999) term referring to the ways in which identity has become far more fluid in late modern life. Further, the idea implies how Western cultures are far less interested in maintaining and reproducing notions of what traditional gender is for people.

Pastiche hegemony: The practice of only finding personal power in localized social settings, rather than having the ability to be powerful across many social settings. Someone who 'does' pastiche hegemony can be a person with great influence and authority, say among one's peers or in one's home, but may work on the lowest rung of the economic ladder at their place of employment.

Residual patriarchy: The trace elements, practices, attitudes, systems of organization and division, ideologies, artifacts, and trappings of patriarchal society that still influence (sometimes in very covert ways) social environments wherein equality is both preached and practiced. Put another way, in countries like Canada residual patriarchy is a socio-cultural condition that still privileges men in sometimes very indiscreet and subtle manners.

1

Men, Power, and Pastiche Hegemony

Chapter Objectives

This chapter introduces and critically explores the following:

- Dominant theoretical links between men and social power
- The concept of hegemony
- An analysis of the concept of late modernity
- How hegemony exists as a process of storytelling
- How hegemony can be won in non political–economic ways

Charlie rises out of bed at the stroke of 7:30 a.m. He's still tired from the three hours of soccer he logged the night before. A competitive player in his youth, he now plays in a men's league four evenings every week. He rambles down the stairs to put on the morning coffee, pondering the day ahead (a quick run, breakfast, work, grocery shopping, dinner, practice, television, bed). Every day is a carbon copy of the previous. He checks his mobile phone for text messages while pouring milk over his gluten-free cereal. Three texts from friends, one from a co-worker. Nothing pressing, nothing significant in them. He crams himself into his expensive car, drives away from the newly fabricated subdivision in which he lives, and scuttles off to work. At the age of 37 he has accomplished much; a successful marketing agent, a gifted athlete, a good friend to many, and a contributor to his community.

But he is alone and confused about how to find a partner, or even how to act in socially mixed company. He wonders if he will ever find love, and whether his successes at work or in sport mean anything. Charlie regularly comes over to my house and plays with my two young sons, and I frequently catch him saying, words barely escaping through tightly pressed lips, 'fantastic'. He spends hours chatting online with potential mates, and then hundreds of other hours on first dates that will never progress past the coffee shop.

'I don't know what women want,' he tells me one day on a run, 'and God, I maybe don't know what I want.' He frets about losing his hair, about looking old for his age and not being fashionable enough, and that no one outside of the tight parameters of his work groups and sports clubs will ever take him seriously as he seems too old-fashioned and out of touch. Work does not define men like Charlie anymore. He is fragmented, self-critical, and plagued with self-doubt despite his ostensible, and traditional, masculine successes. I know hundreds of men like him. They don't seem socially powerful to me . . . at least upon first glance.

When initially considering the substantive contents of this book, I asked myself whether a chapter on power and masculinity should be placed toward the front or somewhere in middle. The analysis of masculinity and power is standard fare within gender literature; and indeed, it is perhaps the launching point for a lion's share of research on masculinity in the social sciences. A chapter on the cultural entanglement of power, men, and masculinity should figure prominently in any text about men in crisis. But as I hope to illustrate throughout this book, power in a late modern ornamental culture is increasingly less defined, nuanced, complex, and negotiated along rigid gender lines. While we have not moved beyond patriarchy in Canada by any means, it is not the same patriarchal, gendered world my father or grandfather experienced. Gendered power for contemporary men in the predominantly residual patriarchy that is Canadian society, is typically achievable. But this is only so in more dramaturgically performed ways, that is, in situations that are reflexive and carefully orchestrated, and situationally constructed ways that are relying less and less on the performance of masculinity. That is, men with access to *hegemonic power* (Gramsci, 1971) are far more likely to maintain it in *pastiche* ways and spotted cultural locations. Being and embodying the hegemonic has little to do with being and embodying a prototypical brand of universally recognized masculinity. Such a realization is one of the important empirical veils lifted through the study of so-called crisis discourses and practices.

Okay, so why is power, and deconstructing how gendered power matters in late modern Canadian society, relevant? At the forefront of the debate about the crisis of masculinity is whether or not men's collective socio-structural positions, statuses, identities, roles, and power chances have altered considerably in a late modern Canadian society. The objectivity of crisis is often accepted or rejected using quasi-objective demographic data on men's access to money, prestigious careers, educational opportunities (particularly university and college programs), and positions of ideological influence. These include ranking office positions such as ranking office positions in government, religion, and even the mass media. Perhaps stereotypically, given mainstream sociology's historical focus on work and occupations (or more broadly, socio-economic status as a predictor of one's power chances across the life-course), sociological constructions and deconstructions of the reported masculinity crisis are concerned with measuring and reducing the complexities of contemporary masculine politics to statistical data and trends. Important patterns about the gendering of work, and the gendering of society, are gleaned from the demographic analysis of who works where and how much they are paid, who creates and enforces law, who interprets and enforces the codes contained in spiritual texts, and who produces and directs television news. Still, those readings of the masculinity crisis that start and end with demographics miss an important point: how situational power and hegemony among gendered people are not explicitly expressed in data regarding the institutional power men and women hold at any given time. As Dunn (1998) argues in his analysis of late modernity, numeric analyses of how institutional positions and status markers are distributed in a society teach us little about how power is linked to identity in incredibly complex ways within a society.

Let's first consider some quality of life data regarding men and women in Canadian society. Standard sociological thinking is that those who hold material or economic power tend to live rather well. If a sexed social category is privileged, its power should be easy to see numerically in objective markers of institutional control and reward. Let's delve a bit into the data, then. As of 2007, Canada was a country with an almost identical sex ratio at the population level (for every 1 woman, there was 0.98 man). According to combined 2007 CANSIM data provided by Statistics Canada, and data released by the World Economic Forum's *Gender Gap* report (in which Canada ranks 18th overall out of 128 countries), fewer women than men dropped out of school prior to, or before the completion of, high school. Women were enrolled in greater numbers of undergraduate and graduate degree programs, and received more degrees in each category than men. These gaps continue to widen almost yearly (crisis advocates almost always cite them!). Men worked in paid, full-time employment contexts more than women and earned more, controlling for employment category or type (women still only earn roughly $0.72 for every dollar a man earns in the same position, and on average $14,000 per year less than men). But these income gaps are slowly narrowing. Women had a 1 per cent lower unemployment rate than men, but proportionally, more men participated in the labour force than women. Since 2001, far more women than men entered the paid labour force. However, more women than men are now working as single parents, and require more flexible (and thus unsecured) work situations. Men were more likely to be entrepreneurs or self-employed in 2007, while women were more likely to be involved in part-time, middle-range service sector posts. Far more men than women held top-level corporate, executive, and managerial positions. Women spent more time doing unpaid housework than men, but these levels are converging. Dizzying, isn't it!

Contrast the above institutional data with other *quality of life* information and reflect on the nature of sexed power in Canadian society. In 2007, men were more likely than women to be obese, dependent on drugs or alcohol, hospitalized for chronic illness, die during adolescence, commit suicide, be victims of crime (with the notable exceptions of sexual assaults), or be incarcerated. On the other hand, boys and men were more likely than girls and women to participate in organized community sport, vote, join a political party or hold public office, or be civically involved in religious or secular clubs and organizations. While more women than men were diagnosed and treated for depression, anxiety, body dissatisfaction, or low self-image (which may have much to do with male medical biases and diagnostic procedures), more men reported overall life dissatisfaction, feelings of alienation, and anomie. Women were more likely than men to have strong and extended friendship networks, and to dabble in the arts. But does any of this teach us about the *gendering* of power or its phenomenological experience?

This very brief and selective numeric view of power, status, and quality of living in Canada paints a complex picture regarding the relationship between the sexing of social privilege, position, authority, and status opportunities. On a strictly economic or numeric basis, men remain in structurally and culturally hegemonic positions in the workforce, and in traditional positions of status and rank. Women, on average, are becoming more formally educated than men, but it does not seem to translate into tremendous economic, social, or cultural capital return. Women continue to shoulder the vast majority of unpaid household tasks (too numerous to list here), even while holding employment outside of the home. To me, all of the statistical trends outlined so far are basic indictors of a *residual patriarchy* in Canadian society—an enduring but fractured and contested institutional structure of political and economic privilege for men. Social roles and access points to power positions in society are indeed shifting within these structures, but perhaps not at the accelerated rate masculinity crisis advocates suggest. This is where many sociologists or gender theorists get off the masculinity crisis train. The show is over, nothing else to see here, keep moving. Think again. Don't pack your analytical bags and go home just yet. Cultural crises are almost never confirmed or rejected by strict demographic data alone.

To begin, cultural theorists often conflate numeric statistical data regarding sex and social power with gendered power. This is lazy. A central focus on material(ist) power between sexed social categories is embedded, either explicitly or implicitly, in demographic and descriptive analyses of contemporary sex (*not gender*) relations. For many sociologists, political scientists, historians, and gender studies researchers who inspect the supposed masculinity crisis, it's *all* about material/economic power. To Johnson (2001), Gordlick-Jones (2002), and Hearn (1999), the masculinity crisis is easily understood, articulated, or negated outright on a starkly socio-economic basis. They claim discourses about masculinity crises emerged in the 1970s and 1980s as women gained inroads into educational and middle-class occupational zones (Allen, 2002). The simple translation is that men's feelings and expressions of crisis are overreactions to perceived economic loss. The crisis involves a decentring of men (mainly White, middle-class men) from structural positions of authority: namely, positions in the service sector and in professional sectors. Women are positioned in such crisis discourses as recent and unwanted members of the patriarchal clubhouse. According to Farrell (2001), even the lightest inspection of economic data suggests no stubborn or objective crisis state exists; women are still, by no means, threatening to men along political-economic lines.

In being mindful of the definition of crisis discussed in the Introduction of this book, there is little merit in accepting or rejecting the existence of a diffuse masculinity crisis as a matter of statistical description or inference. Demographics provide an important window into the sexed structural conditions of late modern, residual patriarchy in Canada, but cannot instruct as to how self/culturally identified males and females negotiate their gendered identities as powerful in daily practice, for example in work, family, political, religious, community, and other cultural settings. Stated differently, rates and figures about men and women do not provide a qualitative, phenomenological feel for how masculinities or femininities are policed, resisted, defended, vilified, celebrated, or ignored as a matter of power in situated contexts. Further still, statistics teach us little about how masculinity may be under pressure or fractured in settings still dominated statistically by men, while revived in other, non-traditional locales. As Baudrillard (2002) remarks, 'like dreams, statistics are a form of wish fulfilment'.

Knowing Masculinity and Social Power

How do sociologists theorize and teach students about the complex relationship between masculinity (and masculinity crises) and social power? Surprisingly enough, not in very nuanced manners. It is neither the place nor purpose of this chapter to talk about all the ways in which masculinity has been linked to power in social life, but a brief excursion into how sociologists generally link the gender category to power is worthwhile.

Within the larger field of gender studies, the idea or identity of masculinity has been traditionally linked to economic, social, and cultural power in countries like Canada. In short, if you are a (at least heterosexual) man you have some semblance of power within this historically patriarchal society. Your identity, quality, morality, and characteristics as male fit well with your ascribed/assumed social roles of power. Full stop. Such an ideology is pervasive in several waves of gender/feminist theories and is replicated generationally in research efforts. Even leading theorists of masculinity like Connell (2005) tend to link masculinity and power somewhat uncritically, meaning they do not question this ideology of power much. The sociological preoccupation with political and economic imbalances in power between men and women, which is so easily (though as we've seen, not unproblematically) encapsulated in demographic data about education, work, occupations, and political participation, encourages a rather simplistic construction of power lines in Canadian society (i.e., people who are privileged institutionally have power while those on the outside do not).

When I teach courses in the sociology of gender, the introduction to sociology, deviance and crime, popular culture, or the sociology of sport, students tend to react and protest vehemently against common sociological constructions of gendered power. For young women in these courses, the constant victimizing of women in sociological theorizations (or their construction as powerful only in the context of minded social resistance) is often out of synch with their lived experiences. In many ways, their protests turn Smith's (1987) classic description of a bisected sociological consciousness on its head. Additionally, many young men (of course in the privacy of my office) regale me with stories of doubt, social impotence, and anxiety about their masculinities in one context or another. Their consistently negative reactions to a range of primary readings on gendered power spurred on my own thinking about men, masculinity, and possible crisis.

The rather blanket connection between men, masculinity, and power stems from a general but not universal tendency to study men in a number of ways. I encourage any reader of this book to reflect on the continuum presented below in Figure 1.1 that depicts the manners by which social scientists come to know masculinity and compartmentalize its connection to power.

The first, and least sociological, way of knowing masculinity relates to the *bio-psychological* study of men. From a host of bio-psychological perspectives, the physiological man and cultural masculinity are practically inseparable (Daly

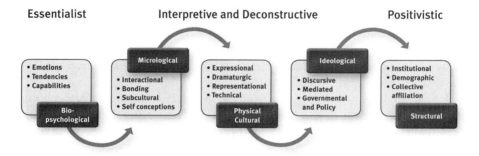

FIGURE 1.1 Knowing Masculinity

and Wilson, 2005). Men are believed to have an innate and unlearned, but socially reinforced, drive for power, domination, violence, and self/other alienation. Even when I write these words, my memory drags me back to first-year psychology and lectures on Freud. Masculinity is simply a cultural catch-all term that refers to roles, statuses, and identities that derive from or serve to support men's natural tendencies. Societies, armies, economies, systems of thought, and modes of cultural expression can all be traced to genetic codes buried deep within men. Men's biologies and psychologies are rarely viewed as progressive or nurturing within bio-psychological research; rather, men need to be civilized for a peaceful social order to appear (Elias, 2004). I am reminded of the 2000 movie *What Women Want*, starring Mel Gibson as a womanizing advertising executive. Gibson's character, through an act of cosmic fate that leaves his brain magically rewired, can listen in on all women's private thoughts. Gibson only now appreciates the tyranny of his genes and their social expression, and becomes a better person/man because his fundamental essence is changed. Maybe my friend Charlie, who I introduced at the beginning of this chapter, needs a similar bump on the head. In moments of popular cultural representation like *What Women Want*, essentialism reigns supreme. And indeed, the late modern renaissance of genetic and socio-biological studies of the relationship between men and crime perhaps foreshadow reinvigorated essentializing on the academic horizon (Atkinson and Young, 2008). I often ponder, like Pease (2000) does in *Recreating Men: Postmodern Masculinity Politics*, and Digby (1998) does in *Men Doing Feminism*, whether we have moved past essentialist ways of seeing masculinity within or outside of the academy.

From bio-psychological perspectives, masculinity is a code and physical cultural practice established on inherently anti-social, pathologically genetic (i.e., violence and aggressively sexual), and cognitive foundations. Even intelligence, rationality, and artistic and spiritual expressions (the so-called hallmarks of Enlightenment masculinity) are applied by men as cunning techniques of dominance. A middle-aged marketing executive from Edmonton named Carl, whom I interviewed in a study of cosmetic surgery, told me an interesting, though horribly depressing, story about the nonchalant ways people essentialize male bodies, and the consequences:

> About three years ago my wife asked me . . . sitting there in the middle of dinner one night . . . if I felt bad about getting old. She held her head sideways when she asked, with her wine glass dangling precariously on the corner of her right palm. 'Should I?', I said. She went on with, 'It's just that, well, I read so much now about how men your age [53] become sad when they mature because their virility and essence is gone. I mean we have our kids, our lives, your work is great, but losing that part of you must be hard.' What part did she mean? 'Cindy, where the thell are you going with this? What are you saying? I'm sort of lost.' 'Exactly, hon. It's what I'm saying. I know you must be getting lost, dear, and if you ever want to talk about it, I'm here. Honey, you know I will always see you as the handsome young man I fell in love with.' We'd spent nearly thirty years together, have shared incredibly intimate and connective times and know each other inside and out. She knows me as a human . . . but at the end of the day still sees my masculinity as flesh and blood. Not as a devoted husband, not as a proud father, not as a friend or anything. She worries about me feeling worthless because my 'essence' is gone. How would she have liked it if, after pouring a glass of scotch one night, I said, 'Cindy, don't feel bad that your tits are hanging past the waistband in your pants. I'm still here for you, love.' It stuck with me. Her words haunt me.

Carl's story is by no means unique. The coupling of youth, genetics, physicality, and a range of essential indicators of masculinity runs as deep in

Canadian society as it does in theoretical analyses of the genetic basis of human sexed behaviours. A fifteen-year-old boy in Ontario sheepishly confessed to me, during an interview about why he stopped taking gym in high school, that he didn't feel as if he belonged in the class because he, like other boys who had quit gym in his school, just didn't have the appropriate genetic gifts to be strong and healthy. Where do boys get these ideas from?

Essentialist codes linking men to power operate overtly and covertly across our social institutions and within popular culture. Massively popular crime or medical TV programs like *CSI*, *Law & Order*, *House*, *ER*, and others remind us of biological essences of men's social behaviours. Bordo (1999) reminds us, however, in *The Male Body: A New Look at Men in Public and Private*, that many men have materially benefited from socio-biological ideologies that have to justify men's positions of authority across North American social institutions. Consider why male professional tennis players often compete in the best 3 out of 5 set matches and women 2 out of 3 set matches. This discrepancy, which builds directly on the enduring historical premise in sports cultures that women do not possess the requisite biological tools to play as long as men, has been used to justify unequal pay, sponsorship, access, and media representation patterns between men and women in the sport for nearly 100 years. Other socio-cultural theorists of sport like Atkinson and Young (2008) note that allowing oneself to be essentialized as a man can generate tremendous social, cultural, and economic capital in athlete cultures.

Perhaps the richest and most compelling studies of men and social power have been conducted via *micro-logical* studies of how men experience and wield social influence *as males* through social interaction. The literature, which cuts across sociologies of work and professions, crime and deviance, religion, war and violence, bodies, sport, media, health, race/ethnicity, and of course gender and sexuality, is absolutely bursting with small-group, qualitative case studies of how normative masculine social statuses and identities are used to create hierarchies of cultural power and control across the social landscape. Duneier's (2000) study of sidewalk culture, Sparkes's (2005) investigations of men with spinal cord injury, Kimmel's (2008) analysis of laddism, Stoudt's (2006) dissection of cultures of school violence, Beal's (1995) work on skateboarding crews, Yeung's (2006) account of being gay in college fraternities, and Schugart's (2008) analysis of metrosexuality at work, each provides compelling micro-testimonials regarding how traditional codes of masculinity and access to social power and authority are intimately coupled, wielded, and resisted by situated men. The above studies and many, many others repeatedly attest to the same thing: how men seek to generationally *dominance bond* (Farr, 1988) within small groups by policing and reproducing normative masculine standards of speech, body style, ideology, and symbolic identification.

Physical cultural studies (PCS) of men and masculinity advance critically and theoretically driven analyses of the relationship between gender codes, power, embodiment, and the representation of identity. PCS research reads gender codes about masculinity through the many ways in which gender ideology is embodied as a public performance of power. PCS research on men and masculinity advances a wide-ranging theoretical vocabulary, using concepts from a variety of disciplines including cultural studies, economics, history, media studies, performance studies, philosophy, sociology, and urban studies, in engaging and interpreting this particular aspect of masculine physical culture.

Johnson and Holman's (2004) work on hazing rituals in sports represents, par excellence, how physical cultural practices are informed by identity codes that must be situated within broader relations of power between people. Physically and emotionally dangerous hazing practices are lauded in sport spaces as important rituals for bonding teammates. Failure to participate in traditional hazing rituals on a team may prove socially disastrous for new members. One's disinterest in embodying masculine sporting codes through forms of tribal self-abuse in a sport subculture can indicate social and ideological difference from the others. In some hyper-masculine sport circles like football, rugby, and hockey, the rejection of hazing is tantamount to a rejection of the sport culture and its established hierarchies of alpha male power. While hazing practices often violate league or organization rules, which explicitly prohibit them, hazing thus serves as a stark, and generally accepted, reminder to rookie members on a team that codes of masculine risk-taking, aggression, and authority abound in the physical practice of sport from beginning to end. Johnson and Holman's (2004) research on the gender-based logic of hazing practices offers critical insight into how hyper-masculine rituals like hazing reaffirm social structural hierarchies inside and outside of sport. This gender logic privileges a particular kind of masculinity over others, and raises serious questions as to why sports insiders continue to encourage young men to participate in hazing practices in the name of group bonding. Through PCS research efforts like Johnson and Holman's and others', several dark sides of masculinity are exposed.

Perhaps two modes of sociological research in studies of masculinity are most popular. One is to expose the ideological dimensions of masculinity as a cultural gender logic. And the other involves structural expositions on how masculinity is embedded in social roles, statuses, and identities which are replete with material, economic and/or political power. In the first, classic Marxist and (pro)feminist analyses of the ideological foundations of patriarchy reign supreme. In the second, masculine ideologies are located within particular institutional zones of power, and interpreted as case studies in how patriarchy is maintained (Pringle, 2005).

As an example of Smith's (1987) *The Everyday World as Problematic* autobiographically reveals how masculine codes and logics are foundational in the operation of modern universities and their departmental systems of knowledge production. Her work in some ways typifies how gender scholars have illustrated how masculinity is (only) a structural ideology (and as such can be decentred), but have rather insufficiently exposed how dominant ideologies and structures of masculinity in countries like Canada may be as exclusionary to (most) men as they are to women.

Ideological and structural–ideological analyses of men and masculinity are rapidly becoming overly mechanistic and positivistic in a traditional scientific sense. That is to say, simplistic and uncritical connections between patriarchy, masculinity, and power are hinged upon demographic statistics, population trends, quality of life indicators, survey results, and anecdotal or other quasi-objective data that seem to expose how men, in particular a few select types of masculinity, remain the ideological and structural norms. Akin to Ashe (2007), I question whether the garden-variety ideological and structural accounts of power that hold firm to binaries like masculinity/femininity, power/powerless, victimizer/victimized, and normative/deviant are reflective of contemporary experiences with gendered power for a range of men. It is precisely from these grounds that quick dismissals of masculinity crises may be launched (i.e., men still hold key power positions in society, therefore masculinity equals power). When my students ask why sociologists regularly offer unilinear and concep-tually flat constructions of masculinity and power, I normally point them in the direction of one preferred concept: *hegemony*.

The Root of It All: Hegemony, Late Modernity, and Fear

Sociological accounts of power are many, diverse, and deep-rooted in the disci-pline. If there is a lingua franca in sociology, one might argue that the majority of us speak in theoretical tongues of power. Among the most commonly used sociological dialect in research and writing on power stems from Antonio Gramsci's (1971) canonical *Prison Notebooks*. Within the study of the gendered power, one would be hard pressed to find a more commonly used theoretical concept than Gramsci's notion of *hegemony*.

Gramsci's construction of hegemony is born from an idea that ruling organ-izational bodies in a society, like a government or a State, cannot enforce control over vast groups of people without ideological convincing. Gramsci, a Marxist-inspired Italian intellectual, predominantly saw the State as a coercive political wing of capitalist industrialists. Yet, the State and the economically privileged classes (comprised predominantly of upper class, White, Christian men in Western nations) do not simply wield ideologically unjustified power over others (e.g., women, ethnic minorities, and members of the working class). This would create largely unstable, and potentially violent, social orders. To Gramsci (1971), socially legitimate and enduring power is established and maintained through subtle interinstitutional and cultural means: a process of hegemony. Hegemony is political, ideological, social, and cultural power that flows from intellectual and moral leadership within a society. A ruling class forms and maintains its hegemony in civil society by creating and enforcing its norms, values, and statuses that are, in turn, promulgated and normalized through political parties, schools, media, the church, and other voluntary associations. These are what Althusser (1971) describes as a society's *ideological state apparatuses*. Power is first grounded in material capital and political authority, but then sustained when members of a society recognize the ways of life of the ruling classes as their own. As feminist scholars including Angela Davis (1983), bell hooks (1984), and Catharine MacKinnon (1989) teach us, such is the historical basis of patriarchy as a form of hegemony.

Gramsci argues in *Prison Notebooks* that hegemony is ultimately exercised through the promotion of an ever-present false consciousness among its targets of power; such that I or you believe the values and life choices we make for ourselves (i.e., to go to school, wear particular clothing, get married, have children, live in a certain area) are indeed our own, and not part of a larger class-based social agenda. Hegemony operates á la *The Matrix*, wherein one is convinced to sleep comfortably in a dream world of false realities, unaware of the power mechanisms underpinning one's existence. Hegemony is also this process to which Gramsci refers when explaining why people seemingly consent to being ruled (under the rubric of our common culture) within a relative state of social domination. Long before the time of Gramsci, Charlotte Perkins Gilman critiqued (masculine) hegemony, and the manners by which patriarchy produces false consciousness among women and men in Western nations. Through the extended parable of *Herland*, Gilman (1951) not only deconstructs and exposes patriarchy as a form of hegemony, but also alludes to the consequences of collective acquiescence to hegemony.

Regardless of the feminist utopia Gilman creates in *Herland*, resisting hegemony and shedding its ideological trappings proves difficult in advanced capitalist societies. Hegemonic cultural innovations such as compulsory schooling, mass media, and popular culture have indoctrinated those outside of power zones to be largely complacent to, or even ignorant of, hegemonic cultural power plays. Instead of working towards a cultural revolution that would truly serve their collective needs, people who are ruled in advanced societies prefer to listen to the rhetoric of nationalist leaders; seek consumer acquisition opportunities and middle-class statuses of success; embrace an individualist ethos of cultural worth through perceived merit-based sports and/or accept the guidance of bourgeois religious leaders. Gramsci (1971) therefore argued for *wars of position* and *wars of manoeuvre* as mechanisms for combating the tyranny of hegemony. Wars of position are culture battles in which anti-capitalist/ authoritarian elements seek to gain a dominant voice in mass media, mass organizations, and educational institutions to heighten class-consciousness, teach revolutionary analysis and theory, and inspire revolutionary organization. Following the success of a war of position, new leaders would be empowered to begin wars of manoeuvre, the actual insurrection against the established power bloc, with mass support.

Feminist and profeminist scholars from the 1980s onward embraced Gramsci's ideas in their respective deconstructions of patriarchy. While Gramsci's analysis of domination was first advanced specifically in terms of economic class domination, it has been readily applied to the study of patriarchy as a mode of structural and cultural domination. From the above, it is easy to understand why gender researchers canonized Gramsci's concept. Following Kessler et al.'s (1982), and Connell's (1987) seminal treatises on the nature of hegemonic masculinity in the West, the term hegemony has been linguistically united with the idea of masculinity for well over two decades. A central problematic in this book, however, is whether blanket constructions of either patriarchy as hegemony or hegemonic masculinity are still viable in a late modern Canadian society.

Connell's (2005) and other standard descriptions of hegemonic masculinity tend to revolve around several core ideas. First, at any given time one form of masculinity is culturally exalted as the ideal-type (Donaldson, 1993). It is the dominant or cultural benchmark of masculinity, but not a statistically prevalent masculinity. In the West, the cookie-cutter hegemonic man is a throwback protagonist from a John Steinbeck or Harper Lee novel. He is John Wayne. He's a frontier 'man's man' who embodies control, confidence, self-importance, and strength through his very swagger. He is Achilles. He is Michael Jordan. He is James Bond. He is the man every boy supposedly emulates and who grown men envy.

Jefferson (2002) challenged the construction of a single hegemonic masculinity in sociological theory, arguing that there is more or less a hegemonic power bloc of many men with different kinds of masculinities. To varying degrees, each of these men may be hegemonic as a power holder in certain corners of their social worlds. But they do not participate in the universal brand of class hegemony that Gramsci articulates, or in broader structural–cultural hegemony as Connell outlines. They have frailties, inadequacies, and impure masculine statuses that exclude them from ideal-type categorization. These men can be dominated, influenced, and stigmatized by other men and women. And yet in other contexts, the type of masculinity they embody has considerable cultural cachet. A Black male in the working class, who is clearly not a part of established hegemony in countries like Canada or the United States, may be hegemonic within his own family or small social circle.

I think my friend Charlie is this sort of man. He is hegemonically powerful in places, but not in all places. His hegemony is *pastiche*; it is put together, mixed and matched. I, too, am hegemonic along these lines. Much of the remainder of this book will focus on how hegemony has become a pastiche micro-logical power play in late modernity for men.

The second core idea of hegemonic masculinity is normally defined as an offshoot of a system of gender codes that legitimates patriarchy, and which guarantees (or is taken to guarantee) the dominant position of some men over others, as well as the subordination of women. What I mean by this is that hegemonic masculinity creates and polices social hierarchies of gender/power. However, Gramsci's description of hegemony suggests that any prevailing cultural norms that cleave people into ruling or ruled groups are not set in stone. Rather, the ideological roots of status hierarchies and the institutions, practices, and beliefs that support them can be critiqued as reversible systems of domination. This means that norms and cultural ways of life promoting men as natural leaders (in any social context) can be destabilized, challenged, and dissected as exploitive techniques of power. Unlike a diamond, hegemony is not forever.

Finally, Gramsci's construction of hegemony has been modified and extended by contemporary gender theorists, who read contemporary power struggles in social life as contests over the ability to define reality. By taking the lead of radical social constructionists and post-structuralists including Foucault (1977, 1980), Pringle (2005) contends that power is more closely linked to a group's access to the production and dissemination of knowledge (i.e., means of representing social truth) than strict membership in elite status or class positions. Individuals who control the process of ontological framing in a society—who Foucault (1978, 1980) refers to as those who dictate discourse within particular social formations, and shape cultural *dispostifs*—are hegemonic in contemporary life. If, as the argument goes, women and members of the heretofore underprivileged masculine under-classes make social inroads into these positions, then the historical ideologies that have served to marginalize them as socially inferior can be decentered and replaced with alternative hegemonies.

Returning back to the main theme of this book, how is hegemony related to a potential masculinity crisis or even a post–masculinity crisis Canada? *Masculine* hegemony has been fractured into a million pieces but not dislodged entirely, nor exposed to its deepest social roots. Crisis and fear about male hegemony and its splintering into a range of situated and contestable forms, however, has cut particular groups of men to the bone. In particular, the death of archetypal hegemonic masculinity hit men the hardest who, as Connell refers to them, were once *complicitly hegemonic males*: men who benefitted from and emulated masculine hegemony, but could not fully achieve hegemonic standing. To understand the complex relationship between the disruption of masculinity and the creation of crisis for these men, we need to understand a bit more about them, and how late modernism severed the umbilical cord connecting them to social and cultural super-privilege.

Late Modernity, Implosion, and Crisis

Who are complicitly hegemonic males? They are men who benefit from being male when patriarchy reigns. But they are not the movers, shakers, and mega-masculine players who establish and police cultural standards. They are everyday guys who have authority in the home, at school, on the street, in the newspaper, or anywhere else, simply because they are male. While they may at times feel twinges of guilt about wielding masculinity to get their way over others who rank beneath them on the social status ladder, they ultimately recognize that membership has its privileges. But through the course of late modernity, membership, we have learned, may actually come with a considerable price tag: at least at first!

Jeb is a 37-year-old data analyzer for a major investment consultant group in Toronto. He's not a principal member of the corporate team, but he loves the power and prestige associated with working for the organization. Jeb spends the bulk of a Friday at work in front of a sparkling new 25-inch computer monitor sorting through the dizzying array of numbers, rates, trends, and pie charts his managers send to him. Parked at his upmarket IKEA desk and surrounded by his beechwood-effect semi-cubicle walls, Jeb pounds down triple espressos and double lattés all day as he manipulates the data. Jeb goes home at 8:00 p.m. to a wife, a child, and a dog. Strung out from work, he crashes on a leather sofa, turns on another monitor (this time a more impressive 50-inch plasma television), and curls up into a comfortable position, while eating a warmed dinner that was ready almost an hour earlier when Jeb swore he would be home. He falls asleep there, and is awakened the next morning by his dog Gem, who needs to be let out. After his brief dog-minding duties are fulfilled for the day, and before anyone else in the house is awake, Jeb is out the door to meet with a running group. It's a Saturday, and he'll spend the morning with his running mates, first trudging through local hills and trails on a ten-mile sojourn, and then poring over the week's frustrations with them at a *trés chi-chi* coffee *boîte*. Later, he takes his five-year-old son Alex to the park for an hour, and then quickly back home for dinner. He watches a hockey game in his basement lair that evening, and then back to bed after the eleven o'clock news and a few emails to co-workers detailing a few loose ends he forgot to tie up yesterday.

Week in and week out, Jeb staggers through the same pattern. Jeb can do this, he has the right and responsibility, he thinks, as a husband, worker, and father to do what he needs first. Wives, computers, dogs, televisions, cars, and even his son, are the accoutrements of his masculinity. He never forces anything as a man, he never fights about his status, and he never has to lay the masculine foot down in an act of declaration anywhere. He gets by most days riding on the coattails of traditional masculinity. No one will ever write a newspaper article about his colossal business acuity, take his photograph and splash it across the evening news, nor will he ever win a community award for being husband or dad of the year. He's not that kind of man. But he gets by nevertheless. That is, until he came home at 9:35 p.m. one cold November weekday in 2005 to find his masculine fortress of solitude empty. Only a few window treatments, a blanket and pillow, and a note left on the kitchen counter, carefully folded into three, remained. The note read, 'Sorry, Jeb, we moved on without you.' Jeb was flabbergasted and rundown for months. He withdrew into himself, and retrenched even further into the last trace of masculine power in his life: his work.

Almost a year to the day later, Jeb is dating again. He tries Internet dating services, blind-date setups with friends, the local bar scene, and even cruising local grocery stores and libraries for single women. He is astonished to learn that the younger women he meets, and initially likes, will not tolerate him. They want him to cook, they themselves want to stay at work late, for him to be up to date with the latest fashion trends, and to place their sexual needs first. They glance with both vitriol and confusion at him when he goes to help them on with an overcoat. They will not entertain discussions of sport, and drag him away from his running group to Saturday morning yoga classes. Jeb is lost. His masculinity was cut off at the knees when his wife Karen left him. He is adrift in sea of nouveau gender codes and he swims without a preserver. Karen's parting words to him were more poetic and prophetic than he realized.

Jeb's narrative of confusion, loss, and identity recalibration must be contextualized within the social environment(s) and time in which he lives. In truth, it's a pretty confusing narrative. Jeb's identity crisis developed at a time when many of the social truths around him were imploding, realities blurring, and social and cultural 'boundary crossing' proliferated. Boundary crossing is a hallmark of late modern Canada. Hardt and Negri (2004) argue that with the ongoing transition from modern industrialism to the late modern, service-oriented, ornamental societies Faludi (1999) discussed, rigid boundary codes of identity (like male/female) have weakened and been penetrated. Adorno and Horkheimer (1944) and Marcuse (1964) predicted that a shift to commodity-fetished and service/knowledge economies would indeed rewrite cultural practice in these ways and others. Lefebvre (1991) concurred, arguing that the molecular features of everyday cultural life (such as the construction of gender or gender power) would be turned somewhat upside down through the twentieth-century progression into a different molar, late modern society.

Late modernist arguments about the fragmentation of culture and boundary crossings are almost universally encapsulated by, in either subtle or overt ways, Jameson's (1991) and Lyotard's (1979) analysis of the death of Western institutional meta-narratives (i.e., as discourses that create and help reinforce social boundaries), and Anderson's (1991) notion of contemporary *imagined communities*. From Jameson (1991), Lyotard (1979), and Borgmann (1993), cultural studies theorists have drawn attention to how the fragmentation of work and the economy, education, religion, health and medicine, the arts, the media, and other institutional spheres produced a zeitgeist of distrust for any culturally overarching truth claim in the latter stages of the twentieth century. Cultural meta-narratives like belief in government, science, God, patriarchy, or other totalizing frames erode in late modernity. The power to know and to produce reality is far more public than private and institutional. The splintering of cultural knowledge production, representation, and dissemination into a billion pieces leads to a looseness of [cultural] meaning in late modern social spaces.

From Anderson's (1991) lead, cultural studies theorists address how concepts like the nation-state, society, or even small group collectivities are more fictional constructions of cultural and structural alignment than empirical realities. For example, Wilson and Atkinson's (2005) examination of Rave and Straightedge online communities in North America illustrates how groups of politically disenfranchised and alienated middle-class boys may actually never come into embodied, face-to-face interaction with one another, yet participants understand members' biographies, lived experiences, and practiced lifestyles as communally bound. Virtual boundary lines provide meaning in the practitioners' everyday lives by creating common bonds and systems of representation with 'others like me, out there'.

Emphasizing the cultural change of any spatially and socially arranged, imagined community such as a nation-state, city, or local neighbourhood, is of course the ongoing process of globalization. Frankfurt School theorists predicted that the mass globalization (read: Americanization) of culture would create new cultural centres and colonies of economic and ideological production (see Wallerstein, 1978). The homogenization thesis reads a one-way cultural flow between global actors; economic and political power centres like the United States and the United Kingdom export cultural products and ideas that undermine local cultures in the Second and Third worlds. In Kenya, Coca-Cola becomes a cultural drink of choice; in Vietnam, Nike becomes a brand symbol of local identity; and in Morocco, Diesel jeans are more coveted than traditional gandoras or djellabas. Local actors become part of the globally imagined (Western) community by consuming images of nations (and their imagined identities) through commodity acquisition, highlighting the fetishization of commodity exchange–value over use-value. This leads to what Maguire (1999) describes as the 'increasing variety of', but 'decreasing contrasts' between, world cultures and their boundaries. Boundaries, at all levels of consumption, prove to be more permeable and expansive in the late-modern, global era (Appadurai, 1997).

Chaney (1994) argues that the global reformation of culture as increasingly post-industrial or late modern opens up personal representation for widespread mixing and matching. Chaney contends that stark divisions between hierarchically organised taste groups within and between societies are not nearly as pronounced as those found in the 'modern' era. Access to a full sweep of visual, material, and ideological sources of cultural production is not owned by the empowered elite, but by cultural omnivores. Logics of neo-liberalism, (mass) market consumption, and reflexive representation extolled in such Western nations each destabilize notions of dominant or authentic cultural identity in any space (Andrews, 2006; Giddens, 1991; Hannerz, 1996). As groups mix-and-match cultural objects, images, and practices as part of establishing unfettered reflexive identity, established-outsider cultural practices bound in (definitive) space and time are replaced by the practice of situated representation and the aesthetics of everyday life. Spivak (1994) argues that the decentring of dominant cultural identities and exploration of subaltern cultures allows for a vast array of representational practices to be deployed within institutional landscapes.

Among the most discussed conditions of late modernity is the contemporary cultural emphasis on doing identity in highly personalized, transitory, and consumeristic manners: what Giddens (1998) and others refer to as *reflexive individualism*. Giddens argues, as Bauman (2000) similarly writes in *Liquid Modernity*, that people in late Western capitalist societies are mobilized by economic stakeholders to view their bodies, selves, and minds as ongoing construction projects. One should continually incorporate commodities into his or her own unique systems of personal signification and representation in order do their own *life politics* of self-awareness (Giddens, 1998). You are never complete, never fulfilled, never finally 'you'. You (the incomplete you) must keep buying products so you can redefine your identity to reflect who you are at the moment. The person who stagnates, who opts out of the endless spiral of consumption and representation, risks ostracism. Beck (1992) writes about the movement to these sorts of ornamental, self-engaging, and hyper-individual 'ME!' practices as part of the movement toward an entirely self-referencing culture. The consequences of living in a self-referencing culture run deep. For example, hyper-reflexive modes of living do not translate well in the reproduction of stable cultural identities, nor do they have a tendency to reify dominant ideologies or *meta-narratives* (like masculine hegemony, or patriarchy) that have historically framed the construction and display of identity. Fornäs (1995) brilliantly captures the experience of living in self-referencing cultural webs by describing how one perpetually lives in the 'crossfire of contradictory messages'.

From the above perspectives on late modernity, doing one's social identity and having power in Canada may be nothing short of the simulacra Baudrillard (1995) outlines. Muggleton (2000), like Baudrillard, describes the contemporary cultural milieu in Western nations as an endless, 24-hour-a-day supermarket of commodity and ideological style; where identities are not anchored in stable cultural images and systems of physical practice, but attached to transitory images of a liquid self. Straw (1991) describes the cultural movement toward reflexive identity construction and boundary disruption as a general movement into diffuse taste culture lifestyles where people care more about how their consumer purchases create their social identities rather than anything else. In a world perhaps oversaturated by global commodities and the cultural flow of consumables, one must thus question whether stable, intersubjective understandings of (gendered) identities are possible (Lash, 1999). If this is the case, how can hegemony be linked to masculine identities in the manners by which Connell (2005) and others have described?

Let's start to answer the question by explaining what may have happened to my liquidly modern, decentred friend Jeb. Given the social trends and breaks in culture I have discussed in this chapter, it seems as if late modernism created what sociologist of health, illness, and bioethics Arthur Frank (1995) refers to as 'narrative wreckage' in his masculine life. Frank posits that all lived experience is a story. We live, breathe, communicate, and perceive through storytelling. It's how we know who we are, and assign meaning to everything we do in life. We simply do not live outside of the language(s) that enframe and mediate our worlds of experience. Patriarchy, hegemony, and masculinity are all narrations codified by social institutions, everyday practices, and forms of physical culture, and are disseminated through media. But as stories, they are vulnerable. Stories are retold, altered, broken, and redefined, and they develop a million fissures over time. New narrations about gender, identity, and power, for example, may be told that push traditional stories about them to the margins. When new stories, new ways of thinking, new ways of telling gender and power emerge, stories of the past may fall to pieces along with the institutional practices that have recounted them for ages. Such is the nature of liquid, late modernity. Many, many, many narrations of masculinity now exist. When there is no longer a standard social script to learn about masculinity and its relationship to power, doubt ensues for some men. This is what Faludi (1999) means when she describes how men lost their moral compass in the world during the last three decades. They are not sure how masculinity fits into social scripts, how it is performed, if it is powerful, and if it is appropriate.

Frank (1995) argues that a major life upheaval or break in identity creates a *narrative rupture* of one's self-image; this is a point from which the life-course is shifted into a new narrative trajectory. In simpler terms, narrative rupture happens when an event or set of events occurs in a person's life that changes social identity permanently. Frank explains how, for example, when a person is diagnosed with a critical illness like cancer, their story as a healthy person is changed forever. From the point of diagnosis onward, they will always be a person with (or recovering from) cancer. The long-term, late modern fragmentation of masculine hegemony and patriarchy in Canada creates sweeping narrative ruptures for particular men. From Frank's perspective, men who perceive a crisis of masculine identity experience a general loss of *author-ity* for narrating their selves as powerful men. Literally, the cultural story about men, masculinity, and hegemony they were taught or read about in early life did not materialize in their adulthood. Jeb is in doubt about who he is not only because he is a product of late modern ornamental cultures, but because complicitly hegemonic male identities like his were the most vulnerable to narrative wreckage. Alternative stories about male hegemony told by women and marginalized men through the 1970s to the 2000s challenged the social privilege of men like Jeb in particular. Reflect back upon the standard-of-living data introduced at the beginning of this chapter. Truly hegemonic men in the upper echelons of political economic power of Canadian society have been (until very recently with the global collapse of the banking industries and the fall of many lending empires), unscathed by late modernism at either a material or an ideological level. But by contrast, the story of normative masculinity for generations of men in the middle (i.e., complicitly hegemonic men in the urban, White, middle classes), has been attacked, deconstructed, and recast from all sides. These men's roles, identities, and statuses were rather loosely and lazily attached to patriarchal authority. Late modernism and the decentering of unquestionable masculine hegemony in most social settings has turned over these men's apple carts. There is narrative wreckage all around. From this narrative wreckage, stories about crisis emerge. Jeb cannot relate to late modern women, for example, because he understands little about the gendering of identity, desire, and power in late modern society. The absence of his traditionally role-bound family and the lingering presence of his loss force him to encounter a culture he had been cognitively and emotionally ignorant of for most of his adult life.

In *Revisions: Gender and Sexuality in Late Modernity* (2002), Lisa Adkins writes that stories about crisis like Charlie's and Jeb's develop as part of a contemporary nostalgia about the 'good old' days of masculine hegemony. Men who fear that their power to narrate male identity and power has vanished experience what Lyotard (1979) articulates as a projection into/from *throwness*: a placement into the void of late modern hyper-subjectivity. Crisis stories are narrations of what Foucault (1981) refers to as the death of the subject in the *History of Sexuality*, and the dissolution of permanent forms of identity within heterotopic spaces—*heterotopia* is a word coined by Foucault (1967) that refers to a space that is outside traditionally normative, or hegemonic institutional zones. Foucault articulates several possible types of heterotopia spaces:

i) *Crisis heterotopias* are separate spaces like a boarding school or a motel room where activities like coming of age or a honeymoon take place out of sight;
ii) *Heterotopias of deviation* are institutions where we place individuals whose behaviour is outside the norm (hospitals, asylums, prisons, rest homes, cemeteries);
iii) Heterotopia can be *a single real place* that juxtaposes several spaces. A garden is a heterotopia because it is a real space meant to be a microcosm of different environments with plants from around the world;
iv) *Heterotopias of time* such as museums enclose in one place objects from all times and styles; and,
v) *Heterotopias of ritual or purification* are spaces that are isolated and penetrable yet not freely accessible like a public place. To get in one must have permission.

A growing number of men in Canada are immersed in Foucault's crisis heterotopias. Being in a crisis heterotopia involves one's social dislocation from a long-term gender story about masculinity and power and where it is appropriately enacted (e.g., social institutions). Crisis heterotopias produce narrations about masculine status, identity, and place in a world marked by blurred socio-cultural boundaries, spaces, and selves. If my standard narrative masculine script is no longer tenable in total in the late modern landscape, and I should/could reflexively create my own, newly liquid masculine self, how do I actually do it? What anchors my identity? How can I enact power if masculinity is no longer my universal ticket into the clubhouse of privilege? Fromm (1941) suggests that when the conditions of (late) modernity exert their force on us, an overall fear of freedom (or too much subjectivity) ensues. When we have too much choice to to make new identities and to search for status and power in new ways, we immediately fear flying without a predetermined cultural script that tells us how to think, feel, and act. The ontological instability of late modernity allows for hyper-individualism and a sense of self-importance in people—what Niedzviecki (2004) calls the 'Hello, I'm special because I am different' generational mentality. This can produce tremendous existential anxiety for many men. Such projection into such existential throwness may explain the nostalgic undertone in crisis discourses. In a world where men are free to redefine the self in multiply masculine ways, logic dictates that more than one man might long for a hyper-simplified and seemingly better hegemonic past.

Although it is a predictably tough French sociological concept to employ, Lyotard's (1989) notion of *scapeland* equally screams out to me when I review my ongoing empirical research on crisis narratives and the narrative wreckage that is late modern masculinity. In truth, my understanding of how crises are comprised of spectacular presences and absences is based on my reading of Lyotard. Scapeland is an experiential state of radical impermanence, emptiness, and unmarked space. Lyotard's scapeland is that which 'is' before description and definition; it is that which appears as the erasure of an ideological or narrative support (Lyotard, 1989: 216–17). Scapeland is the absence of direction and destination provided by cultural scripts or modes of thinking and understanding. With reference to the masculinity crisis, it is a generational mode of experience based on a mindset of masculine emptiness (absence of surety about what is masculine), mixed with a longing for the known and stable hegemonically real space of the past; it is a desire to remedy feelings of a 'present absence'. The scapeland of late modern life forces some men to enter a gender frontier that needs to be written. Encountering the openness and emptiness of frontier scapelands can be seriously frightening stuff!

Jock Young's 2007 book, *The Vertigo of Late Modernity*, also captures what is frightening about living in a cultural scapeland for men like Jeb and others. Young explains that the looseness of meaning and identity in scapelands breeds a pervasive zeitgeist among men, of the fear of losing all of one's social statuses and sources of cultural power, and thus being cast out of social networks. It is the fear of losing one's seat at the head table of society. Young's thoughts draw into sharp relief the ultimate paradox of late modernity, and for me, one of the defining reasons why (gender) crisis discourses emerge. Despite our collective participation in and celebration of self-obsessed late modern liquid societies, the thing we all fear the most is losing our most valued collective identities, and of being too alone with our own hyper-subjectivities. Freud's (1962) social psychological classic explanation of life in modern society, written as *Civilization and its Discontents*, has been turned on its head. We no longer hate our cultures because they force us to be social and to lose our individual sense of self. Being left alone to construct one's own individual (gender) identity and the severing of traditional sources of social power and status is what men in crisis fear. Underpinning the bulk of masculinity crisis discourse is, then, a desire for identity fusion and the reconnection of masculinity to stable forms of identity as sources of power. Such men in crisis are the new discontents.

Summary

The solutions men have developed to combat or manage masculine hegemony/identity crises in Canada and elsewhere are fairly common. Most have come to terms with the idea that if late modernism will not allow one to be a universally masculine/hegemonic/authoritarian subject, one can strategically use a range of hybrid masculinities to become quasi-hegemonic in different situations of interaction. A growing number of men learn that there is a deepening and widening of the 'lived milieu of power [chances]' (Grossberg, 1997) in countries like Canada. This is the lynchpin for our analysis of masculinity/power crises offered in the remainder of the book. Contemporary male power is no longer derived primarily at the socio-economic level, but is rather found in one's ability to be a flexible male figure and to recognize and embrace the ontological instability of any identity in late modernity. Power is based, then, on being able to frame one's (masculine) identity in a chameleon-like way, and to embrace, incorporate, and reorder all identities that are struggling for cultural legitimacy. Such men realize that aligning one's sense of performed masculinity, for example, with insurgent gendered, racialized, working class, and other heretofore marginalized identities and related physical practices can make one appear as culturally progressive, cool, sensitive, moral, genuine, correct, or liberal in one context or another; each of these become techniques for achieving power in a liquid modern, reflexive identity–based society. An individual man listens to rap music and wears hip-hop clothing, engages in a full range of hyper-feminized body grooming practices, and fleetingly participates in neo-working class subcultures like Straightedge. The ontological instability of late modernity creates the possibility for men in crisis to seize any and all forms of identity as a means of gaining cultural power. The decoupling of political economic hegemony from men/masculinity has created social locations where being ornamental, in Faludi's (1999) terms, actually works as power. Such is the nature of *pastiche hegemony* in late modernity. What is once perceived as a culture of crisis (i.e., the implosion of dominant masculinities) is transformed into practices of power. These men are far, far beyond the masculinity crisis.

They resemble Neo, the protagonist in the movie *The Matrix*, who learns he can actually stop bullets with his mind after he finally understands how to manipulate structural conditions underpinning the make-believe computer world.

Pastiche hegemony is power earned bit by bit, metre by metre, interaction by interaction in the scapeland of late modern life. It is, as Andrews (2002) notes, a 'radically contextual' form of power. Pastiche masculine hegemony draws on and seeks to exploit the structural and cultural conditions of residual patriarchy in countries like Canada (i.e., enduring forms of material, political, and cultural privilege for men, in general), but equally takes advantage of new and socially lauded forms of doing reflexive identity to win power. The late modern man is powerful when he finally accepts and wields his ability to change the nature and performance of his masculinity when need be, when emergent situations demand him to enact gender in a variety of ways. This type of hegemony is power through the exercise of flexible identity within small group contexts. It is never fully fixed, stable or uncontested. Pastiche hegemony operates by incorporating and co-opting the widest range of gendered identities and performances possible. This includes a full range of femininities and heretofore marginalized masculinities. Through the remainder of this book, we examine and explore the boundaries of crisis narratives in a range of social settings, and contextualize within them attempts to win pastiche hegemony by men. In these discussions, we uncover how men narrate masculine anomie, nihilism, escape, indifference, hyperbole, and recycling as physical cultural techniques for doing pastiche hegemony.

Discussion Questions

1. Do you think men still have the majority of social power in Canada because they still tend to dominate the upper echelons of the business world?
2. Do you think the truly hegemonic man exists in Canadian society? Why or why not?
3. Who is the most powerful man you know, personally, in your life? What makes him powerful in your eyes?
4. Is a sociological statement about the relationship between men, masculinity, and power incomplete if it totally ignores the biological and psychological characteristics of men? Why or why not?
5. If you had to design a study of men in Canadian society, what main sociological problem would it involve and why?

Key Readings

Adkins, L. (2002). *Revisions: Gender and Sexuality in Late Modernity.* New York: McGraw-Hill. This book is a critical text in contemporary feminist social theory. It brings together recent sociology of late modernity, particularly sociologies of

1 MEN, POWER, AND PASTICHE HEGEMONY

reflexivity, aesthetics, and de-traditionalization, with a consideration of transformations of identity, especially transformations of gender identities. In so doing it puts
forward a distinctive thesis, namely that within late modernity gender and sexuality
are being reworked in terms of categories of reflexivity and risk.

Connell, R., and J. Messerschmidt. (2005). 'Hegemonic masculinity: Rethinking the
concept.' *Gender & Society*, 19: 829–59. Connell and Messerschmidt's article
engages in a comprehensive review of the major debates and controversies surrounding the use of the concept of hegemonic masculinity in contemporary sociology. The authors revisit the genesis and canonization of the concept, and suggest
critical points of revision given current social trends and forces. Its importance is
in its outline of how traditional modes of doing hegemonic masculinity have been
partially fractured and destabilized.

Frank, A. (1995). *The Wounded Storyteller: Body, Illness and Ethics*. Chicago: University
of Chicago Press. Frank's widely acclaimed book focuses on how social experience
is made and defined as meaningful through the process of story-telling. The book
focuses on how the normative story of peoples' lives is broken when illness strikes,
and how their identities become subsequently framed by bio-medical stories and
discourses. Contained across the pages of the work is a sensitive and powerful
account of how social stories about illness rarely openly reflect the lived experiences,
emotions, and identities of those living through illness.

Giddens, A. (1998). *The Third Way: The Renewal of Social Democracy*. Cambridge: Polity.
Giddens' book is one of the most important statements in the 1990s on the rise of
neo-liberalism in Western societies. In the book, Giddens also makes a contribu-
tion to the debate now going on in many countries about the future of truly social
democratic politics. Giddens discusses the dissolution of the welfare consensus
that dominated in industrial countries up to the late 1970s; the final discrediting
of Marxism; and the profound social, economic, and technological changes that
helped bring these about. Giddens subtly links arguments about the rise of neo-
liberalism to the notion of a risk society.

Gramsci, A. (1971). *Selections from the Prison Notebooks*. London: Lawrence and Wishart.
This selection of Gramsci's writing contains his most important thoughts that were
written during his imprisonment during the Italian fascist regime. It includes 'The
Intellectuals', 'Texts on Education', 'Notes on Italian History', 'The Modern Prince',
'State and Civil Society', 'Americanism and Fordism', and notes on the philosophy
of praxis, together with an informative introduction on the Italian Communist movement in the first decades of the twentieth century. In this collection, Gramsci's theory
of hegemony in class societies is fully presented, together with his interpretation of
Marxism both in philosophy and in his analysis of the modern world.

Web Links

Statistics Canada (www.statcan.gc.ca/start-debut-eng.html). Quite simply, the starting
point for anyone interested in doing macro-level analysis of sexed and gendered
power differentials in Canadian society.

Men's Bibliography (http://mensbiblio.xyonline.net/). The best online resource for academic information on men's issues and the sociology of masculinity.

Key Terms

Essentialism: A commonly held socio-cultural belief that one's biological character-istics are, or should be, linked to one's cultural identities, statuses, and roles. In relation to the study of gender, essentialist ideas hold that your attributes and social positions as a gendered (male or female) person are directly correlated with sup-posed 'natural' strengths and weaknesses you possess as a sexed (man or woman) person.

Heterotopia: A term coined by Michel Foucault referring to a place, state, or process in which a person or a group of people participate with uncertain, unknown, and unfamiliar feelings. The notion of heterotopia is similar to Victor Turner's (1969) notion of liminality; a process or situation someone enters without knowing the outcome, and in which one's identity may significantly change as a result of the process.

Life politics: Literally the policies, rules, and reflexive practices organizing one's life, or the lives of a group. One's life politics can refer to the styles of living one chooses and how these styles of living are intended to communicate one's sense of self-identity to others.

Meta-narratives: A grand story or set of cultural beliefs structuring social practices and ways of thinking in a society. Examples of traditional or modernist meta-narratives in society are religious ideology, capitalism, and science, each of which became ways of seeing, organizing, and knowing the world.

Residual patriarchy: In basic terms, the trace elements of historical patriarchy in Canada, as evidenced in often hidden or silent ways in social institutions, cultural practices, or mass media representations of life. Residual patriarchy is an enduring but fractured and contested institutional structure of political economy of privilege for men in Canadian society. Social roles and access points to power positions in society are indeed shifting within these structures, but perhaps not at the acceler-ated rate masculinity crisis–advocates suggest.

2 Violence, Residue, and Pastiche Hegemony

Chapter Objectives

This chapter introduces and critically explores the following:

- ⊛ The debated relationship between sex, gender, and violence
- ⊛ The moral panic regarding young men and violence in Canada
- ⊛ The physical cultural 'hidden curriculum' linking masculinity and bullying
- ⊛ The habituation of violent spectacles in contemporary popular cultures
- ⊛ The proliferation of 'self-violent' mindsets and activities among men

Phil was a friend of mine in Grade 8. I say 'friend' in that we knew each other, rode the same drab bus back and forth to junior high school, shared several classes, and cheered for the Montreal Canadiens. But we were not good mates. Like clockwork, Phil and I, and other classmates, would wait for fifteen minutes or so every afternoon for the school bus to gather us and shuttle us to our nearby suburban homes in Bedford, Nova Scotia. Small flocks of us would wait patiently for our number 24A bus to Eaglewood, peppered across a small hill full of moss and rock at the end of the school's circular driveway. Our school bags were neatly and hierarchically lined along the sidewalk as a makeshift queue. Every day, an oily-haired Elvis impersonator of a bus driver named Cecil would wheel his orange bus around the school parking lot, thrust open the rickety door, and shout at us to scuttle in as fast as possible in his raspy, rattly, smoker's voice. But as the sun beamed down on a Thursday afternoon in late May of 1984, Cecil's bus did not arrive at 3:26 p.m. as it usually did. Even by 3:45 p.m., no Cecil in sight. To alleviate the angst and boredom, one of the senior bullies in the school's pecking order, a curly-haired, 15-year-old fear captain named Henry, decided he would pin down my friend Phil on the grass and paint a white, Liquid Paper moustache on his upper lip. Anyone could have been Henry's target. Phil was most likely separated from the herd by misfortune alone. Within a minute and without a word of resistance, the degradation ceremony reached its inevitable conclusion. Phil escaped during a chorus of laughter from Henry's henchmen, and he ran in tears to the school. 'Asshole,' I remembered uttering, barely loud enough to be heard. Henry caught the insult and I immediately materialized on his victimization radar screen. 'Shit,' I remember thinking to myself, 'now I'm going to get it even worse than that poor bastard Phil.'

Henry was in love with my sister Bronwyn (he would sing a television commercial jingle to her on the school bus—from an A&W hamburger advertisement from the early 1980s that proclaimed 'Achin' for the Bacon'), so I normally carried a flimsy sort of diplomatic immunity amongst the ranks of junior thugs in our school. But I had always been an easy target for bullies. I have the slender build and bone structure of my Irish mum's side of the family. I had a flair for British, romantically *avant-garde* fashion as a young teenager and was the first boy of my age in the school to pierce his ear. I gelled my hair before the other boys did, wrote poetry before I was twelve, and never wished to participate in sports involving power or aggression. I had always been top of my class academically, involved in drama, and loved student council. Despite the fact that I chased and dated about two dozen girls in junior high and played on several sports teams (like soccer and hockey), I was targeted and harassed on a weekly basis. I supposed the simple appearance of my quasi-feminine masculine difference had been enough. I never experienced anything physically violent or terribly abusive, just constant belittling and badgering. I've been called 'fag' about seventeen million times in my life—even to this day, when some of my students learn I'm married with children, they pull a very puzzled look. Henry, in fact, called me 'King of the Fags' on a regular basis.

Henry turned on his heel after hearing my 'asshole' utterance. As he prowled by, deliberating over what torture he would inflict and the speed of the kill, I completely froze and turned my gaze the other way. The physical punishment I would receive did not frighten me. I only prayed that everyone else was looking away. His cold, nicotine-stained right hand grabbed me by the back of the neck and he sat down beside me on the edge of the sidewalk. The force of his arm pressed my head downward, and he said, 'kiss it, kiss the ground'. I did, he released me and walked away without another word. The next day he sat on the bus beside me asking if I had watched the hockey game the night before. Phil, by contrast, did not show up for school until Monday. I went on as if nothing happened, because that's what kids like me did, and still do today.

Kissing the proverbial ground is a masculine rite of passage in a million different contexts. Whether one playfully learns to submit to one's father while wrestling on the living room floor; to not speak back to a male teacher; to accept the orders of a sports coach; or to walk down the opposite side of the hallway from older boys, part of the learned code of masculinity is deferral to those who are in some manner above you on the hegemonic masculine ladder. Such is the lesson Sutherland (1947) exposed in his theory of *differential association* many decades ago. Feminist scholars since the 1960s have equally noted how the power mongering, resource gathering, commodity accumulating, and sexual conquesting that comprises everyday life might be categorized as the social practice of (male) *bullying:* of acquiring one's wants, needs, or desires, or extending one's will over others through aggressive, exclusionary, or quasi-exploitive social means. Social order, cultural norms, rituals, and mores governing social practice are largely established through explicit and implicit forms of bullying. The practice and purpose of bullying is generationally similar, but those in charge of socially legitimate bullying and the discourses framing its practice shift; such, one might argue, is the basis of the 1990s masculinity crisis.

As noted in the Introduction and chapter 1, traditional masculine power and authority is largely earned by the deployment of accepted social, physical, mental, and emotional bullying by males. Such is, as Elias (2004) writes in his treatise on the civilizing of Western men, one of the bases for establishing a hierarchy of order within a species seemingly preoccupied with violence. Pastiche hegemony is won on large or small scales through one's ability to bully first men, and then women in a socially accepted—or at least tolerated—manner. 'Healthy' bullying sorts the herd and inspires greatness in others. In one context, bullying may be construed as economic leadership and representative of an entrepreneurial spirit, in another the drive to find love, in another it stands for sporting drive and prowess, and in yet another it is constructed as part of one's role as a mythic family or community protector. Therefore, bullying is a personality characteristic associated with one's gender, and is part of any accompanying role set. Hegemonic men are, traditionally, the types of men who bully and 'get away with it'. Farr (1988) argues that male superiority and privilege is often won when men bond with the strong, while avoiding and deriding the so-called weak. Such links between violence, bullying, masculinity, and power are enduring and historically prevalent in Canada. One might suggest they comprise part of the meta-narrative of masculine power and authority. The meta-narrative of divine hegemonic masculinity in countries like Canada has been seriously questioned. Feminist scholars like Catharine MacKinnon (1989, 2005) and Dorothy Smith (1987) illustrate how rigidly guarded hierarchies of power within business are referred to as natural, or colloquially laughed about as the old boys' club. As such structures of patriarchy were increasingly challenged, we used catchy terms like the 'glass ceiling' as a means of objectively documenting oppressive power structures within the economy. Today people refer to these imbalances and blocks in more aggressive political terms, calling them systematic discrimination, or outright violations of human rights. The ability for men to economically, politically, and culturally bully (*qua* masculine right) is no longer a universally accepted part of the social script, and discourses about gendered power expose those inequalities as deeply intolerable.

Indeed, as Faludi (1999) documents, one of the primary lines of male backlash in the 1980s and 1990s centres on the discursive (i.e., framed by language) link between hegemonic masculinity, bullying, the victimization of women, and violence. While our teachers, parents, and brothers knew about kids like Henry in our school, these boys were largely tolerated in my era. Today they are the targets of expulsion, psychological counselling, ostracism, folk devilling in the media, and police monitoring—often simply for what they 'might' do to others (Acland, 1995). Criminologists, sociologists, psychologists, social workers, and journalists use terms like sociopath, 'lost boys', and 'super-predators' in reference to boys who are at risk or on the edge of losing control in a world that no longer tolerates their testosterone-infused incorrigibility (Fox and Levin, 2004). The general exposure of patriarchy as a bullying, alienating, and far too often violent culture of social order has transformed into a general discourse about masculinity as inherently violent and bully-oriented (Tiger, 2000; Hise, 2004). A massive jump in prevailing discourses about bullying and its link to power achievement has been made. Perhaps the ghosts of Columbine or Montreal's École Polytechnique still haunt public consciousness and spread fear about what young boys may do next in their unbridled quest to assert themselves in a cultural milieu that defines them as social junk.

Through and past the masculinity crisis of the 1990s, the subject of boys, men, and violence has been much debated, hyberbolized, and showcased as a symptom of the need for cultural gender reform. Studies directly linking the social performance of a stereotypical, bullying-based masculinity with violence are both extensive and almost singular in their gender analysis. School violence, gang violence, knife and gun violence, drug-related violence, sexual violence, sports violence, theft-related violence, domestic violence, crowd protest violence, violence against the environment, faith-related violence, violence against children, war and genocide, violence against animals, violence at work, hate crimes, and homicide (Collier, 1998; Hearn, 1998; Walklate, 2004) have all been theorized as essentially male-perpetrated acts. As Belknap (2006) reminds us in her book *The Invisible Woman: Gender, Crime and Justice*, even the idea that women can be violent like men is often forgotten in Canadian society. Crisis advocates have been quick to dismiss unilateral depictions of violence as a problem of masculinity. As a result, what 'male' violence means and indicates has become a battle of language, a discursive war illustrating the instability of many historical truths about what counts as legitimate social behaviour for males where the nature of male bullying as a means of securing power has been interrogated at length. To initially interpret how the discursive war regarding male power/violence/bullying has been cast, the work of post-modernist theorist Jean-Francois Lyotard is especially helpful.

Critical sociologists of the 1980s and 1990s used Lytoard's work in the general analysis and deconstruction of historically dominant truths underpinning modernist ways of thinking, about such themes as progress, universal truth, and biological essentialism. Lyotard's (1979) work is generally characterized by a persistent opposition to universal truths and *meta-narratives* that served to create and reinforce false and oppressive categories of difference between people (i.e., men/women, White/Black, upper class/working class, etc.). He is fiercely critical of many of the universalist claims of the Enlightenment, and those who have adopted Lyotard's thinking argue how many modernist ways of living are predicted on exploitive false realities (i.e., such as the natur-alness of patriarchy and male domination). Most famously, in *The Postmodern Condition: A Report on Knowledge* (1979a), he argues that postmodern times are marked by a diffuse incredulity toward such meta-narratives. These meta-narratives (also called *grand narratives*) are large-scale theories and philosophies of the world, such as the progress of history, the knowability of everything by science, and the possibility of absolute freedom. Lyotard argues that we have ceased to believe that narratives of this kind are adequate to represent and contain us all. We have become alert to difference, diversity, and the potential limits of our grand human aspirations, beliefs, and desires, and for that reason the postmodern age is characterized by an abundance of micro-narratives: claims to knowledge and truth at a far more local and temporary level. The masculinity crisis, we have already seen, is arguably a symptom of the break-down in the collective trust in the hegemonic masculine meta-narrative.

According to many advocates of postmodernism, meta-narratives have lost their power to convince. They are only stories told to legitimize various versions of 'truth'. As such, what we now see as masculine bullying can no longer be reconciled as part of teaching boys and men to be dominant or normative authority figures. The meta-narrative of the natural patriarchal order has been symbolically dismantled. With the transition from modern to postmodern, Lyotard (1979) proposes that meta-narratives like patriarchy must give way to *petits récits*, or more modest and tentative narratives. For a theorist such as Lyotard, then, discourses about violence, bullying, and masculinity are 'language games' (sometimes also called 'phrase regimens'), played between multiple communities in the struggle for social power. So, the masculinity crisis has been fuelled by an inability to own systems of language, or put another way, the representation of traditional masculinity (and power) in countries like Canada as normative, beneficial, and impervious to criticism. As Lyotard argues in *Just Gaming* (1985) and *The Différend* (1983), universal statements of truth about masculinity are not allowed in a world that has lost faith in meta-narratives.

The battle over the bully-essence of Western patriarchy is a discursive language game waged by those who have been traditionally victimized by domi-nant constructions of masculinity. Micro, or 'petit', discourses about social practices as illegitimate forms of male privilege (or bullying) are part of what stirred the masculinity crisis of the 1990s in schools, churches, government offices, businesses, families, leisure spheres, and elsewhere. Increasingly inter-rogated was the link between male bullying as an ideology of power, and its manifestation through physical violence. As someone whose vocation includes studying masculinity, I am overwhelmed by how quickly and deeply academic discourses about masculinity from the 1970s onward easily coupled the vast majority of masculinities in Canada with violence and crime. Academic and popular discourses about the culture/order of male bullying in the West became fixated on the supposed interrelation of *physical violence, crime, and exploitation*. Late-twentieth-century backlashes against feminism, a full spate of men's movements, and crisis advocates often cited the irresponsible empirical association between men and violence as a stimulator of growing alienation, resentment, and frustration among men who felt unjustly stereotyped as bullies and aggressors (Pease, 2005).

The purpose of the rest of this chapter is twofold. In the first instance, I examine the sort of moral panicking about masculinity and violence that peppered media and criminological discourses in the first wave of male crisis (circa the late 1980s). Portrayals of men as naturally violent beings are frequently cited by crisis advocates as symptoms of a culture symbolically and discursively at war with men. The purpose of the discussion is not to document, in any empirical or objective manner, correlations between men and violence, nor is it to legitimate crisis sentiment. The aim is to discuss how discourses of men as inherently or naturally violent (re)emerged *prior* to the claimed masculinity crisis. No group or category of men escaped scrutiny. Men on the fringes of the social order and power structures, though, were more heavily criticized than others. At the crux of the matter are the masculine language games played regarding patriarchy, bullying, and violence in Canada, and how the deconstruction of the first term lead to the discursive amplification of the second and third.

In the second instance, the chapter questions the physical cultural *hidden curriculum* linking masculinity and bullying, which endures in Canada despite the ongoing academic and popular cultural deconstruction of hegemonic masculinity. Despite a multitude of interinstitutional discourses about bullying, it is still a central physical cultural technique for 'doing' a range of masculinities. But strangely enough, burgeoning self-violent male subcultures have cropped up through the crisis as aggressive technique for winning pastiche hegemony in micro spaces: that is, for securing a hegemonic masculinity in one small part of one's life. In simple terms, cadres of young men now do violence against their selves, or select others, as a way to reassert control over what counts as healthy post-crisis masculinity. As I argue in the chapter, the culture of male self-bullying has blossomed as a *spectacle* (Debord, 1967) of residual patriarchy and is potentially symptomatic of generations of young men who are convinced that violence is the solution.

Masculinity, Violence, and Moral Panicking: The Usual Suspects

An undergraduate student of mine once asked, as part of the preparation for his fourth year honours thesis on men and violence, where he should begin reading in the subject area. What a daunting task. For well over a hundred years, academics have scrutinized the professed biological, psychological, and sociological links connecting men to violence. No single subject, save for work and economics, receives as much attention in masculinity literature as violence. For gender theorists and criminologists, the concepts of masculinity and violence are practically intertwined. Cohen and Harvey (2006) point out that in the 1990s masculinity/violence/crime literature, too often is the precise link between masculinity and violence rigorously explained or understood to be there. Academics, social control agents, and everyday citizens may offer theories as to why, on average, men are far more likely to engage in physically violent behaviours than women, but no one seems to have isolated the precise way that gendered identities become linked with violence. Popular theories range in scope and detail from genetic 'bad seed' arguments to over-socialization to criminal values in small, hyper-male groups. Data from the Uniform Crime Reports in Canada consistently reveal that boys and men are more likely to be both the perpetrators and victims of violence than girls or women, with notable exceptions like sexual assault in the case of victimization. But what such trends mean with regard to gender socialization, identification, performance, and representation are neither clear nor consistent.

Socio-cultural accounts of masculinity and violence can be lumped quite crudely into four conceptual camps. The first, and most traditional, set of accounts come from theories that link masculinity and violence to *structural and cultural pathologies that prohibit men from fulfilling their social scripts as providers, caretakers, and authority figures. Social disorganization theories, anomie and strain theories,* and *conflict theories* each present, at their very core, a portrait of male perpetrators as those who have failed to become normative, economically and culturally integrated members of society (Gomme, 2006). These men are not born bad, but they engage in interpersonal violence (e.g., fist-fighting, partner abuse, property destruction) as a response to alienation from the structural and cultural mainstream. Accounts of rising rates of violence against women in the 1990s were explained by crisis theorists as unfortunate side effects of the structural and cultural displacement of men from positions of power (White-head, 2002). While their use to explain theories of white male violence wanes in the sociological literature, their deployment in the study of violence among ethnic minority males in Canada and elsewhere continues with great legitimacy (Awkward, 2002; Hatty, 2000).

A second set of accounts regarding masculinity and violence is, according to a majority of my students, the most sociological. Learning theories depict the male perpetrator of violence as one whose understanding of masculinity, and the set of behaviours accompanying it, includes belief in the ability to wield violence against others. Men who abuse violently have been beaten by their fathers, socialized within communities beset with male role models who are violent, watch large amounts of male violence on television or in movies, or exist in cultures where the right to be violent as a male is linked to a sense of mythic patriarchal power and control (DeKeseredy and Schwartz, 2005). In brief, they roughly imitate what they have learned to be male-appropriate violence. Therefore, these explanations of aggression and violence address issues of gender-centric attitudes, and maintain that these behaviours are learned and brought about by a combination of contextual and situational factors. The social context of the dysfunctional family, for example, produces stress, aggressive personalities, and violent behaviour. Or the situational factors like alcohol or drug abuse, financial problems, or marital infidelity accommodate the use of aggression and violence. Probably the most familiar of these social learning theories is the 'intergenerational transmission of family violence' explanation, which contends that people who have witnessed or suffered physical family violence when growing up will have a greater likelihood of living in a violent domestic situation later on in life. There are also associations between those people who have been sexually abused, especially boys, becoming sexually abusive teenagers and adults. Dating back to the early 1920s, sociologists have also argued that violence may be learned intimately as part of the ethos of distinct subcultures or gangs. Many different studies illustrate how male violence becomes part of the deliberate signifying practices of self-labelled male outsiders (for specific examples, see Sutherland's [1947] classic theory of differential association, or the style-subculture research of Hebdige [1979]).

Third, fields of psychology and social psychology, perhaps the two most influential in shaping public opinion about the link between masculinity and violence, contain dozens of theoretical explanations linking men to violence. They are too extensive and diverse to detail here. Suffice it to say that each has, at its base, a construction of a man who engages in patterned or repeated violence as one who possess a psychopathology (Flowers, 2003). Whereas social psychologists have clearly accounted for the situated contexts giving rise to relatively unique instances of the loss of impulse control (i.e., frustration-aggression theory; relative deprivation theory), a majority of existing popular theories in this area portray the male perpetrator as one who has an inability to identify with others, a hatred or disgust for women, experienced abuse himself, a strong need to control others, a borderline personality, an anti-social personality, or a psychological disorder such as post-traumatic stress, poor impulse control, low self-esteem or substance abuse (Copenhaver, Lash, and Eisler, 2000). Even the most influential theory of violence and crime in the second half of the twentieth century, Gottfredson and Hirschi's (1990) *general theory of crime,* sees poor impulse control and self-regulation abilities as common in young boys (and future criminals), as a pathological masculine state of being.

Finally, toward the end of the twentieth century, sociobiological theories of violence made a triumphant comeback within the academy. The term *sociobiology* was introduced in Wilson's *Sociobiology: The New Synthesis* (1975), in the application of evolutionary theory to social behaviour. Sociobiologists claim that social behaviours have been shaped by natural selection for reproductive success, and they attempt to reconstruct the evolutionary histories of particular behaviours or behavioural strategies. Sociobiology is based on the idea that behaviours like violence are at least partly inherited at the level of one's genes and can be affected by Darwinian natural selection. It starts with the idea that these behaviours have evolved over time, similar to the way that physical traits are thought to have evolved. Therefore, sociobiological theories generally predict that humans will act in ways that have proven to be evolutionarily successful over time, which can among other things result in the formation of complex social processes that have proven to be conducive to evolutionary 'fitness' (i.e., successfully passing on one's genes to another generation). Therefore, when one engages in violence it is both a genetically inherited disposition, and is a behaviour that makes sense in a given context because it will allow survival of the gene pool. Thus, violence makes sense because it is an environmentally adaptive strategy that ensures genetic fitness.

Sociobiologists are quick to cite how, across time and national boundaries, males are consistently found to be more violent than females by a very, very large margin. The essential and reductionist sociobiological explanation accounts for the sex difference in violent behaviour through the apparent asymmetry in fitness variation between the sexes. Male fitness is limited by access to fertile females and female fitness is limited by access to resources. A female could copulate with a different partner every night without increasing her fitness, whereas a male doing the same would increase his fitness tremendously. This is why males throughout most of the animal kingdom seek copulations with multiple partners despite the risk of injury and death from competitors and why they have evolved the mechanisms (most specifically, testosterone-driven size, strength, and aggression) to pursue that strategy. This is also why female animals have evolved tendencies to choose the males most likely to provide them with the best genes and the ability to provide parental investment; which may have been achieved through violent means. Given our evolutionary history of much greater parental investment by females compared with males and our sexually dimorphic reproductive strategies, it is almost impossible to imagine human males and females *not* evolving widely different propensities to engage in violence. Dawkins (1976) added to this thinking by introducing the idea of the 'selfish gene' as the basis for violence in males. Alongside sociobiological (by the end of the twentieth century, called 'evolutionary psychology') accounts of violence in men arose more aggressively biological theories that cited gene problems in men such as the Dopamine Receptor (D4), Serotonin, and MAOA genes as key predictors of violence (Rowe, 2002). At the same time, thinly veiled sociobiological theories of the 'superpredator' killer or family annihilators located the propensity toward violence in men at genetic rather than environmental or social roots (Fox and Levin, 2004).

Crisis theorists tend to have strong affinities for any and all of the clusters of theory outlined above. Violence among men in a cultural time of male crisis can easily be reconciled and justified using any of the above theoretical frameworks. Each of the above clusters of thinking provide rational theories for explaining male violence, as they are largely equation-based, positivist, control-oriented ways of thinking about violence and aggression. Violence is almost always a solution to a problem that helps a boy or man alleviate isolation, anger, doubt, or anxiety. Whether men are violent because they are pushed out of power positions in society, exposed to pathological cultural conditions in impoverished communities, mentally and emotionally victimized in a culture which preaches an impossible standard of male hegemony and embodiment on the one hand while castigating it on the other, or ascribes male violence to uncontrollable genes, the science of male aggression certainly fits in well with crisis mentalities. While criminologists and deviancy theories have on the one hand overly, and empirically inaccurately, theorized violence and aggression as a male phenomenon, the overemphasis is substantial fodder for crisis subjectivities.

Violence, Men, and Media Panics

Stanley Cohen (1972) describes a *folk devil* as a person or group of people who are portrayed in the media as cultural outsiders, and who are blamed for crimes or generally scapegoated for other sorts of social problems. The description of folk devils though the media as miscreants, and their subsequent targeting by social control agents, frequently intensifies into a mass movement that is called a *moral panic*. When a moral panic is in full swing, folk devils are the subject of loosely organized but pervasive campaigns of hostility through gossip, the spreading of urban legends, shunning, and even arrest for anti-social behaviour. Cohen's description of the 'folk devils and moral panic process' has been used extensively by sociologists to account for how cases of male violence have been over-amplified in the mass media and heralded as signifiers of inherent pathologies in gender socialization processes in Canada and the United States (Young and Craig, 1995).

Consider several of the major moral panics about violence involving young men in Canada in the past decade and a half. In the 1980s and 1990s, criminologists and gender theorists widely promoted the notion of a sexual assault cultural pandemic among young men (Davidson and Moore, 2005). Whether one attributes the spike in reported sex assault cases to new modes of reporting sex crimes or actual numeric increases in their incidence is irrelevant to the disturbing crime data of the era. What crisis advocates including Hoff Sommers (2000) and Tiger (2000) lament, however, were the manners by which sex crimes were linked to a mainstream masculinity in a blanket fashion. Despite what men and women often read from certain academics, not all men are either

Box 2.1 ❄ Canadian School Shootings

Few instances of youth violence in the last decade stirred as widespread a moral panic as school shootings. If you were an historian in 2089 reading media accounts of youth violence in the twentieth century you might be lead to believe that students in Canada were at a serious risk of being shot at school. Since 1975, there have been eight reported school shootings. While the events are always tragic and in most cases deadly, it is still an incredibly statistically rare form of male-dominated violence.

Table 2.1 Canadian School Shootings since 1975

School	Location	Date	Persons Killed
Centennial Secondary School	Brampton (ON)	28 May 1975	2
St Pius X High School	Ottawa (ON)	27 October 1975	1
École Polytechnique	Montreal (QC)	6 December 1989	14
Concordia University	Montreal (QC)	24 August 1992	4
W.R. Myers High School	Taber (AB)	28 April 1999	1
Dawson College	Montreal (QC)	13 September 2006	1
C.W. Jefferys Collegiate Institute	Toronto (ON)	23 May 2007	1
Bendale Business and Technical Institute	Toronto (ON)	16 September 2008	0

inclined or predisposed to sexually offending. Easily constructed were assessments of the crimes as prototypical examples of the male quest for dominance over women. Date-rape cultures in high school and universities, along with highly mediated cases of 'sex points gangs' in Canada who emulated the Californian 'Spur Posse' (i.e., subcultures of young men who kept score of how many women with whom they interacted sexually, competed amongst themselves to accumulate the most points), became battleground panics in popular and academic writing. Critical criminologists including Dutton (2006) do not discount troubling rates of sexual assault across North America, but question if the increased attention and potential over-amplification of the crimes as a masculinity issue in the 1980s.

At the same time White Canadian young males were increasingly scrutinized as potential sex criminals, young Black, First Nation, and Asian boys were being progressively portrayed as the face of hedonistic gang violence in Canada. The media, panicking in the late 1980s, described ethnic minority youth as having fully contracted the American gang disease. A 2004 study of youth gangs in Canada conducted by the Astwood Strategy Corporation (*Canadian Police Survey on Youth Gangs*) documented that Canada now has 434 youth gangs with roughly 7,000 members; a huge preponderance of these gangs date back to the early 1990s. As of this study, Ontario accounts for the heaviest gang activity with 216 youth gangs and 3,320 youth gang members. Saskatchewan is second (28 youth gangs and 1,315 members), followed by British Columbia (102 youth gangs and 1,027 members). The vast majority of youth gang members are boys or men (94%) with almost half (48%) of them under the age of 18. The largest proportion of gang members are African-Canadian (25%), followed by First Nations (21%). Normally inferred from these patterns is that young males who are most at risk of joining gangs suffer from the greatest levels of social inequality and disadvantage. Discourses continue to suggest that young males from ethnic minorities that are structurally and culturally discriminated against will engage in gang violence as a means of doing a particularly fatalistic and exaggerated masculinity. These discourses also suggest that these young men's hyper-violent street hegemony compensates for their inability to achieve politically economic male hegemony in 'normal' (i.e., White) male society.

Other criminologists portray these young males as people with nothing to lose, with learned tastes and dispositions for violent thrill-seeking (Katz, 1988; Tittle, 2000). Young men on the fringe with nothing to lose often fight, exhibiting little foresight or concern, with rival crews from neighboring communities. These boys are the most likely to be involved in knife and gun violence in Canada, or associated with drug dealing either directly or indirectly. Indeed, the moral panic about minority masculinity in Canada is flavoured by a focused attention on the links between masculinity, minority membership, and drug-related violence through the use of weapons (Gurr and Ross, 2003). They are the new Skinheads or Crips and Bloods without the publicly lauded subcultural styles or cachet. Not only do gang panic discourses further marginalize young men in minority communities as fringe, at-risk members of the community, they further stereotype masculinity in these communities as atavistic and universally uncontrollable. The young minority male who is integrated into mainstream Canadian society is the wonderful exception rather than the rule; his primitive masculinity is, by some stroke of cultural fortune, 'cured' (Welch et al., 2002). Such discourses are, by even the least critically trained socio-logical eye, products of inferentially racist and xenophobic concerns about increased multiculturalism, immigration, and the changing demographic composition of a Canadian society that is the least 'middle-class White' that it ever has been in its history.

The moral panics about boys and violence in the past 20 years have also been peppered with a popular and academic sentiment that growing numbers of at-risk youth have learned penchants for 'senseless violence', malicious anti-social behaviour, and public disruption (Acland, 1995; Wilson, 2006). What is particularly troubling to youth violence researchers is the degree to which affective (i.e., 'heat of the moment' or emotionally driven) versus instrumental violence (i.e., planned or calculated violence used in furtherance of a personal goal) is seemingly prevalent among 'troubled' young men in urban and suburban areas. Violence predicated on little instrumental or rational grounds is typically baffling for sociologists of crime, gender, and violence. Owing largely to the positivist legacies in the sociology of crime, deviance, and violence, acts that appear to have little economic, cathartic, social-status, or subcultural capital still tend to be theorized rather poorly; frameworks like Tittle's (1995, 2000) control-balance theory are notable exceptions. Schinkel's (2008) analysis of 'senseless crime' similarly argues that burgeoning moral panics about youth violence question how and why young boys are socially driven to experiment with (or merely release) their so-called natural compulsions toward aggressive impulses for little other than a momentary destructive thrill.

The type of organized underground 'fight clubs' portrayed in Chuck Palahniuk's 1999 movie (and 1996 book) of the same name, *Fight Club*, have existed in Canada for the better part of a decade. Beginning in early 2002 with the advent of Web platforms such as MySpace and later YouTube, parents of the boys involved became increasingly aware that organized fist-fighting groups were scattered across their neighbourhoods. Residents in Vancouver, Toronto, Regina, Montreal, and Halifax respectively notified the police and local school authorities that fight clubs, drawing in some cases dozens of participants, were held on school grounds, in local fields or parks, and in mall parking lots. A rash of media articles highlighted the issue as yet another symbol of a generation of 'lost boys' in Canada. A 21 September 2006 television segment on CityTV's (Toronto) six o'clock news portrayed fight clubs as dangerous social outlets for boys with no life aspirations or normative social bonds. The rash of newspaper articles on fight clubs appearing between 2006–8 in the Canadian press suggested this brand of senselessly violent behaviour might foreshadow long-term behavioural problems among legions of boys who feel that overt aggression is acceptable (Purdy, *Regina Leader-Post*, 29 January 2008).

Instances of *happy slapping* are statistically rare forms of violent behaviour among disaffected, bored, and self-indulgent teenage boys. Nevertheless, they too were subjects of brief moral panics in the 2000s. With subcultural roots in the United Kingdom, France, and Germany, happy slapping involves committing a random act of violence (e.g., hitting, punching, kicking, or pushing) against a random person in public. A 8 March 2007 CBC story on happy slapping depicted those responsible as urban vigilantes on the path of wanton terror. Similar case examples of, and moral panics about, 'boys gone bad' cropped up in newspaper articles during the mid-2000s. *Flash mobs* and *flash mob banging* were regularly documented in Toronto and Vancouver. Flash mobs are organized public gatherings involving hundreds of strangers, in some cases, who meet at a designated place and time to engage in a disruptive act. Flash mobs are arranged through virtual means (Internet or cellular networks) and are generally intended as disruptions of the public order. At times, the acts may be as simple as holding up red umbrellas at a crowded intersection on a sunny day, or walking across a private golf course and interrupting play. Other times, as in the case of flash mob banging, the events might have aggressive undertones. Flash mob bangs are staged events where youth (predominantly male) arrive at a busy urban space and pretend to engage in a shootout with either pantomime or plastic guns. The mob ends when everyone is symbolically murdered, and prostrate on the sidewalk. Flash mobbing has been described as yet another empirical reminder of how young boys in Canada seem to have little better to do than behave in aggressive, socially bullying manners.

There is little empirical, theoretical, popular cultural, or commonsense reason to believe that masculinity and violence will be either disentangled or disambiguated in the near future. Discursive battles about the aetiological (or causal) role of masculinity in the social experience of violence are unlikely to end any time soon. What is surprising is how frequently these battles reflect lines of thinking that are decades old. In the next section, we consider potentially new ways of thinking about the complex relationship between violence and bullying in times of perceived crisis.

Spectacle, Self-Violence, and Crisis Subjectivities: Project Mayhem

Few sociologists of gender would disagree that the global political landscape changed dramatically after the multinational invasion of Afghanistan in 2001 and Iraq in 2003 (Beasley, 2008). The softer and gentler era of diplomacy, border-dismantling, and coalition-building so characteristic of the culturally global 1990s gave way to a resurgence of neo-conservative and territorial bullying, following the tragic events of 11 September 2001 and the subsequent military invasions engineered by the United States. It is easy to understate the ways in which traditional hegemonic masculinity resurfaced from 2001–3 as part of the ethos of Western jingoism and xenophobia spurred on by the global 'war(s) on terror'. Despite overt Canadian resistance to the culture of terror and fear promoted largely by the Bush administration in the United States and its British Blair counterpart, North American culture became saturated with revitalized discourses about the need to 'man up' (a term I heard about a million times while living in Calgary) and confront adversity with aggressive resolve. New binaries of good/evil, friend/foe, patriot/terrorist, strong/weak, democratic/totalitarian, and just/unjust were circulated through governmental and social institutions. Unapologetic hegemonic masculinity rose from the ashes.

Risk theorists including Seidler (2006) classify the post-9/11 2000s as a decade where alternative masculinities have become narrowed or remarginalized within a reinvigorated neo-conservative culture of White male resisters and warmongers. In *The Terror Dream: Fear and Fantasy in Post-9/11 America* (2007), Faludi argues how 'crisis' males on the political right seized the cultural *terrorscape* of the early 2000s as a platform for quashing the counter-male hegemony movement of the 1980s and 1990s. Using mantras and symbols of preservation, resolve, freedom, progress, humanism, and religious fundamentalism, Western leaders including George W. Bush and Tony Blair discursively reframed a military offensive as a convoy of global perfectionism (Atkinson and Young, 2003). Even in the face of scathing critique from the left and military scandals including the Abu Ghraib and Guantanamo Bay torture and humiliation cases, support for the military offensive remained somewhat stable until the latter part of 2006. At the same time, critics in the academy like Gill and McLean (2002) were dismissing the masculinity crisis as theoretical fabrication or male backlash. Their academic positions were understandable given the resurgence in male bully culture in global foreign policy and 'homeland' practice in North America. On a continent where male-dominated governments and institutions now surveilled, targeted, detained, disrobed, invaded, and documented citizens in the name of international security, it is difficult to see a culture of men in crisis.

Not completely unrelated to the neo-conservative war on terror, key social institutions, including the educational system and the medical establishment, did well in the early 2000s to promote a full spate of health crises and panics. Epidemiologists, surgeons, psychiatrists, and others clamoured to call attention to skyrocketing rates of obesity, drug addiction, attention deficit disorder, and autism (among others) in young boys and men especially (Campos, 2004, Evans and Rich, 2006). Not since I was a young boy in the 1970s did so many fear and risk discourses abound about being a young man in Canadian society. I cannot remember a time where one was at risk of being a soft or potentially victimized male. The now iconic court scene and diatribe from Rob Reiner's 1992 movie *A Few Good Men* in which Daniel Kaffee (Tom Cruise, dressed in his 'faggoty white' Navy uniform) grills hardened Marine Colonel Nathan Jessep (Jack Nicholson) about his bullying tactics against other Marines predicted well the 2000s' call to hegemonic male arms. Nicholoson's unabashedly irreverent response to Cruise's in-court challenge of his masculine authority signalled a general call for men in crisis to emerge from their slumber of risk and self-pity, and claim their birthright as traditional social leaders. Nicholson decries the emasculation of the American male, and reminds audiences that without loutish, violent male hegemony, crisis ensues:

You can't handle the truth! Son, we live in a world that has walls, and those walls have to be guarded by men with guns. Who's gonna do it? You? You, Lieutenant Weinberg? I have a greater responsibility than you can possibly fathom. You weep for Santiago, and you curse the Marines. You have that luxury. You have the luxury of not knowing what I know—that Santiago's death, while tragic, probably saved lives; and my existence, while grotesque and incomprehensible to you, saves lives. You don't want the truth because deep down in places you don't talk about at parties, you want me on that wall—you need me on that wall. We use words like 'honour', 'code', 'loyalty'. We use these words as the backbone of a life spent defending something. You use them as a punch line. I have neither the time nor the inclination to explain myself to a man who rises and sleeps under the blanket of the very freedom that I provide and then questions the manner in which I provide it. I would rather that you just said 'thank you' and went on your way. Otherwise, I suggest you pick up a weapon and stand the post. Either way, I don't give a damn what you think you're entitled to!

The 'truth' to which Jessep refers is the social need for bullies, for men who are unafraid to take charge and aggress others for the greater social good; a difficult truth for men like Kaffee and those who stand up to hegemony in the name of political correctness. Jessep is stripped of his rank, thrown out of the Marines, and goes to prison in the movie. Herald the death of hegemonic masculinity in the story, and the triumph of alternative men. Flash forward a decade in real North American culture, and the Nathan Jesseps of the world multiplied by a factor of ten thousand and were deployed into the streets of Baghdad and hills of Kandahar. Viva bully culture and the discursive reinvention of masculine authority.

Bullying is a technique of doing pastiche hegemony that is always about fear-mongering, risk (creation), and surveillance, as Colonel Jessep reminds us all. Playground bullies like my childhood nemesis Henry struck fear by creating a constant risk of explosion on the playground. Each one of us knew he was always present, always watching, always circling to find a victim. His bullying was panoptic and omnipresent. From time to time, patriarchy may be deconstructed as a bully culture, its victims exposed, and male crises produced, but its ideology lingers in both subtle and flagrantly resistant ways. For many men in crisis, the reclaiming of the right to bully and the right to be justifiably violent is the pastiche formula for salvation. Between 2001 and 2008 I met dozens of men who 'found' late-modern forms of aggression and violence in life after slipping into a crisis mentality. When I first encountered men who 're-bully' as a means of alleviating a perceived masculinity crisis, I struggled to make sense out of why they embraced rather than rejected aggression and violence as a solution. Many of these men had been bullied extensively in their youth and had been socially defined as lesser males. Are they simply part of a Neanderthal backlash culture? Are their forays into bullying culturally vacuous and immature? Or, do their newly found appetites for bullying represent a reality about the deeply embedded and resilient nature of pastiche hegemony in the West? While concurrently rereading Guy Debord's (1967) *Society of the Spectacle* and Jean Baudrillard's, *Cool Memories IV* (2003), I had a revelation.

As a major intellectual influence on the French neo-Marxist, Situationist movement of the 1960s, Debord wrote scathing critiques of the capitalist, bourgeois, middle-class hegemony in France. His 1967 landmark book, *Society of the Spectacle*, is a rejectionist and rebellious tome that eviscerates normative modernist cultural ideologies of economic production and social order. At the heart of Debord's analysis of modern French life, he sees that all of everyday experience is geared toward the worship and reification of the capitalist social modality of living, from the production of commodities, to their consumption and display, to their lauding as evidence of Western progress. Debord (1967), like Heidegger (1954), contends the humans become willing but unwitting drones to capitalist production and commodity fetishism. Think about that the next time you fork over $5 for a latté at Starbucks. The capital-S *Spectacle* of life is capitalist order, reason, and social organization (e.g., the form and content of our social structures and our cultural ideologies). Meanwhile, small-scale *spectacles* (i.e., the practices of buying commodities, showcasing them on our bodies, and mediating them through television) become the fabric of everyday life. To Debord (1967) we might add that hegemonic (male) capitalist order is historically achieved through both overt and covert instances of force and bullying, and as such are foundational aspects of the Spectacle and of spectacles. Patriarchy is an essential component of the modern Western Spectacle, and micro-spectacles of male hegemony are traditionally replete with instances of bullying and violence, as I have argued in the previous chapter on social power. In Debord's terms, our gendered Canadian history has been one that evidences quite clearly an iron heel of the (male) Spectacle and spectacles.

What first, second, and third waves of feminism in Canada have accomplished, though, is a general disruption of the masculine-capitalist Spectacle as a take-for-granted social teleology. Andrews (2004; 2006) illustrates that complicity in a gendered, Spectacle-based society produces hegemonic masculinity, arranges social relationships around male hegemony, and aggressively silences alternative constructions of reality. If, for the sake of argument, the perceived masculinity crisis of the late 1990s and early 2000s is an empirical reality, then it surely rests in part on the collective realization that bullying-based hegemonic masculinity is no longer a pristine or irreversible meta-narrative of/for/through/underpinning the Spectacle. If hegemonic masculinity is secured through an uncritical acceptance of the gendered Spectacle, then awareness of and resistance to a gendered political economy of the Spectacle can indeed be crisis-producing! At the ground level of everyday life, if men can no longer *(re) produce* hegemony via tactics of exclusion, exploitation, bullying, and violence in the society of the Spectacle, what then of hegemonic men? Men in crisis have long lamented that their removal from social seats of power (i.e., as producers of the Spectacle) will be the death of traditional masculinity in Canada and elsewhere, and will give rise to soft men. I'm not so sure about that claim.

A science teacher once told me that if 10,000 nuclear bombs simultaneously exploded on earth, the only creature capable of surviving the blast or the resulting nuclear winter is a cockroach. I hope we will never be in position to test the veracity of such an empirical claim. But hegemonic masculinity is like a cockroach in the face of 100,000,000 challenges to its legitimacy. Deeply seated in Canadian cultural practices, it is also entwined with the structures and logics of our Spectacular social institutions. Hegemonic masculinity mutates, hides, reclassifies, incorporates, and rejects itself in order to exist in new forms (Connell, 2005). Think about our concept of pastiche hegemony. In returning to the substantive focus of this chapter, bullying and violence still abound as part of winning and doing local, pastiche forms of male hegemony. What has potentially changed, however, is what counts as legitimate or tolerable male bullying and violence: what one may participate in as pastiche hegemony. I argue below that hegemonic masculinity for men in crisis is won in a pastiche manner by *consuming virtual forms of hegemonic masculinity through self-bullying and violence*.

Debord, again, helps to illustrate why bullying the self can be hegemonic in a society of crisis. He maintains that the Spectacle is reproduced by the creation of false needs and desires in a culture that encourages the pursuit of constant production and accumulation. An economy can only grow, and the male power structures underpinning it solidify, if we constantly 'give' our minds, energies, and souls to the Spectacular. To the men who perceive their position in the Spectacular society to be at risk in late-modern Canada, it signals an end to their ability to use gender as a tool for bullying and gaining traditional forms of male power. Think of Tyler Durden's (Brad Pitt) now infamous speech in the holy grail of masculinity crisis movies, *Fight Club*:

> I see in Fight Club the strongest and smartest men who have ever lived. I see all this potential, and I see it squandered. Goddammit, an entire generation pumping gas, waiting tables, slaves with white collars. Advertising has us chasing cars and clothes, working jobs we hate so we can buy shit we don't need. We're the middle children of history, man; no purpose or place. We have no Great War, no Great Depression. Our Great War is a spiritual war. Our Great Depression is our lives. We've all been raised by television to believe that one day we'd all be millionaires and movie gods and rock stars. But we won't; and we're slowly learning that fact. And we're very, very pissed off.

If power/pastiche hegemony through bullying and masculine aggression can no longer be secured by all men, then how do these men actually secure traditional maleness if they desire it? They can't, right? Wrong. Small-scale, localized, traditional hegemonic masculinity is achieved through a consumption of selected forms of self-violence and bullying. If hegemony cannot be produced through structural and cultural bullying, *it can be purchased and consumed as a technology of the self*, or in Foucault's (1988) terms, as an 'ethic of self care'. This is not historically new (Jeffords, 1989). Men in crisis meet crisis with an ultra-aggressive, problem-smashing approach that embodies a quintessential masculine ethos of 'taking on the self' (or others) through bullying-based and violent physical practices.

LeBreton (2000) documents the growing interest for some men in the symbolic play of violence and death through extreme sport. For them, this is a means of achieving a sense of hyper-masculinity. By laughing in the face of risk and playing on the physical 'edge' (Lyng, 2008), middle-class men in crisis celebrate the thrill of (potentially complete) masculine erasure. By pushing the self physically to the limit and walking the edge of catastrophe, one engages in a gendered territory-marking of the highest consumer order. Spectacles of potential self-destruction connote a crisis-based fatalism on the one hand and yet a sense of hyperbolically hegemonic masculine resolve on the other. As women have made inroads into practically every (hegemonic) male cultural preserve in Canada, self-aggression against the body in exaggerated ways is a gesture of masculine capital. Intensely attacking the body in aggressive, injury-producing, and dramatic ways signifies that 'even though you are encroaching on my social terrain and our physical cultural practices as men, I can be more physically aggressive, powerful, and in control than you'. While one cannot socially bully with impunity, one can certainly aggress the self in increasingly flamboyant manners in the name of leisure, recreation, self-expression, reflexive individualism, or personal identity exploration. Quite simply, these men are becoming self-violent risk-takers in order to be heard as hegemonic men. This oeuvre is a retrenchment into hyper-real hegemonic masculinity that anchors the self in a form of embodiment and praxis that women still do not venture into with great gusto.

For men in crisis who use self-bullying as a means of winning pastiche hegemony, a desire to consume violence is often evident. This is in order to ensure the hegemonic male's place as head at the Spectacle table without forcing the position by aggressing others. The response cannot be divorced from a broader culture in which women's dieting, plastic surgery, psychotherapy, and other pain-producing modes of self-work receive considerable attention and accolade. Late-modern life is arguably one in which such self-aggression is lauded as self-investment and self-care. So, for men in crisis, hyperbolic forms of self-aggression/bullying jive well with current sensibilities to consume social power through painful bodywork. This also fits nicely with contemporary preferences for the return of the Marlboro man in a risk- and fear-saturated world. A few examples help to illustrate.

I. Backyard Wrestling

I met a nineteen-year-old young man named Jonas in 2000 during a study of tattooing in Canada. He had a series of interconnected Japanese tattoos on his arm, and I interviewed him twice about his constructions of the body project. Jonas, a self-identified Goth death rocker (not too common in rural Brooks, Alberta where he lived) stood about six feet tall and was incredibly muscular for his age. At the time of interview, Jonas and 13 of his friends organized and operated a backyard wrestling league in Brooks, out of Jonas's house. He wrestled under the name Dr Destructo. Three times a week, Dr Destructo and his friends and enemies staged shows for neighbours in a ring made of mattresses, wooden planks, clotheslines, and garden hoses. Over the course of two years, Jonas broke three ribs, his nose, his right arm, and his clavicle, and he knocked out three of his teeth in the name of his passion for wrestling. He only retired from the league because he decided to pursue post-secondary education in 2001 at a university in Ontario. During many of our interviews he waxed poetic about backyard wrestling, and expressed how much he enjoyed the thrill of pain, and the joy of pushing his body beyond normal male boundaries.

The late 1990s and early 2000s witnessed a minor moral panic over backyard wrestling in North America. *Backyard wrestling* is a general term used to describe the controversial practice of professional-style wrestling as performed by usually untrained fans in an unsanctioned, non-professional environment. Backyard wrestling is also a title applied to underground filmed and produced wrestling shows, videos, and matches carried out by mostly untrained athletes, usually comprised of males between the ages of 13 and 30. Though backyard wrestling was not unheard of prior to the 1990s, the modern backyard wrestling craze lasted from roughly 1996 to 2003, during a time when televised professional wrestling was enjoying a period of unparalleled popularity (Atkinson, 2003b). Local Canadian federations included the Backyard Wrestling Federation, Sarnia Wrestling Alliance, Backyard Juggalo Wrestling, Tecumseh Wrestling Federation, Saskatoon Xtreme Backyard Wrestling, McLuhan Wrestling Federation, Renegade Wrestling Federation, Obviously Bad Wrestling, and Jonas's Extreme Western Wrestling. These clubs were included in the mass-mediated moral panic about the dangers of backyard wrestling and the inherent pathologies of its enthusiasts. Many of those who practice backyard wrestling embrace a style that emphasizes risky high spots (which can involve diving or taking bumps from rooftops or ladders) and the liberal use of weapons (e.g., baseball bats, chairs, barbed wire, metal pipes, and construction tools) in matches. Even among participants who shy away from this, there is still a considerable level of inherent risk involved.

The Canadian backyard wrestling movement was an outgrowth of the American scene. In August 1997, a backyard promotion originating from Vallejo, California, began filming the television/Internet backyard wrestling show called 'CWF Devastation'. The program aired between 1997–2000 on California public access stations (and then on the Internet), and has often been cited as the inspiration for the legendary west coast backyard movement of the late 1990s, the influence of which stretched to (primarily) southern Alberta and southern Ontario. CWF Devastation was celebrated among underground wrestling communities for its original writing and innovative cinematography, as well as its brutal violence and its cutting-edge wrestling style. With the advent of open access and personal media production websites in the late 1990s, backyard wrestling found a stable and more permanent home on the Internet; websites became places where youth across the North American federations could attempt to out-do one another with increasingly extreme forms of wrestling violence. Through the early 2000s, backyard wrestling became infamous for its out-of-control, unregulated, and dangerous stunts. Many people, most commonly male teenagers like my friend Jonas, frequently risked their lives in attempted dives, jumps, falls, and bumps in the ring. Many others would use harmful weapons, performing matches with flaming tables, barbed wire, light tubes, thumbtacks and sharp metal tools such as cheese graters.

Jonas's backyard wrestling exploits of the late 1990s and early 2000s were, of course, the physical cultural cousin of 'jackass culture' in North America. The MTV television program *Jackass* aired between 1999 and 2002. The show featured a cadre of cast members including Johnny Knoxville, Bam Margera, Steve-O, Wee Man, and Chris Pontius participating in humourous, albeit extreme, stunts of self-abuse. While *Jackass* drew a massive audience in its three seasons, it also drew a full spate of influential critics. On 29 January 2001, for example, United States Senator Joseph Lieberman publicly condemned MTV, *Jackass,* and the culture of dangerous masculinity it encouraged, in connection with a dangerous copycat stunt in which a 13-year-old Connecticut teenager was left in critical condition with severe burns after a stunt gone wrong. Lieberman followed up with a 7 February 2001 letter to MTV's parent company Viacom urging the company to take greater responsibility for its programming and do more to help parents protect their children. MTV responded to the criticism by cancelling all airings of *Jackass* before 10:00 p.m., but Lieberman's continued campaign against the show led to MTV refusing to air repeats of the later episodes.

Akin to Lieberman's condemnation of *Jackass*, major professional wrestling federations including World Wrestling Entertainment and the now-defunct World Championship Wrestling decried rogue backyard wrestling as unsafe and unrepresentative of the culture of pro wrestling in North America. Wrestling pundits closely linked the development of these 'bandit leagues' to the ethos of spectacular risk-taking and recklessness in quasi-mainstream wrestling promotions such as Extreme Championship Wrestling, Xtreme Pro Wrestling, and Combat Zone Wrestling. When these promotions closed and/or toned down their extreme nature, a majority of the backyard wrestling leagues followed suit. Increased media attention, local policing of backyard leagues, and reforms within the professional wrestling promotions toward toning down the violent nature of the shows led to a generally unpopular view of wrestling and unprofessional stunts, which in turn led to a decline in the popularity of backyard wrestling. In addition, globally circulated stories about injuries produced from copycat backyard wrestlers—including one about a five-year-old boy who performed a 'pile driver' move on his 22-month-old cousin, severely injuring the toddler's spine—raised public ire about backyard wrestling and highlighted its danger (Huggins, 2002).

Jonas and his mates remained indifferent to the moral panicking and stereo-typing of backyard wrestling. To this group, who are all lower-middle-class boys who would admittedly never fit in with mainstream culture, dangerous backyard wrestling antics provided them with a sort of masculine 'subcultural capital' (Thornton, 2005) that other boys simply could not attain in rule-bound, affectively-contained dominant sports cultures. In particular, as the world of sport has been encroached upon by women and varying codes of femi-ninity, the excessively misogynist world of backyard wrestling advocates clichéd forms of risk and self-injury in the name of good show as a valued masculine enterprise. To this end, Jonas and his crew routinely described feeling more like 'real men' than the ice hockey or football players in their high schools. Partici-pation in this hyper-violent recreational culture afforded them an opportunity to self-bully as a means of living up to a mythologized masculine attitude, process of self-objectification, and territorial male-marking.

II. Laddism

Laddism (conceptually related to *mimboism*) is a model and lifestyle of mascu-linity that diverges significantly from the image of the late-modern man in crisis. Laddism is a stereotypical and *atavistic* (i.e., a biological throwback to a more primitive human being) style of life embracing the hedonistic consump-tion of risk through drug and alcohol consumption and sexual conquests. Emerging from the United Kingdom in the 1990s, laddism spread through the early 2000s to countries like Canada. Among its devotees it is character-ized by an obsessive-compulsive focus on male youthfulness, consumption, and bachelorhood. Lads characteristically objectify women in a manner that smacks of a backlash against prevailing political decrees of gender sensitivity and correctness in Canada (Attwood, 2005). To these lads, the purported masculinity crisis has been associated with a dismantling of traditional gender roles, and the overturning of the hegemonic labour force composition and family responsibilities (Benwell, 2003; Ferree, Lorber, and Hess, 1999; Heart-field, 2002; Kimmel, 2000). As such, their laddism has been described as an outright protest against feminism and images of the 'new man' (Nixon, 2001). Lads reject gender equality and instead advocate returning to a more sexist and sexualized view of gender relations (Benwell, 2004). However, they do so not through institutional political tactics or cultural policy reform, but through (what might be argued) highly immature and tantrum-esque forms of corporeal indulgence. For the new lad in Canada, consuming images of the traditionally powerful male authority figure through Dionysian consumption is a model of crisis protest and resolution. Laddism is, then, strictly a model of *consum-erist masculinity* that renounces self-responsibility, celebrates binge drinking, and encourages boyish ego stroking (Whelehan, 2000). The lad embraces and surrounds himself with signifiers of stereotypical hegemonic masculinity such as sports, cars, and video games, while indulging in alcohol, drugs, and promiscuity (Jackson, Stevenson, and Brooks, 2001).

The lads I have come to meet through my research on masculinity are primarily white, upper-working-class or lower-middle-class young guys aged between 15–30. They are defined through their defiant and humorous opposition to the traditional Protestant work ethic and middle-class respectability (Weber, 1958). Laddish values such as 'having a laugh', engaging in disruptive behaviour, and objectifying women are justified by them as logical outcomes of living in a society in which boys are generally expected to be 'bad' (Francis, 1999). Laddism is in this respect an outcropping of a present-centred and fatalist mentality among a growing number of young boys who believe the best way to gain power and attention as young men is to live harder, faster, and more recklessly than even the most traditionally hegemonic male. They are not subculturally affiliated with others in the Canadian milieu of style-oriented and consumption-obsessed neo-tribes (Maffesoli, 1988; Wilson, 2006) like Ravers, Goths, Skaters, and others, as they interpret most of such subcultures as definitively non-masculine. Gill (2005) argues that laddism is only a media construction, and that empirical studies have not shown either boys or men straightforwardly inhabiting a pure laddish identity. Still, there is evidence of laddish values becoming hegemonic among boys in crisis.

Martin is a 28-year-old car salesman living in Montreal. I followed Martin and three of his best friends for a month in 2006 in order to understand the lifestyle and ethos of living like a lad. This short ethnography turned into the most physically and mentally taxing 30 days of my life. Each of the lads scurries home from their dead-end 9-to-5 jobs every day to quickly shower, grab a ready-made meal from the freezer, down a cocktail or two, and head out to a bar. Evenings typically begin with a subdued round of watching hockey or basketball at a local sports bar, accompanied by three or four pints of beer. From there, the lads head out to a singles bar where they ply their respective 'sure-fire' pickup techniques within a gathering of completely suspecting women. Surprisingly or not, at least one of them normally returns home with a woman for an anonymous sexcapade. These are the evenings of lad legend. The unlucky others pile into a cab between 2:00–3:00 a.m., fall into their single bed studio apartments, and wake up the next morning at 7:30 a.m. to reproduce, like a scene from the movie *Groundhog Day*, the events again and again. A couple of them may meet for lunch to recount the night's dirty details and to strategize about the evening ahead. They revel in the lack of seriousness and industry with which they approach life, and cherish the moments where they can escape the necessary trappings of day-to-day subsistence work.

Martin describes laddism as a culture of 'living within but not for the system'. Laddism is a style of 'making do' for him, putting in the least amount of effort required to fund his extracurricular activities. Laddism ventures far beyond Peter-Panism, as it borders on the self-congratulatory apathetic. Martin's life, quite to his own admission, is flavoured by a sentiment of defeatism and self-loathing. He sees no prospect or hope in trying to be conventional as he sincerely believes the system is against men like him and that no matter how much effort he devotes to being accomplished in business, family, or social terms, he is set up to fail. His close friend Sam, a car park attendant in north Toronto, said to me, 'some people never get on the social ladder of success. But you can still have fun on the ground. I can go out, get drunk off my tree, and maybe get into a fight on the way home. That's living, because I don't have to worry about my precious image or that my boss or wife might get mad about what I got up to the night before. Total freedom, dude, freedom'. Guys like Martin and Sam express an acute disinterest in emotional attachment with women, or fail to exhibit even a basic emotional awareness. Part of their carefully fabricated bravados and ethos of 'living for the day', they view emotional sensitivity as a characteristic of the weak. The rail against such emotionalism especially in the presence of their non-lad workmates and friends, boasting that they do not need to be sensitive, aware 'new men' in order to live like 'proper men'. Not included in these narratives are accounts of the myriad sexually transmitted diseases each have contracted over time, their bloating bodies and failing health, or their sense of loneliness and isolation each feels when the rest of the lads are not up for a night on the town. Nevertheless, men like Martin celebrate their own boorish brand of laddism as self-reflexive and free, in opposition to older, less narcissistic forms of masculinity; and, in opposition to new, more nurturing and caring ways of being men, as refreshingly honest, sexual, and smart.

III. Bugchasing

Bugchasing is part urban myth and part reality in contemporary Canadian society. Bugchasing is a queer version of 'straight' lad culture in certain respects. Bugchasers are gay men who seek HIV-positive sexual partners for the purpose of having unprotected sex and sero-converting. In short, bugchasers actively engage in unprotected sex with other men in order to become HIV-positive. *Giftgivers* are the HIV-positive men who comply with the bugchasers' efforts to become infected with HIV. Both are widely disdained and stigmatized in gay communities (Moskowitz and Roloff, 2007), and their prevalence has been much exaggerated by the Canadian conservative media. Bugchasers indicate various reasons for their desire to contract HIV, including fluid-bonding, and a sense of inevitability combined with a desire to take control by being active in their sero-conversion. For some gay men, the process of *gifting* resounds with Mauss and Hubert's (1966) understanding of the gifting process as a symbolic social act of power. Bugchasing is often linked to gay men's feelings of inevitability toward HIV contraction, the empowerment of choosing when to contract the virus, and a general resistance to being overly targeted and pathologized by the Canadian medical community.

The bugchasing phenomenon gained critical press coverage and notoriety after the American pop cultural monolith *Rolling Stone* magazine printed an article in 2003 by a freelance journalist, Gregory Freeman, entitled 'Bug Chasers: The men who long to be HIV+'. The article provoked a storm of controversy in North American media because it suggested that the practice might be relatively common in the gay community. Public concern over bugchasing amplified when American film director Daniel Bort released a 2003 short film on the subject called *Bugchaser*, which premiered at the 16th Annual Austin Gay and Lesbian Film Festival. Another film, called *Gift* by Louise Hogarth, also documented the subculture of bugchasing and added to a mini panic regarding the practice. The moral panic about bugchasing was swift and predictably severe. Following the *Rolling Stone* article, sexuality researchers inside the academy quickly turned attention to bugchasing. Since the late 1990s researchers have documented, explained, and looked for a solution to 'the problem' of bugchasing. Gauthier and Forsyth (1999) published among the first academic accounts of bugchasing, in which they explored the genesis of the American barebacking (unprotected sex) subculture. Tewksbury (2004) followed suit by studying the role of the Internet as a social facilitator of bugchasing and the crystallization of gifting networks. Grov and Parsons (2006) extended Tewksbury's research and used Internet profiles of 1,228 bugchasers and giftgivers to identify six types of community participant: the committed bugchaser; the opportunistic bugchaser; the committed giftgiver; the opportunistic giftgiver; the serosorter; and, the ambiguous bugchaser or giftgiver. While each of these studies provided initial insight into the phenomenon, few actually document the meanings associated to bugchasing or giftgiving for those involved.

Blechner (2002), by contrast, argues that bugchasers are lonely and alienated males who view HIV contraction as a path to becoming part of a community that elicits public sympathy and caretaking. Other bugchasers, he argues, are so overwhelmed by the anxiety of contracting HIV that they decide to be proactive and contract the disease on their own terms. This, they feel, leads to a sense of relief from that anxiety that they will eventually become HIV-positive by 'getting it over with'. Most recently, Moskowitz and Roloff (2007) attempt to quantitatively explain why bugchasers chase HIV. They claim individuals who look for HIV are pathological sex addicts with measurable impulse control disorders. These individuals are preoccupied with sexual highs (via risk-taking), and now turn to bugchasing to achieve the ultimate risk-oriented sexual high. LeBlanc's (2007) survey of bugchasers illustrated a more nuanced understanding of bugchasing as an erotic and emancipating *technique of the self* (see chapter 4 for a more detailed discussion of this concept). I met a bugchaser named Ewan in the summer of 2005, and his personal narrative reflects relatively little about the practice documented in the academic literature to date.

Ewan is a 33-year-old property developer who lives in the heart of downtown Toronto. I first met him through a friend of mine from graduate school.

A self-confessed relationship junkie, Ewan struggled to find Mr Right for the better part of his twenties. A series of either dead-end or vitriolic relationships later, he committed himself to the fact that he might not ever find his soul-mate. His sense of relationship fatalism was hardened by the loss of several close friends or former partners in the 1990s due to AIDS-related illnesses. Because Ewan is an emotionally open, empathetic, and nurturing soul, he would often act as a caregiver and nurse for his friends in their last days. He grew progressively frustrated and embittered by how their families, friends, and doctors infantilized them. His irritation for their treatment as medical specimens swelled, and his contempt blossomed for the passive-aggressive manner by which men living with HIV/AIDS were stigmatized as victims of their own 'pathological' desires. His experience with the illness process smacks with Frank's (2004a, b) articulation of the medical 'ride' and the loss of self/ agency through illness diagnosis and treatment. He rants about the ways in which the Canadian media continues to portray gay men as a 'special risk' population, and rails against social discourses about the need for the gay and lesbian community to live in a state of fear, surveillance, and self-monitoring.

Ewan and I met on many occasions to discuss how common AIDS discourses offend his sense of empowered (gay) masculinity. 'It's so typical', he told me one day, 'that gay males are portrayed as weaklings. Other men fight disease, own it, live with it, and stand up against it. Gay men are told to run and hide.' Through a series of interviews with Ewan, his confusions about being and feeling strong and proud as a male became evident. Like other gay and straight males of his era, Ewan argues that with the increased awareness of multiple masculinities in Canada and promotion of gay men's rights, the practices of the gay community have ironically come into far greater social, cultural, and medical scrutiny and control. As a bizarre offshoot of the masculinity crisis in straight communities, alternative masculinities may have won cultural space to varying degrees but they have also been forced, as Foucault (1983, 1988) might predict, to become more confessional to hegemony and subject to insti-tutional pathologizing. He says, 'with every year as gay men become ingratiated in Canadian straight society, gay identities change. They become as narrowly defined as straight men. This is so true the minute you are diagnosed [with HIV]. You don't own your body anymore, and the freedom to be without being shamed. You talk of crisis, that, for me, is one of the biggest crises facing the gay community today . . . defining it from within, from the body out.'

As an extreme gesture of defiance against increased colonization of gay bodies from the cultural outside, Ewan became a bugchaser. He found and joined an Internet group who specialized in holding 'bug parties' and within a year, he became HIV-positive. He lives to this day without fear of his body or when he will die. He refuses to receive conventional medical treatment, preferring to 'treat his body' with an intensely strict raw, whole-food nutritional regime. He is open and out about his HIV status, and now lives with a gifter he met at a bug party. While seemingly incomprehensible to some, Ewan's embrace of HIV in the face of crisis is a rather stereotypically hegemonic response to feelings of victimization and oppression. He has claimed the right to 'be' physically and emotionally in a community where such rights are continually eroded along several lines. Ewan's self-aggression and bullying is a (literally) fatalist strategy of self-emancipation from a gender/sex crisis, but also a quintessentially male 'shove' back against a culture that routinely picks a fight with him. Like other bugchasers I met through Ewan, they find pastiche hegemony within their own communities by engaging physical cultural risks that mark their identities with signifiers of strength, bravado, desire, irreverence, dominance, power, and personal control.

IV. Ultra-Endurance Running

You stop a horse that is bolting. You do not stop a jogger who is jogging. Foaming at the mouth, his mind riveted on the inner countdown to the moment when he will achieve a higher plane of consciousness, he is not to be stopped. If you stopped him to ask the time, he would bite your head off. He doesn't have a bit between his teeth, though he may perhaps be carrying dumb-bells or even weights in his belt . . . Like dieting, bodybuilding, and so many other things, jogging is a new form of voluntary servitude. Decidedly, joggers are the true Latter Day Saints and the protagonists of an easy-does-it Apocalypse. Nothing evokes the end of the world more than a man running straight ahead on a beach, swathed in the sounds of his walkman, cocooned in the solitary sacrifice of his energy, indifferent even to catastrophes since he expects destruction to come only as the fruit of his own efforts, from exhausting the energy of a body that has in his own eyes become useless. Primitives, when in despair, would commit suicide by swimming out to sea until they could swim no longer. The jogger commits suicide by running up and down the beach. His eyes are wild, saliva drips from his mouth. Do not stop him. He will either hit you or simply carry on dancing around in front of you like a man possessed . . . In a sense, he spews himself out; he doesn't merely expend his energy in his running, he vomits it. He has to attain the ecstasy of fatigue, the high of mechanical annihilation, just as the anorexic aims for the high of organic annihilation, the ecstasy of the empty body and the obese individual seeks the high of dimensional annihilation: the ecstasy of the full body. (Baudrillard, *America — Excerpts 1,* Verso Books, 1989)

I started running in 2002 as part of a regimen to get back into shape and lose the spare tire I built while doing my Ph.D. in the late 1990s. I hated it at first, and even running a thousand metres proved draining. In April of 2009, I ran four fell races (running events held across mountains or dales) on consecutive weekends, varying in length from five miles to 30 miles. I love running now. I love running long and I love running until my limbs can no longer move and my mind is pushed almost to the point of hallucination. I know scores of men who feel the same. Like Baudrillard's (2003) runner, there is a strange ecstasy in the self-punishment and aggression associated with this form of self-flagellation. This is definitely the case for me in the context of running ultramarathons.

Rising in prominence within global sports and leisure cultures over the last ten years, ultra-endurance sports are those that exceed, through either time or distance measures, standard running or cycling races. A running race, for example, is considered an ultra-endurance event when it exceeds marathon distance (26.2 miles) or when the race is stretched out over the course of several days. 'Ultramarathons' vary from 50 to 1,000 miles and may take days to complete. The booming interest in ultramarathon running is perhaps attributable to the spread of extreme sports cultures in North America and around the world. From the 1990s onward, serious, recreational, amateur, and elite athletes have explored high-risk sports such as bungee jumping, skydiving, tunnel snowboarding, kite surfing, BASE jumping, and helicopter skiing as extreme, thrill-seeker sports. Risk or extreme sports subcultures challenge traditional cultural understandings of sports as safe leisure, and principles of strict self-care and health safety in recreational pursuits. Extreme sports culture is dominated by White, middle-class males and is underpinned by a credo of pushing and testing the body's limitations in physically hazardous or emotionally draining contexts.

A sport such as the ultramarathon well qualifies as a nascent extreme, post-masculinity crisis sport with deep cultural roots. The global cultural ascendance of extreme sports is interlaced with the blossoming popularity of its older extreme sports sibling, the marathon; which used to be the sole terrain of hegemonic men, but since the late 1970s, is now also the domain of women. Prior to the 1970s, marathon running was once a sport for an exclusive cadre of elite male athletes. However, amid a surge in health concerns among the baby boomer populations in Canada and elsewhere, training for and running marathons caught on in the late 1970s. Although the precise cause of the peak in interest is debated, notable influences included the generational popularity in aerobic exercise among women in the middle class, and the establishment of major 'cause related' marathons across North America that centrally involved women participants. These include races such as the 'Canadian Breast Cancer Foundation CIBC Run for the Cure' series (to promote fundraising for and awareness of breast cancer). A second renaissance of marathoning occurred in the late 1990s, with new generational interest in long-distance running spawned by new public health concerns among 'out of shape' or obese populations in the West.

At the same time that marathons were including more and more members of the global population, ultramarathons were increasingly sought out by men wishing to push self-identity envelopes. As marathon culture became more socially inclusive and evolved into a de-gendered sport less concerned with records than participation and fun, some of the more 'serious' male runners became engrossed with ritually punishing races covering, at a bare minimum, 30 miles. In quintessential hegemonic masculinity crisis form, as marathon running was no longer the benchmark of male athletic excellence, social competitiveness drove male athletes to fabricate races that would challenge even the most conditioned runners; the hegemonic male wing of running culture once again had a club for its elite. Not surprisingly, during the late 1970s and early 1980s, when ultramarathon germinated, other sports such as the Ironman Triathlon (1978) in Kona, Hawaii (a 2.4-mile swim, 112-mile bike, and 26.2-mile run) and cycling's Race Across America (1982) emerged as more men experimented with distance sports.

In his book, *Hello, I'm Special* (2004), Niedzviecki underscores how hyper-consumerist, middle-class, Anglo methods of being 'special' in countries like Canada propel many men of my generation to seek out novel rituals and corporeal performances. With the overarching pressure to be unique in late-modern middle-class cultures, saturated by ideologies of consumption and reflexive individualism, males (in crisis) are encouraged to constantly work the self through liminal pursuits. This is especially true for male ultra runners in crisis who heavily associate their public image of masculinity with their abilities to endure more than other men and women. Because Canadians often value doing 'whatever it takes' to be special, punishing the body through ultra sporting practices can be a marker of achieved male identity.

In 2007, I met a 39-year-old legal assistant named Pete who is an avid ultra runner and Iron-distance triathlete. Pete is not a traditionally 'masculine' man in most respects, but has found a way to receive kudos from the men and women in his life through endurance sport exploits. To him, endurance sport is a signifying practice of masculine resolve, and it is shared among those who are collectively disaffected with, and alienated from, mainstream, nouveau, or soft constructions of masculinity in Canada. Ultra endurance running is also a magic gender elixir for him because no one, other than himself, is physically or socially implicated in his resistance against soft masculinity. His endurance pursuits are defined as meaningful at a time when he feels that masculinity is less framed by physically oriented ritual experiences of pain and suffering, and more by what clothes you wear or music you listen to. Pete also expresses a level of frustration with the type of work he, like other males in his social network, does every day and the drain it has on his embodied masculinity. He explains:

> I spend every day of my life behind a desk or [on] the phone or perched at a computer. I drive a two-hour commute daily and spend my entire lunch waiting for a table, and then sitting down eating. The clock bangs 5:00 p.m. and I feel like Clark Kent ripping off the suit and bursting out of the phone booth into the Superman costume . . . Guys like me turn 30 and look down and see a gut for the first time and hate life. Blasting the body through hard training and racing is the yin to the office yang and the best medicine to ritual boredom I know. Maybe

being in the zone at work is a thrill, okay, but I feel the most keyed up in life when the kilometres feel like metres in the middle of a run. At work I'm a name on the door, or at the bottom of a page, but in a race, it's just my body, the elements, and me. Whatever I've lived through is related to how I pushed my limits.

It is precisely the ability to aggressively persevere through forcing one's body through pain that guys like Pete interpret as a source of masculinity; a kind of power absent to him in most other social settings. Ultra runners' abilities to persevere through scripted forms of athletic suffering and 'sporting' self-abuse are mutually recognized social bonding capital among them; inasmuch, it adds another layer of exciting significance to the process. The capacity to withstand long periods of sports-related suffering secures them a degree of pastiche hegemony. Quite predictably, as Maffesoli (1998) and Muggleton (2000) would point out in their studies of subcultures, ultra runners tend to label outsiders as 'wimps'. Day to day, week to week, men like Pete lead rather unimpressively masculine lives, but on the weekend they are hegemonic male warriors. They run, kilometre after kilometre, in private battles with their bodies and male identities.

Summary

We live in a society beset with a constant fear of the male perpetrator who is progressively annoyed by his symbolic emasculation in late-modern Canadian society. Studies of violence and male bullying proliferate within a series of sociological subdisciplines. The twentieth century might be remembered by gender theorists as a point in time in which male bullying (across the social landscape) experienced its conclusive deconstruction. But still, violence, bullying, and pastiche forms of masculine hegemony are alive and well. The discursive battle about the role of bullying and gender in society continues. Even for men in self-perceived crisis the gendered ideology linking bullying to winning social power endures as a form of residual patriarchy. De Certeau (1984) describes how the world of everyday life is full of remainders of the past, of the unspoken yet present. Such is the case with the image of traditional male hegemony and its procurement through bullying amongst many men who feel their masculinity is in crisis. The desire to self-bully as a technique for doing hyper-real masculinity seems to be a collective solution to these men's common status problems.

Crime, violence, aggression, and bullying, therefore, all take place subjectively and experientially in situated contexts. Each may be tied conceptually to cultural residues of patriarchy and traditional male hegemony in Canada. Men who consume rather than produce (self)violence may do so as pastiche hegemony and find fleeting moments and feelings of power while bullying. This tendency toward consumption can be parlayed into symbolic capital of the hegemonic as it celebrates a decisively (albeit rejected in many spheres) risk-filled, crisis-embracing masculine unapologetic. Viewed from this perspective, the myth of masculine hegemony has never faded away. In Baudrillard's (2001) terms, the crisis might be considered a perfect conceptual example of a *non-event*. A non-event is that which actually occurs but is more of a media fabrication than a common, lived reality. The non-event fails to live up to or fulfill its promise, or as something which has no singular cultural meaning or importance (Baudrillard, 2001). Most of the moral panics of the twentieth century can be classified as non-events as we tend to erase them from collective memory or eschew them from our everyday cultural practices once the media shifts its gaze to an alternative problem. The masculinity crisis may be among the latest of non-events. Patriarchy's residues are present even when they are rejected overtly, the image of the hegemonic male is resurrected in leisure and self-work settings, and the ability to be stereotypically hegemonic is more open to consumption than in any previous era. One might ask, then, whether or not hegemonic masculinity is more of a lived reality for men in post-crisis Canadian society.

Discussion Questions

1. Do you think the media play a central role in perpetuating the idea that men are naturally more aggressive than women?
2. What do you think explains the high rates of patterned male violence in Canadian society?
3. Consider some of the forms of crisis alleviation I presented in this chapter. Do you think that involvement in any of these actually produces a long-lasting, positive outcome for the men?
4. Do you think the desire to self-injure is a practice only engaged in by men? Can you think of other physical cultural practices of self-harm with more socially 'feminine' roots?
5. From your own experience in sociology, could you employ another set of theoretical ideas to offer a different interpretation of men and violence than the one I presented in this chapter?

Key Readings

Acland, C. (1995). *Youth, Murder, Spectacle: The Cultural Politics of 'Youth in Crisis'.* Boulder, CO: Westview Press. I had the pleasure of meeting Charles Acland years ago, and he introduced me to the idea of youth 'in crisis' long before most people in the academy had even given the idea a first, let alone second, thought. In this book, Acland examines the late-modern culture that has produced a heightened state of awareness of youth violence in North America. Beginning with a critique of statistical evidence of youth violence, Acland compares and juxtaposes a variety of popular cultural representations of what has come to be a perceived 'crisis' of North American youth. Acland predominantly argues, like other cultural studies researchers, that the crisis tends to be more of a media myth than an empirical reality.

Debord, G. (1967). *The Society of the Spectacle*. Paris: Black & Red. *The Society of the Spectacle* remains today one of the great theoretical works on modern-day capitalist, cultural imperialism, and the role of mass mediation and commodity fetishism in social relationships. While Debord is often difficult to read, the book is ultimately worth it for anyone interested in the male-controlled, techno-capitalist domination of everyday life. His insights are penetrating, remarkable, and have proven to be more acute with the passing of time. Debord illustrates how private and public overconsumption has become the hallmark of an age that has debt-financed its way into history.

Gottfredson, M., and Hirschi, T. (1990). *A General Theory of Crime*. San Jose: Stanford University Press. Few books have made as immediate and enduring an impact on a sociological subdiscipline as Gottfredson and Hirschi's *A General Theory of Crime*. The text outlines what is now popularly known as the 'self-control' theory of criminal behaviour, and points to key bonding and social-psychological developmental processes in youth as prime predictors of future deviant behaviour. The book pays considerable attention to the gender-crime-deviance link by addressing how and why boys tend to be at greater risk of criminal pathways than girls.

Hise, R. (2004). *The War Against Men*. Oakland, CA: Elderberry Press. This book will enrage proponents of the masculinity crisis thesis. Hise's account of masculinity in late-modern America claims that extant theories of social inequality, which situate men at the top of the economic food chain, must be revisited. *The War Against Men* also decries the portrayal and treatment of men across a vast array of other institutional and popular cultural sites in North America. For crisis theorists it offers documented evidence of a systematic gender discrimination against fathers, sons, and brothers.

Lyotard, J-F. (1979). *The Postmodern Condition: A Report on Knowledge*. Manchester: Manchester University Press. Lyotard's text is canonized by many contemporary thinkers, and vilified by more classically oriented sociologists. The book brings to the fore issues in the transformation of modern to postmodern culture. The book principally introduces and defines postmodernism in society by looking at the status of science, technology, and the arts, the significance of technocracy, and the way the flow of information is controlled in the Western world.

Web Links

Bugchasing commentary (www.alternativesmagazine.com/15/hill.html). This article was written by an author who became a bugchaser and was 'gifted'. In the article, an insider account is given regarding the politics, practices, and psychological impacts of bugchasing.

Dean Karnazes (www.ultramarathonman.com). One of the world's foremost ultra runners. This website provides key links to the world of ultrarunning, and insight into what it takes to be a competitive ultra runner in society.

FHM Magazine (www.fhm.com). One of the flagship magazines in lad culture. FHM is an unapologetically laddist trade publication, and is cited among masculinity authors as one of the defining tomes in the life politics of the contemporary lad.

Situationalist Interational Anthology (www.bopsecrets.org/SI/index.htm). An online repository of Situationalist writing from the early days in the movement. Links to web articles are provided along with primary texts from figures like Debord and Jorn.

Key Terms

Bugchasing: The act of intentionally seeking HIV/AIDS through sexual encounters with others who are HIV positive. Bugchasing is defined by a small minority in the gay community as an act of resistance against medical definitions of the body and sexual identity. Critics of bugchasing decry the practice as a fatalistic response to the medicalization process in society.

Folk devils: People who have been targeted and publicly labelled in a society as 'bad apples' and are scapegoated for wide social problems. Folk devils are publicly condemned by authority figures in order to show audiences which social activities should be avoided and which should be emulated. Those groups seen as folk devils, of which society disapproves, stand as a constant reminder of what we should not be in everyday life.

Laddism: A way of life among young, urban, relatively affluent men who resist the late-modern death of traditional masculinity. These men embrace and hyperbolically embody the characteristics of the dominant teenage male and resist adopting adult male roles and statuses. The young men drink a lot of alcohol, and are mainly interested in sport, sex, and music.

Moral panic: A set of discourses and practices of widespread concern whereby members of a society and culture become hyper-sensitized to the challenges posed to apparently accepted moral and ethical values and ways of life by the activities of troublemaking folk devils. A moral panic is largely promoted and spreads through mass mediation (i.e., on television and in the newspaper) of the public issue at hand. The process of moral panicking underscores the importance of the mass media in providing, maintaining, and policing the available frameworks and definitions of deviance, which structure both public awareness of, and attitudes towards, social problems.

Sociobiology: a synthesis of scientific disciplines that attempts to explain social behaviour in animal species (including humans) by considering the Darwinian advantages specific behaviors may have. It is often considered an integrated branch of biology and sociology, but also draws from ethology, anthropology, evolution, zoology, archaeology, population genetics, and other disciplines. Within the study of human societies, sociobiology is closely related to the fields of human behavioural ecology and evolutionary psychology.

Situationalists: A restricted group of international revolutionaries founded in 1957 by Guy Debord and Asger Jorn, whose influence peaked during the unprecedented general wildcat strikes of May 1968 in France. With their ideas rooted in Marxism and the twentieth-century European artistic avant-gardes, they advocated experiences of life being alternative to those admitted by the capitalist order, for the fulfillment of human primitive desires and the pursuing of a superior emotional quality. For this purpose they suggested and experimented with the *construction of situations*, namely the setting up of environments favourable for the fulfillment of such desires. Using methods drawn from the arts, they developed a series of experimental fields of study for the construction of such situations, like unitary urbanism and psychogeography.

3 The Lost (and Found) Boys

Chapter Objectives

This chapter introduces and critically explores the following:

- A review of the 'war on boys' thesis
- Selected indicators of a supposed masculinity crisis among boys
- Arguments regarding how subculture resistance has become involved in masculinity crisis politics
- An extended case of male crisis subcultures called 'Straightedge'
- Questions whether resistance to male hegemony is ultimately a struggle to be hegemonic after all

Mother I tried please believe me,
I'm doing the best that I can.
I'm ashamed of the things I've been put through,
I'm ashamed of the person I am.
Isolation.
Isolation.
Isolation.

(from the song 'Isolation' by Joy Division)

A good friend of mine named Andy has a young son named Gareth. Andy grew a bit concerned several years ago when, by age three, Gareth showed only slight developmental progress with his speech. I know Gareth well, and he seems like a normal little boy to me; he's a bit on the shy side, but hey, so was I at his age. After reading about speech delay over several days of Internet browsing, Andy and his wife Claire concluded their son might be autistic. I don't remember hearing much about autism in the popular media until about ten years ago. Who knows why, but an entire generation of millennial children suddenly became autistic as pop psychologists fired out medical warnings to parents regarding their shy, inattentive, and easily distracted children. Convinced by the medical data available, Andy and Claire dragged Gareth to a gaggle of specialists. Sure enough, their do-it-yourself diagnosis was supported by most of the autism experts. Gareth is now enrolled in a school for special-needs children and takes medication to help him concentrate and communicate. One day out of the blue, Andy said something to me that I will never forget: 'Mike, did you ever notice that most autistic kids are boys?'

Andy's observation is bang on the money. The imbalance between autism diagnoses among boys and girls is incredible (Sicile-Kira and Grandin, 2003). Boys are over 30 times more likely than girls to be diagnosed with most autism-related disorders. While researchers are struggling to explain how genetics, physiology, social environment, psychological conditioning, nutrition, and cultural role imitation might contribute to the disorder, few have convincingly explained why autism tends to be a boys' problem, or the sudden jump in cases in the past decade. The curious medical relationship between boys and autism is not the only one to catch the attention of sociologists of health in the 2000s.

Medical sociologists also question why boys are more quickly diagnosed with attention deficit hyperactivity disorder than girls. Biederman et al. (2002) note that the relative speed with which ADHD is discovered in boys is a risky and biologically unfounded convention. I cannot help but think of young Gareth when I read about contemporary diagnostic practices. Is he truly a little guy struggling to find his voice in the world, or is he a victim of new gender biases in the medical system? Crisis advocates staunchly profess how there is no coincidence between diagnoses of autism and ADHD among North American boys and the general war on men. Christina Hoff-Sommers is among the leading, and most controversial, neo-conservative proponents of a thesis that articulates a failure on the part of multiple institutions to medically and socially protect boys in a left-wing, anti-male, 'feminist world'. In *The War Against Boys* (2000), Hoff-Sommers works to deconstruct feminist agendas in contemporary education and medical spheres. She notes several alarming trends: boys drop out of school, are diagnosed as emotionally disturbed, and commit suicide four times more often than girls; they get into fist fights ten times as often; they murder 20 times more frequently and are 15 times more likely to be the victims of a violent crime; boys are six times more likely to be diagnosed with developmental disorders; boys get lower grades on standardized tests of reading and writing, and have lower class rank and fewer class honours than girls. Hoff-Sommers sources these problems to a basic discounting of boys' biologies and developmental patterns within school settings. Elementary schools are essentially anti-boy because they emphasize reading (a skill, like speech, that develops faster among young girls than boys) while restricting the movements of young boys as a matter of daily convention. Boys are given tasks they are not ready for at an early age, or are immobilized in class (forced to sit still at their desks, for example) and thus become frustrated. They grow bored and inattentive, and so they lash out. To Hoff-Sommers (2000) schools effectively feminize the curriculum around girls' developmental patterns, forcing active, healthy, and naturally rambunctious boys to conform to a regime of gendered obedience. The result are institutional policies and modes of teaching that take what is normal behaviour for boys and pathologize it—that is, treat it as a symptom of a disease. Gurian (1997) similarly argues in *The Wonder of Boys* that regardless of how testosterone is surging through their little limbs, we demand that boys sit still, raise their hands, and take naps. The ultimate message is that boyhood is a defective state of being and that autism or ADHD must be the root cause. To scholars like Hoff-Sommers and Gurian, there is absolutely no question how and why our modes of education lead to the identification of autism and ADHD in young boys like Andy's son Gareth.

It is difficult to further reconcile these gender trends, but Hoff-Sommers (2000) proposes a value-laden set of answers. According to Hoff-Sommers, a culturally enforced 'misguided feminism' has been spreading such slander about boys. Boys face a chilly classroom climate. Schools are an inhospitable ground for boys whose propensities for rough and tumble play, competition, aggression, and rambunctious violence are cast as social problems. If it sounds biologically essentializing, that's because it is; for me, it is one of the most interesting gender battlegrounds in our culture. According to crisis theorists, misguided feminists have ignored the natural biological differences between boys and girls, and in their fear and loathing of all things masculine, they have demeaned an entire sex-based mode of education. The masculinity crisis is to Hoff-Sommers a politically correct failure to recognize basic biology. Boys, she argues, are simply different from girls, and efforts to transform time-tested and beneficial definitions of boyhood and masculinity will run counter to nature's plan.

Hoff-Sommers is not alone in her critique of the treatment of boys in school, or in the recognition of the widening educational gaps between males and females. Although he disagrees with Hoff-Sommers about the need to embrace essentialist masculine biology, Pollack (1999) argues, in *Real Boys*, that that being a boy in late-modern life is not all hegemonic fun and games. As co-director of the Center for Men at McLean Hospital and Harvard Medical Center in the United States, Pollack works to reveal what lies behind the stoic masks of troubled, modern boys as they struggle to cope with the mixed messages, conflicting expectations, and increasingly complex demands they receive in a hyper-sensitive gender culture. Kindlon and Thompson (2000) paint an equally depressing portrait of life for many young boys in North America in their book, *Raising Cain*. Through accounts of how young boys become emotionally scarred in a culture that is wrestling with the definition of appropriate masculinity, they expose a generation of boys who are sad, afraid, angry, and silent, simply about being boys. Kindlon and Thompson (2000), for example, point to chilling effects and outcomes in the cultural contestation about what it means to be male, such as demographic spikes in number of boys at risk for suicide, alcohol and drug abuse, violence, and loneliness.

Masculinity crisis theorists might be quick to jump in precisely at this juncture of the discussion with other 'hell in a handbasket' type comments. Along with the trends noted above, they point to the far greater likelihood of North American boys to be in gangs and go to prison, be overweight, or die in automobile accidents than their female peers. As I have documented elsewhere, they ask serious questions about why skyrocketing rates of body dissatisfaction, anorexia, and over-the-counter exercise supplement usage among boys tend to be unnoticed or explained away as anomalies by gender researchers (Atkinson, 2007).

Despite all of the trends noted above, we might do well to look beyond 'boy crisis' discourses in Canada and elsewhere. Students in sociology classes always ask: why don't we look for something positive in the world for a change? Yes, mushrooming rates of 'boy problems' in North America are important, but so are the new ways in which boys in crisis are managing their identities and social conditions of risk. I came across (well, sought out, really) a group of these boys in 2000, and studied how they engage in a subcultural brand of self-protectionism in the face of risk and crisis culture. For the remainder of this chapter, I examine their post-crisis lifestyles and highlight the potential for youth to fashion their own forms of risk intervention. What immediately struck me about the group is how, in a culture of extremely prone to risk, they become empowered through a spectacular physical-cultural practice of absence (well, abstinence, really). What I argue below is how their collective solution to crisis rests on the rejection of both traditional and crisis masculinities. At once, they decry traditional hegemonic masculine identities and practices (to which they simply do not have access), as well as soft, self-victimizing masculinities focused on doubt and risk. Through a resistance against both masculinity types, they engage in subcultural lifestyles as a pastiche hegemonic manoeuvre. In the previous chapter I discussed how some boys respond to crisis by consuming the image of masculinity; in this chapter we examine how boys respond to crisis by rejecting consumption as a technique for doing pastiche hegemony. They are modern day ascetics, and they call themselves *Straightedge*.

Finding Boys through Straightedge

At a time when boys who are supposedly in crisis are demonized, medicalized, or criticized for hyper-individualistic and fatalistic consumption ideologies, we often ignore how small clusters of boys actively resist consumption pressures through physical restraint. Sociologists have studied, for instance, how esoteric religious groups reject mainstream forms of consumption and bodily indulgence via the practice of *asceticism,* or through morally grounded lifestyles based upon intense body purification and control. Ascetics approach the body as a natural entity needing protection from 'noxious' physical pollutants (e.g., drugs, alcohol, disease, and, in some cases, medicines) or risks to its moral integrity created by cultural standards (e.g., sexual or eating norms and preferences). Often, an ascetic philosophy is buttressed by a belief that it is one's duty to align pure body practice with pure spirit. Recent sociological analyses of ascetic lifestyles have focused on the ways in which cultural messages regarding self-control, mind/body unity, and social interdependence are purposefully embedded in ascetic practices.

Here is, once again, where I have to offer a bit of academic confession. I am irredeemably fascinated by secular and non-secular forms of asceticism in subcultural settings. My intrigue hastened when I met a group of Neo-Primitives in Toronto in 1996. Neo-Primitives are, in general, enthusiasts of intense 'rituals' of the flesh including tattooing, piercing, branding, scarification, 'flesh hook' suspensions, and other radical modifications of the flesh. Among the Neo-Primitives I studied are hyper-body purists who tightly control everything to which their bodies are exposed, and who engage in symbolic rituals of the flesh (i.e., body cutting, branding, or flesh-hook hanging) to cleanse their bodies from time to time. I have also met and shared academic research time with young, ascetic yoga practitioners and Parkour enthusiasts who similarly see the body as a physical entity to be guarded with extreme vigilance. I started to scour academic literatures on asceticism in poplar culture, and surprisingly found only a handful of contemporary case studies. Shepherd's (2002) analysis of the Australian anarcho-environmentalist movement, for example, suggests how political resistance to environmental degradation may be waged through asceticism among like-minded young rebels. This young group of environmental protesters rejects capitalist philosophies of mass consumption in favour of a 'less is more' approach to resource use. In the hope of minimizing their collective environmental footprint, members practice Spartan discipline over their own consumption practices and attempt to initiate 'a moral [environmental] regeneration of the social world' (Shepherd, 2002: 142). Sociological analyses of ascetic lifestyles like anarcho-environmentalism are, however, very rare.

Like the anarcho-environmentalist lifestyle described by Shepherd, Straightedge asceticism is founded upon principles of intense self-restraint and personal responsibility, culminating in the practices of abstinence, sobriety, and protection of the body from noxious or addictive agents (Atkinson, 2003a; Irwin, 1999; Wood, 1999). Straightedge enthusiasts commonly reject hedonistic body pleasures and vices, and instead advocate ongoing self-improvement through body purification. Amazing in a cultural time and space when precisely the opposite is advocated as the norm! I quickly became fascinated by how their position on physical consumption and corporeal practice starkly opposes expressions of self-indulgence and hedonism common in other North American youth groups 'in crisis' like Skaters (Beal, 1995), Goths (Tait, 1999), Ravers (Wilson, 2006) and Hip-hoppers (Martinez, 1997).

The cultural origin of Straightedge in North America is pivotal for understanding their logic(s) of asceticism, and the group's relative 'uniqueness' among youth in crisis. In 1981, an American punk rock band called Minor Threat wrote a song titled 'Out of Step (With the World)'. The song extolled the virtues of self-restraint, personal responsibility, and social awareness. By rejecting the largely nihilistic messages offered to youth by other punk rockers of the day, Minor Threat challenged their (mostly male) fans to embrace more positive social attitudes about the body, spirit, and mind (Wood, 1999, 2001). Specifically, instead of being encouraged to aggressively resist their own working-class disenfranchisement and cultural dislocation through body hedonism (e.g., through sexual practices or consumption of drugs), a new generation of male punks was asked to adopt strict corporeal practices that would socially and psychologically enrich their lives. The credo of this inverted punk philosophy became 'Don't drink, don't smoke, don't fuck. At least I can fucking think' (from the song 'Out of Step [With the World]' by Minor Threat). These underlying ideas suggested that if young people could take control over their own bodily impulses through asceticism, they could then collectively bring about positive cultural change (Irwin, 1999). In effect, Straightedge evolved into an ascetic lifestyle of rebellion against the physical excesses asso-ciated with male-dominated youth cultures in North America. Through the early 1980s, the first and second waves of Straightedge practitioners created brands of punk music, clothing, and language to represent their philosophies of corporeal asceticism. Closely aligned with more traditional punk styles (e.g., ripped clothing, Mohican hairstyles, shaven heads, thrasher music, and Doc Marten boots), physical Straightedge style drew attention to an alternative message of walking 'the edge' through ascetic self-restraint. By the mid-1980s, Straightedge had developed into a fully subaltern lifestyle of ascetic resistance, with practitioners' alternative physical styles entwined with messages of phys-ical purity (Wood, 2001). Reaching the apex of its initial popularity during this period, the lifestyle waned in appeal by the latter part of the decade as Rap, Grunge, Goth, and other socially rebellious (and more nihilistic) male-in-crisis style cultures blossomed in suburban scenes.

However, a new generation of North American males started to explore the viability of Straightedge during the apex of the first wave of the masculinity crisis in the 1990s. Tired of the nihilistic messages offered by other youth subcultures in the era, the new cadre of Straightedgers sought proactive solu-tions to their feelings of (largely class) disenfranchisement, risk, and anxiety. Straightedge spawned a variety of ideological offshoots during this time, and practitioners often incorporated Vegan and/or Animal Liberation Front ideolo-gies into the lifestyles. Groups of Straightedgers in the United States (New York, Utah, and across southern California), and Canada (British Columbia, Ontario, and Newfoundland) adopted militant positions regarding physical purity, claiming 'absolute purity' to be the hallmark or true subcultural unique-ness of Straightedge. An even smaller number of extremist Straightedgers began to use violence against non-believers as a means of illustrating commit-ment to their morally superior ascetic lifestyle.

With the slow movement of Straightedge through Western nations, the Straightedge 'figuration' (Atkinson, 2003a, 2004) has grown and splin-tered into a series of factions (Wood, 1999, 2006). As a result, Straightedge asceticism is not a universal regimen among young boys, but rather engaged on a continuum. On one end of the Straightedge ascetic spectrum, some partici- pate in the lifestyle recreationally by adopting the principle of self-restraint, but do not become involved with many other enthusiasts, politically or otherwise. They believe in a plurality of Straightedge lifestyles and do not castigate those who do not practice ascetic philosophies. In the middle of the spectrum are the majority of Canadian Straightedge enthusiasts, whose asceticism organizes most daily rituals, social interaction choices, and leisure pursuits (e.g., going to local Straightedge concerts, spending time online with other Straightedgers, and promulgating the lifestyle). On the other end are a small number of 'Hate- Edgers' or 'Hardcore' practitioners who aggressively incorporate Straightedge into everyday life. Hate-Edgers are uncompromising with regard to asceticism, occasionally wielding violence against targeted non-believers. They are the hyper-political faction of the subculture, accepting only ultra-pure Straightedge ways of life as the truth. These enthusiasts internalize the common Straight- edge mottos 'Down for Life' and 'True Till Death', sayings that represent an eternal and uncompromising belief in Straightedge asceticism to the extreme (Atkinson, 2003a).

Differences between the signifying practices of Straightedge enthusiasts and those in other youth figurations are not inconsequential for understanding the social politics of asceticism. Much of the subculture literature in North America and the United Kingdom points to the dissenting, fatalistic, and present-centred mentalities adopted by young males in crisis or by at-risk groups (Brake, 1995). Subcultures (youth or otherwise) typically share political orientations of resis- tance to traditional social constructions of gender, structural constraints over social power chances created by class position, and educational disparity, but rarely coalesce around secular ascetic practices. Very few case studies document how secular youth groups embrace, rather than aggressively reject, (dominant male) cultural norms regarding the consumption of drugs and alcohol, the avoidance of physical risk, or sexual restraint (see Wilson, 2002a). Even fewer (outside the literature on environmental or religious social movements) docu- ment how asceticism and self-protection are employed as resistance strategies among socially labelled boys either in crisis or at risk of losing their masculine identities as part of a larger gender 'war' (Acland, 1995).

For the remainder of this chapter, Straightedge asceticism is analyzed as a conceptually novel form of young men's resistance that practitioners under- stand as a collective 'calling' (Weber, 1958) during a time of political economic gender crisis. The sense of Straightedge calling emerges out of, and is medi- ated by, a learned cultural *habitus*. *Habitus* can be defined as a socially learned personality structure that directs, but does not determine, one's tastes, prefer- ences, or lifestyle choices. (We will discuss habitus in greater depth later in this chapter.) The habitus experienced by Straightedgers is contoured by anxiety, suffering, and overexposure to late-modern crisis practices of self-indulgence, which have hegemonic male roots at their core. It is a habitus formed in cultural environments replete with perceived risk. In this context, practitioners of Straightedge strive to protect themselves through self-discipline and corporeal control, and they encourage others to recognize the tacit ideological contradictions and self-destructive outcomes associated with so-called mainstream male body practice in Canada. Straightedge teaches us that male crisis subcultures may adopt asceticism as a collective solution to widespread consumption pressures. Straightedge, while being labelled alternative or resistant by both insiders and outsiders in this way, is still a rather traditional or conservative approach to corporeality. However, the emerging popularity of Straightedge asceticism as socially 'resistant' may point to how self-indulgence and risk-taking are perceived to be normative by pockets of young men in Canada, and how traditional body practice is constructed as 'alternatively' masculine.

Crisis, Callings, and Boyhood Masculinities

Max Weber's (1958) landmark analysis of Protestantism as a foundational influence on Western capitalist practices includes one of the most theoretically lucid and relevant expositions of ascetic lifestyles. I remember reading Weber as an undergraduate student, thinking I would never, ever see his ideas again; how wrong I was! Through his theoretical deciphering of Calvinism, Weber outlines how, in this faith, religious asceticism is practiced as a means of demonstrating total acceptance of the will of God, in particular the notion of *predestination*. Importantly, while the Calvinist cannot actually buy his or her way into the chosen kingdom through ascetic performance, he or she may adopt inner-worldly discipline to illustrate submission to God. Inner-worldly asceticism is consciously undertaken as part of a divine 'calling' by the Calvinist and is emblematic of a strict commitment to renouncing, among other things, physical temptation. Protestant asceticism organizes a daily regimen and exemplifies what may be accomplished through divinely inspired self-mastery. Calvinists believe in the doctrines of predestination and unconditional election, which mean that throughout his or her lifetime, the Calvinist believes that only God's mercy will be grounds for his or her salvation, and he or she does not know if salvation is at hand. Consequently, following an ascetic path helps to alleviate the psychological stress involved in not knowing whether one is among God's elect (Weber, 1958).

Building on Weber's work, Harpham's (1987) analysis of religious asceticism as a form of social resistance underlines how ascetics in Western nations tend to renounce dominant norms regarding body performance. Through an understanding of the world mediated by religious doctrine, practitioners of asceticism both condemn the apparent leniency of prevailing moral codes dictating appropriate ways of using the body, and encourage others to engage religiously grounded techniques of ethical body performance. Indeed, ascetics often justify their life/body choices as morally superior to dominant cultural practices. According to Harpham, asceticism involves reflexive self-work in everyday life and a conscious attempt to proselytize others to the ascetic way. Part of the cultural logic of ascetic ways of life is, then, to set a community example for others to follow.

I first met Canadian Straightedgers during my doctoral ethnographic venture on tattooing in Canada, conducted principally in Calgary. Upon completion of the study, in which I met 31 Straightedgers, I decided to explore the cultural significance of Straightedge with greater focus as a separate ethnographic study. I remembered back to my fascination with Neo-Primitive ascetics and simply had to pursue this group as a matter of both personal and sociological curiosity. In drawing upon contacts I established with tattooed Straightedgers, I interviewed and hung around with a collection of 23 of them in Calgary in early 2001. By May of that year, I had completed my Ph.D., packed up house, and moved to St John's to take up residence as a professor at the Memorial University of Newfoundland; all the time I was wondering if I, as an 'older' male who is clearly not Straightedge, could secure entrance to their hangouts in a city I barely knew. I lived in St John's for only three months before I met Jane, a 25-year-old clothing retailer taking undergraduate courses at the university, and her self-employed artist boyfriend Darren. By late autumn of 2001, I was spending time with a group of four Straightedge enthusiasts in St John's; two members of the group were my initial sponsors Darren and Kate, while the other two were aspiring Straightedge musicians seeking to form a local band named Quinn and Chris. Over the next five months, I interacted with the group at local coffee shops, their homes, music concerts, and through a variety of leisure activities. Through the aid of these four sponsors I encountered 59 Straightedge practitioners in St John's.

With a population of fewer than 100,000 and a shrinking youth community, the number of Straightedgers in St John's is astonishing. Even in large urban areas in Canada, the Straightedge population is modest at best, so the presence of Straightedgers in the area surprised me. Most Straightedgers I encountered were between the ages of 16 and 25, male, working-class, and of Anglo-Saxon heritage. Their levels of education varied, with some still in high school, in university, or completely out of the educational system. A very small number were self-proclaimed militant Straightedgers, but they did not identify with Hate-edgers. They knew one another well and used several all-ages hangouts around town as their weekend clubhouses. As the research progressed, I devoted more time to interacting with a core group of them at local hangouts and solicited respondents for interviews. In two years of field research, I interviewed 42 Straightedgers in St John's.

The results of my research in St John's were consistent. Straightedge asceticism is based on a series of simple tenets: avoiding drugs, sex, and physical risk while promoting morality, discipline, and self-awareness. Straightedge is based upon Spartan corporeal practice involving intense restraint. It is predicated on the rudimentary idea that self-protection is uncomplicated: avoid what will harm you physically and reject any cultural influences, practices, and commodities that place bodies in jeopardy. Indulgence is for those who place importance on upholding middle-class ideologies of conspicuous consumption, and not for anyone seeking to achieve harmony in body and self. The coupling of consumption to middle-class hedonism struck me immediately. Most of the discourses about men and boys in gender crisis pertain to men in the Canadian 'middle'. Here, I had found a group who claimed to be at once in crisis but did not look as if they fit in the Canadian middle classes in any manner. Brian (age 19) describes his condemnation of conspicuous consumption and the brand–self image link in the following way:

> How much booze is enough to convince you that you're killing yourself? No one from Molson comes to help you out when you're dying from alcohol poisoning. . . . But they advertise in every corner of the world, and beer is really becoming a part of our culture. My friends drink because they think they have to [to conform]. It's a pretty fucked up society we live in when having the right beer is more important than seeing your life clear and treating your body well. You decide for yourself, will I buy everything that is going to poison me to live up to ideal[s], or do I walk away from that crap and live clean.

But unlike what Brian suggests, the task of staying Straightedge is complicated and taxing. It is a personal test of will one engages on a daily basis. Weber's seminal analysis of the Protestant ethic in Western societies drew attention to the ways in which myriad social tests underpin action, especially ascetic action. These tests become even more crucial in times of diffuse social crisis in which the will and the spirit are taxed considerably. As Elias (1983, 1996) confirms, much of social life revolves around the public performance of ritual tests in the pursuit of distinction (vis-à-vis the display of self-restrained behaviour). The ability to pass these tests on a daily basis is what grounds some Straightedgers' sense of moral superiority (and thus pivotal in their securing a kind of local, pastiche hegemony); being able to 'walk the edge' and not succumb to weakness is a mark of masculine distinction for them. But if the Straightedge calling does not arrive from religious or spiritual faith (as in the case of other ascetic lifestyles), how are the origins of the calling explained? If we cannot ascribe a sense of metaphysical calling to the practice of Straightedge, from where inside does the impetus to 'do' asceticism spring?

Perhaps one of the most neglected concepts in Canadian masculinity crisis research is that of *habitus*. Sociologists interested in the politics and practices of male subcultural life in Canada often fail to interrogate how and why young boys in crisis enter subcultures in the first place. Despite the volumes devoted to youth pathways into deviance (see Tanner, 2001), and research on the career contingencies involved in becoming a member of an alternative group, we know relatively little about how youth are socially and psychologically prepared to be in subcultures. While biographical information about subculture participants may be provided in extant research as a descriptive tool or as a causal predictor, rarely are subjects' *socially learned personality structures* (i.e., habituses) prior to subculture involvement critically inspected. While cultural studies research has championed how a working-class, present-centred fatalism among males motivates subcultural membership (Hall and Jefferson, 1976; Willis, 1978), and feminist research focuses on the ways female marginalization precipitates women's subcultural resistance (Garrison, 2000), few have studied how broader cultural habituses condition youth for subcultural membership.

A specific cultural habitus in Newfoundland prepares selected youth to participate in Straightedge. The habitus orients the boys toward understanding the ascetic lifestyle as a social calling. In the face of massive social and personal risk, and accompanying masculine anxiety, Straightedge (sXe) youth in St John's understand Straightedge asceticism as a means of protecting themselves and morally educating several generations of local males in trouble. Even more specifically, Straightedge derives meaning in St John's because of the cultural contradictions posed in this environment. On the one hand, St John's, Newfoundland, is part of a prominent G8 nation, one progressively recovering from economic hardships in the 1980s and 1990s. Canadians, until quite recently, have become accustomed to an incredibly high standard of living and this is apparent in cultural emphases on consumption and resource use (Suzuki, 2002). Yet St John's, and the rest of the province of Newfoundland and Labrador, continues to experience regional disparity in the form of economic neglect and decay. The accompanying despair often impacts young boys' masculinities in profound ways. Newfoundland is still very much a province steeped in traditional gender codes and cultural practices, especially as they pertain to breadwinning roles. Although Newfoundland youth realize they are members of an affluent nation where financial ability is tied to achieved masculinity, they do not participate in this masculine prosperity at a local level. The resulting division of consciousness has a series of consequences.

First, let us begin by considering from where most practitioners of Straightedge emerge in Newfoundland and Labrador. Overwhelmingly, Newfoundland Straightedgers have both rural and working-class backgrounds. Unlike fellow ascetics in other cities like Toronto and Calgary, Straightedgers in St John's typically emerge from contexts of pervasive economic suffering and receive ongoing generational blows to their public masculinities. Since the first (1992) and second (2002) cod moratoriums in the province, that have all but annihilated the fishing industry, towns and villages have 'closed' in the province (see Mason, 2002). While some Newfoundlanders 'emigrate' to other Canadian provinces, many families find their way to the capital city of St John's. Aaron (age 21) states:

> We left [the town] two years ago when it just wasn't good for us to stay no more. St John's is small for Mainlanders, but it's a huge city from a movie to a guy like me. . . . And when you're my age, and the place where people drink is the best place to be [George Street], you feel out of place right away, you know. At least back home I didn't have to put up with dat all the time.

In a culture steeped in the traditions of community pride, family heritage, tight clan boundaries, and masculine authority, the diaspora experienced by moving even within the province has dramatically altered the feel of life for young males in Newfoundland. By leaving their places of birth and their cultural networks, young men from 'around the bay' (i.e., anywhere in Newfoundland outside of St John's or Mount Pearl) often experience lingering alienation and cultural confusion when they move to the city. In St John's, the economic and cultural situations are only moderately better than in rural outports of the province. The unemployment rate in the city is nearly twice the national average at 17 per cent, and the median income in 2007 for all persons above the age of 15 was only $20,842. Emigration rates in the city (and throughout the province) continue to climb (an 8 per cent loss of the total population in Newfoundland and Labrador since 1996), fertility rates are the lowest in the country, and divorce rates have sharply risen in the past few years to nearly 30 per cent, the highest in the province's history. Despite the incredible resilience of the city and province in attracting new economic development and investment from oil companies, tourism industries, and the public sector, generations of young male Newfoundlanders are faced with grim economic and social prospects.

Second, the cultural character in Newfoundland has suffered from the fragmented nature of the economy. Given the lack of permanence young Newfoundlanders encounter in a country promising economic prosperity for all, it is understandable that some would understand this contradiction and respond through subcultural critique. Even though the trappings of middle-class culture encroach on the city—new cinema multiplexes, bistros, Starbucks, Land Rover dealerships, and cigar bars—most working-class males simply do not have access to, or an interest in, such Mainlander cultural forms. Some feel oversaturated by such commercial influences and over-socialized by outsiders telling them to consume more, and not to worry about the future. Jim (age 25) said to me:

> How the hell can I hang around here [St John's] and spend all the time when I got nothing. . . . I need my community back, I wants to go home but that ain't

gonna happen. I feel pressure to have the right shirt or drink the right beer in St John's, and when you don't, you feel like you out of touch. I don't needs that shit anyway, 'cause it fucks with your mind. It ain't my culture, it don't reflect me.

For many of the young men with whom I interacted, it is ultimately alienating to be in a context in which conspicuous consumption is important (if nothing else, just to stimulate the local economy). Youth who have matured in St John's have witnessed first-hand the economic and social fragmentation of the last two decades. They feel a suffocating lack of personal efficacy and argue that the structure of the community is pathological. Phil (age 24) suggests, 'Here, I have almost no chance to get a good job, and so the feeling is go out and get piss drunk and screw girls. Since you aren't going nowhere you might as well feel good. You get screwed all right, screwed for life'.

One of the most common themes in interviews with Straightedgers in St John's is their perception of a lack of access to structured or institutional avenues of male success. They are bombarded with encouragement to stick around, work hard, prosper, and consume, and yet the institutional means are simply unavailable. Rather than responding to the strain that results from the recognition of this contradiction with a deviant adaptation as Agnew (1992) might predict, Straightedgers seek out more personally and socially beneficial solutions to their masculinity crises. 'There's more than one way to stand up and be counted. My difference is shouting, at the top of me lungs, this [a lifestyle of consumption] don't make no sense' (Lenny, age 23).

Third, the notion that one should 'stand up and be counted' reflects an enduring sense of masculine duty, responsibility, and purpose common in Newfoundland history and culture (Byron, 2003; Ommer, 2002). In the face of seemingly insurmountable economic and political odds, Straightedge youth in St John's respond by holding firm to a tradition of persistence valorized within Newfoundland, but in their own uniquely accessible, pastiche way. Couple this with a strong work ethic in the Newfoundland working class (see Ommer, 2002), and it is easy to grasp why Straightedgers in St John's understand perseverance to be a test of personal will and cultural resilience.

Fourth, and in some ways most consequentially, 82 per cent of the Straightedge practitioners I interviewed have personal histories peppered by acts of violence, sexual disease, alcoholism, or physical and/or sexual abuse. While the vast majority of them have not experienced these processes first-hand, they have been privy to the trials of family members or friends. Alan's (age 19) narrative included the following:

OK, how 'bout this. . . . When I was 12 years old I saw my best buddy's mom and dad duke it out. My sister got pregnant at 14, and my buddy from school has got like eight STDs since we were 16. Half my old friends get shit-faced three or four times a week at least, and smoke a couple of packs a day. Little girls from my high school knew how to shoot heroin or take E [ecstasy]. . . . You're either blind or a moron not to want to avoid it. I don't want to be dead before I'm 25.

For Straightedgers like Alan, asceticism is a natural choice in cultural contexts of depressed excess. Rather than respond to the strain via forms of self-numbing indulgence, these youth pursue self-protective lifestyles. They realize that defiling the body through risk processes is merely a *magical resolution* (Cohen, 1955; Hebdige, 1979) to their collective material and status problems. Such a response contrasts sharply with youth responses to disenfranchisement and anxiety found in identity crisis subcultures like Rap, Hip-hop, Grunge, and Skater, wherein magical resolutions to status problems often involve retreatism and self-indulgence. According to Alan, one cannot alter the structure of the economy or turn the political tides, but one can protect oneself from, rather than wallow in, physical risk-taking. In de Certeau's (1984) terminology, they revert to protecting 'what they have' and can ultimately control their male bodies.

In sum, when exploring the social biographies of Straightedge practitioners in St John's, narrative similarities emerge. The youth grew up in increasingly stressed communities wherein economic uncertainty, cultural disruption, and physical/health risks were widespread. Mixed with these socializing influences were generational lessons about the resolve and doggedness of Newfoundland men. The desire to do something, the search for personal agency, and the rejection of culturally and individually noxious influences from the outside are at the forefront of Straightedge mentalities in St John's. They describe these interests as their calling to the lifestyle and as the foundation of their belief systems. Carl (age 20) believes the lifestyle is something one does not need to search for, but rather he views it as a calling he has always felt; in other words, it is his destiny to be an ascetic:

A [Straightedge] friend, who grew up about 500 kilometers from me, told me one time that he always felt different. He found power from being himself and not just getting gunned [drunk] because all the 'right kids' were doing it. Talk to anyone in the city who's 'down', and they'll tell you the same thing . . . we've all felt that way. It's true what some people say, 'if you're not Straightedge now, you never were'.

For Carl and others, heeding the call and seeking one's destiny as an ascetic is empowering. It reflects, in many ways, a sense of spirituality that underpins most ascetic lifestyles, in that practitioners envision their lifestyles of physical purity as divinely inspired and morally uplifting to other young men in crisis. To successfully protect oneself from destructive influences while seeking physical purity is a cultural vocation performed on a daily basis. Group members coalesce around and relish their collective abilities to 'walk the Edge' as ascetics in Newfoundland.

'Doing' the Straightedge Vocation

The Straightedge ascetic is not simply about self-improvement and personal empowerment. For some youth practitioners in St John's, the lifestyle is not silent social commentary. Their mission is to lead by example in the youth community, to attempt what Shepherd (2002) describes as a moral regeneration of the world. Importantly, although others might not be 'chosen' or experience the innate Straightedge calling (as it is perceived), other boys in crisis may be encouraged to 'consider how they live dead-end lifestyles . . . how gobbling chemicals, fucking and eating fast food means nothing' (Matthew, age 25). Therefore, Straightedge is practiced as a pastiche hegemonic vocation along two lines; in the one instance it is a quest of self-protection and salvation, and in the other it is a journey to rekindle morality in a cultural space plagued by collective male frustration, anxiety, and avarice. As documented by Lupton (1999), these types of subculture/social movements arise as deeply rationalized responses to risk cultures. The Straightedge lifestyle is novel in this context, however, as practitioners are seeking to highlight perceived cultural problems of immorality through their asceticism; it is not, in this case, hyper-individualistic bodywork, but bodywork given to be read and emulated by other young boys.

Elias (2002) and other figurationalists might have predicted the ascetic response among youth to adversity and anxiety in St John's. The push toward self-restraint and self-discipline, even through the articulation of social resistance, is all part of 'civilizing' processes in Canada, wherein groups seek status distinction through tightly regimented corporeal performance (Atkinson, 2003b). Given the economically disempowering conditions in the city and the hedonistic/nihilistic response among other male-dominated youth groups, the Straightedge ascetic becomes predicated on the use of 'restrained' behaviour to engage a lifestyle of moral/physical superiority. It is reflective of a habitus characterized by an impetus to maintain (perhaps stereotypically male) personal control and efficacy in contexts of relative deprivation. To experience Straightedge calling as a form of moral regeneration in depressed social contexts requires action in a range of spheres. Beck (1999) argues, the notion of immanent risk permeates all spheres of social life. As such, it is understandable why some groups develop entire lifestyles of risk management. In Weber's (1968) terms, there are several social spheres wherein one's calling is practiced, including: the aesthetic, the erotic, the economic, the intellectual, and the political. For a Straightedge practitioner in St John's, each is consequential in promoting ascetic lifestyles and inscribing morality into everyday physical behaviours.

The youth subculture literature is full of analyses of how youth signify in-group membership and ideological positioning through physical style

(Wilson, 2002a). In the pursuit of social distinction, subcultures often find it to their advantage to distinguish members from the mainstream. To perform one's calling in everyday life involves 'doing' identity in the aesthetic sphere. Among Straightedgers, outwardly identifying their bodies as different would make tactical sense in their pursuit of moral distinction. However, unlike other forms of youth lifestyle subculture or movement, there is no uniform Straightedge style. Curiously enough, practitioners of the ascetic see little merit in fashioning elaborate costumes to distance themselves from others:

> Part of the lifestyle is about not buying into the needs and goods we are told to buy. If we develop a unique style, then people might be tempted to buy into that only; to steal our clothing from us and forget the message. Straightedge isn't about making up a fashion people can mass produce and make money off of, right, I look like other kids, I wear t-shirts, ball hats, and jeans all the time because I don't want people my age to think I'm weird. It's easy to ignore someone if they look like a freak. It's my message people should hear and it shouldn't be drowned out by fashion. . . . There are some group tags we have like 'XXX' or 'sXe' that I wear on my clothes or get tattooed with, but the tags can't get in the way. (Dan, age 24)

Dan's comments suggest that while the boys share several communally defined logos and tags, these do not facilitate the type of distinction their vocation stresses. Instead, Straightedge is worked through alternative and more civilized social manners. For them, it is a socially superior position that articulates their desire to drop out of supposed mainstream (i.e., middle-class) cultures of masculine consumption and branding.

Of more consequence than commodities to Straightedge enthusiasts is the actual physical shape and performance of Straightedge bodies. Many Straightedgers prefer slim, fit, and fat-free physical forms. Overweight bodies, cigarette-stained fingers, sallow faces, and genitalia scarred by sexual disease are not aesthetically pleasing, specifically because they connote moral laxity and a lack of self-care. Undisciplined, unhealthy, and immoral bodies are emblematic of what Straightedgers perceive to be uncivilized yet hegemonic male norms. Roger (age 18) proclaims:

> The end of an 'eat, drink and be merry' philosophy is ugly. Canadians eat like pigs and no one seems to mind how all the popular foods and drinks slowly kill bodies. A fat, hooked-on-beer body is gross, and when I see one all I think is that the guy is a fucking lazy degenerate. . . . Never mind the fact that we look like hell as a total group of people, and not even natural anymore. . . . Have some self-respect, 'cause you have only one body in life and the harder you treat it the weaker it is.

Roger's words smack of a Straightedge preference for outwardly disciplined male bodies as markers of personal power and integrity. These starkly disciplined bodies are juxtaposed against the expression of sheer physical *jouissance* (playful joy) in appropriate settings like music clubs. All-age music clubs are hubs in local Straightedge communities, wherein practitioners collectively advocate unrestrained physical performance like slam dancing as a vehicle for releasing emotional impulses. A Straightedge concert—a key place for members to coalesce in any city—commonly includes extremely physical and pseudo-aggressive styles of dance:

> Slamming allows me to get rid of a lot of frustration. The pure rush of hitting other people in a small space, but not hating the people I'm dancing with, makes it a wicked experience. The music is pumping and the people are all jacked up with incredible energy. Sometimes my head feels like it's gonna explode, I get so excited. . . . But there's rules, right, like don't go and try to hurt anyone like a dickhead. Even in the chaos of the [mosh] pit, keep the Edge and stay in control. It's our Fight Club—I can get right nasty with other Straightedge kids and no one walks away with a stupid fucking grudge or something.

In these contexts, pogo dancing, windmilling, and other forms of 'contact' dancing provide what Elias and Dunning (1986) describe as a *mimetic* social experience. Mimetic social behaviours are generally those that stand in for, in physically and emotionally controlled contexts, risky social behaviours. Aggressive forms of physical interaction stand in for the unbridled release of desire that is deeply taboo in other Straightedge vocational spheres, thus providing a temporary 'decontrolling of emotional controls' (Maguire, 1993) that are rigorously upheld by practitioners. Their ability to control emotionality and bodily impulse displays a sense of social superiority among them, and starkly juxtaposes their behaviours against those groups who embrace and rationalize 'real' risk in the pursuit of sensual pleasure (see Vitellone, 2003). Of far less mimetic value is the strict regimen of abstinence many Straightedge enthusiasts in St John's practice in the erotic sphere. While disagreements in the community abound as to what is ruled out by pure abstinence (i.e., kissing, oral sex, and intercourse before marriage or after), Straightedgers generally concur that undisciplined sexual practice runs counter to the ascetic emphasis on responsibility and risk awareness. Leading in the youth community in St John's by not succumbing to physical temptation is a defining component of the alternatively masculine Straightedge vocation:

> I find it tons tougher to not have sex than drink or smoke dope. I don't grab a bottle of vodka and get turned on. But when I hug my girlfriend or kiss a bit, I mean, I want to have sex with her. But if I do, then I'm no better than any other

guy who lets their dick call the shots. My self-will is more important, my ability to hold onto a set of principles making my whole life better and safer. . . . [We] still have fun together and love each other, but don't risk disease or pregnancy to prove it. . . . Kids should wait 'til they're older and more mature to enter into a sex relationship . . . and that's what I hope other kids get from what I do. (Carl, age 20)

For Carl, as in the case of other Straightedge ascetics, the community example is more important than his immediate physical needs or impulses. The body's natural desires are significantly 'pushed behind the scenes of social life' (Elias, 2004) as an integral part of the vocation. This is required, according to many Straightedgers in St John's, because Canadian youth do not receive this message sufficiently via other institutional discourses and ideologies (for example in school or at home). Dan (age 24) argued: 'In school they teach little kids how to be sexually active, not how to say no. Every movie or TV show is about sex from the start. The 'learning' channels on cable show sex shows all day. Magazines, videos, and even my textbooks are full of sex. We have a culture that talks a good talk about safe sex, but the safest kind of sex is no sex until you're ready. I don't see nobody selling that message.'

While Straightedge ascetics do not deny the sexual component of humanity, they prefer to devote waking energies to discipline and self-respect in this vocational sphere. For them, the sacrifice of open sexuality is socially beneficial if understood by audiences as a sweeping moral lesson. In Hebdige's (1979) terms, their abstinence is 'given' to be read by others as a conscious gesture of moral regeneration in youth culture. The Straightedge ascetic is also given to be read in the economic sphere, as Straightedge performance includes a strong anti-consumerism stance. Young boys in St John's, for example, emphasize a 'do-it-yourself' philosophy of material and cultural production common in other punk rock and anti-mainstream subcultures (Leblanc, 1999). As they link status achievement through wealth and mass consumption with middle-class gluttony and moral degeneracy, Straightedgers advocate a less-is-more position on consumption, including emphases on green or organic products, generically named rather than corporately branded products, and the local sharing of goods:

Maybe being in Newfoundland, out here in this island, makes you realize how precious natural resources are. As people, we must come to grips with it, and it's nuts Newfoundlanders don't see this more, how scarce natural resources have been. . . . I do my part by growing organic food and avoiding a lot of stuff I can do without, like new Gap jeans, or new shoes every week, or a new ball hat. What you put in your head is the measure of your character, not what you put on your head. (Ryan, age 25)

Dissimilar to other male-dominated youth subcultures like Hip-hoppers (Martinez, 1997) who use symbols of conspicuous consumption as a method of alleviating status frustration as economically underprivileged or disenfranchised men, Straightedgers deny any social merit in consuming more than you need in the search for masculine distinction in times of crisis. Pete (age 22) claims:

> I watched a young guy at a restaurant last week order a $30 steak. What the Christ did he need a $30 steak for? What, so he can brag about how good it tastes? I've eaten steak, and can't tell the difference between a $2 and $20 steak. Bragging about the quality of animal you killed and ate is not worth very much in life. Spending hard-earned money on expensive meat just to brag about it is fucked. . . . I don't have to kill animals, destroy the world, and buy expensive food I don't need just to feel important.

As Pete's narrative implies, the Straightedge economic position also places importance on the protection of animal rights and related environmental concerns. Here, their ascetic position not only includes the moral and physical protection of people, it extends the ascetic boundaries to the broader environment. In this way, Straightedge asceticism resembles in form and content the type of anarcho-environmentalism Shepherd (2002) and Atkinson (2003b) outline. The protectionist mentality also makes sense given their cultural habitus and surrounding crisis socio-economic conditions.

The Straightedge vocation, with its emphasis on self/environment protection and integrity includes a push toward enlightenment through the intellectual sphere. By confronting the contradictions they feel are inherent in dominant cultural logics, Straightedge ascetics encourage others to be more self-aware of the causes and consequences of consumption (and in many ways, why men in the middle class feel crisis when they are not able to gain hegemony economically). Their rationale is hinged upon the idea that if individuals are self-aware, they will try to stimulate greater social awareness. Consequently, enhanced social awareness will lead to the exposure of cultural pathologies that are 'supposed' to be normative; thus people will be motivated to engage social resistance though education and lobbying. Jason (age 24) tells us:

> For me, education is not the same thing as socialization. When a kid grows up, he learns how to operate in society and how to make his way over the social obstacles he encounters. Education is about learning why we do the idiotic things we do, and how we call them our 'culture'. I never really learned anything until I questioned why people drink so much or why they do drugs, it's because of culture, it's because we try to be these kinds of people who don't get along and feel bad while doing it . . . The minute I got unplugged from the mainstream and did what makes me strong, I felt like I was truly an individual . . . I try to

teach people this every day, I think it's my responsibility to share my insights. Why not, why wouldn't I?

For Jason, and ascetics in other cultural groups (Shepherd, 2002), it is through the confrontation of hegemonic capitalist male logics (e.g., hedonism, consumption, risk-taking) and the rejection of their power that enlightenment occurs. With such enlightenment comes a great social mandate to proselytize and educate; this is part of the reason why one interprets the ascetic way as a calling. Some Straightedgers envision themselves as morally gifted and enlightened male teachers responsible for pointing out the pathologies in dominant body/social norms, and suggesting more civilized alternatives. Unlike esoteric groups of ascetics like those described by Iorio (1999), Straightedgers in Atlantic Canada see little merit in concealing their revelations about the masculine self in and out of crisis.

The role of social education is unquestionably a distinguishing characteristic of Straightedge enthusiasts in Atlantic Canada. Straightedge in other parts of Canada tends to be more esoteric and privately (even individually) meaningful, perhaps in reflection of the heavily upper-middle class composition of the group in these locations (see Atkinson, 2004). By contrast, Straightedge in Newfoundland is tied to the local politics of working-class youth activism, consciousness-raising, and pastiche hegemony-securing. In some respects, Straightedge is a political youth party with no voting rights in government, a lifestyle of persuasion led not by casting ballots but by practicing a policy platform in everyday life:

> I wear my politics on my sleeve. What you see is what you get. There ain't no hidden messages in my speech, I tells it like it is. Someone has to stand up and try to save the kids around the city, 'cause no one on the Hill [Confederation building] is up for it. There ain't no membership fees in my club, and my people spends time talking about the truth, my son, not hiding it. (Jim, age 25)

Summary

Straightedge is a novel case example of asceticism in Canada, especially among male youth cultures increasingly labelled as at risk, in trouble, or in crisis. Whereas researchers in the social sciences meticulously document how young boys 'go bad' and get violent in the face of daunting cultural pathologies that place their masculinities at risk, the case of Straightedge suggests how certain youth consciously choose an alternative masculine vocation grounded in individual and collective protection via Puritanical lifestyles. In doing this, Straightedgers tend to see the middle-class mainstream (who they perceive to be hegemonic) as uniformly consumption-oriented, hedonistic, and unrestrained. Such a categorization establishes the masculinities they achieve as ascetics as morally superior and culturally different. The sociology of the gender reveals few empirical examples of how boys' groups use ascetic body practices as social resistance in an era of supposed masculinity crisis. Further, it is rare that empirical case studies of subcultural body work evidence how young boys attempt to 're-civilize' cultural norms and values by returning to 'traditional' or ascetic lifestyles. Their nostalgia for the so-called 'conservative' (in many ways a hegemonic masculine) past is, however, predictably hegemonic in itself. What Straightedge can potentially teach us is that, while the turn to excess among male youth subcultures as a collective response to risk and crisis is well-documented in the sociological literature (Wilson, 2006), as is the development of so-called 'slacker' lifestyles, not all youth groups in contexts of doubt and anxiety develop fatalistic ideologies. Straightedge is not simply a blind response to cultural conditions; it is instead reflective of how young males themselves collectively understand and develop solutions to conditions of self-perceived risk based on their collective social-environmental experiences. In the end, regardless of the broader socio-cultural impact of Straightedge in St John's, Newfoundland, and elsewhere in Canada, we should remain attentive to how the gendered meaning of Straightedge is framed by practitioners as a civilized vocation that emerges from a perceived calling during crisis.

Discussion Questions

1. Do you agree with Hoff-Sommers that schools generally discount the biologies of young boys in classroom settings?
2. Can you think of any other social problem that seems to be more prevalent among young boys than girls? Can you explain, sociologically, why this might be the case?
3. Why do you think asceticism has not blossomed in racial minority male subcultures in Canada?
4. Do you think that the Straightedge writing of alternative masculinities through asceticism is actually an alternative masculinity at all? Could it not be, for example, considered hegemonic in its own way?
5. Why do you think Straightedge has not been attractive to young girls who wrestle with gender doubt and anxiety?

Key Readings

Gurian, M. (1997). *The Wonder of Boys: What Parents, Mentors and Educators Can Do to Shape Boys Into Exceptional Men.*. Los Angeles: Harcher. In considering the cultural effects of heightened gender consciousness, Gurian warns of the dangers of enmeshing male development with a female culture in late modernity. Outlining biological differences, he explains in *The Wonder of Boys* that boys are 'hard-wired' to possess certain traits. Because of male brain chemistry and the hormone testosterone, boys are apt, for example, to relish risk-taking and to be physically aggressive and competitive. *The Wonder of Boys* is a persuasive summons to society, specifically parents, educators, and communities, to unite to channel these traits in positive directions.

Hebdige, D. (1979). *Subculture: The Meaning of Style.* New York: Semiotext(e). In every subject area, there are landmark texts which are 'must haves'; such is the nature of *Subculture*. Hebdige's text launched a thousand research projects from the 1970s onward regarding the genesis and meaning of countercultural lifestyles. Anyone seriously interested in understanding how youth at risk/in crisis form into style cultures as a response should start with this book.

Hoff-Sommers, C. (2000). *The War Against Boys: How Misguided Feminism Is Harming Our Young Men.* New York: Simon & Schuster. *The War Against Boys* is arguably the most controversial and widely debated book on the masculinity crisis in the popular literature. We must question how or even if public discourses about the crisis might have formed outside of the academy if Hoff-Sommers had not written this text. She offers highly contentious and in some cases compelling evidence of a general problem with how boys' bodies and minds are developed in major public institutions in late-modern life.

Wood, R. (2006). *Straightedge Youth: Complexity And Contradictions of a Subculture.* Syracuse: Syracuse University Press. Robert Wood is most likely the leading academic authority on Straightedge culture. This book is the culmination of a decade's worth of research on a male subculture that, until only a few years ago, most people had little knowledge of or concern for at all. In *Straightedge Youth*, Wood meticulously documents the meaning of the practice for youth in Canada, and adds considerable insight into how different varieties of masculinity are part of the Straightedge ethos.

Wilson, B. (2006). *Fight, Flight, or Chill: Subcultures, Youth, and Rave into the 21st Century.* Montreal and Kingston: McGill-Queen's University Press. Wilson's book is one of the first in Canada or elsewhere to provide a sustained analysis of the Rave scene. The book details in part the notion of middle-class youth in crisis, and reviews subcultural theses regarding the manners by which young people seek out hedonism in the leisure sphere as a means of coping with late-modern social strain and malaise.

Web Links

Green Anarchy (http://greenanarchy.org/). A website and related magazine devoted to anarcho-environmentalist philosophy and practice. It provides a socially militant look at anti-capitalist and green practices.

Sociology, University of Birmingham (www.sociology.bham.ac.uk/). While the Centre for Contemporary Cultural Studies is no longer active at the University of Birmingham, its Sociology department website contains key links relating to the CCCS and stencilled occasional papers that were prominent in its development.

Straightedge (www.straightedge.com/). The widely accepted beacon of subcultural information regarding the history and contemporary practice of Straightedge. For well over a decade, the site has been an initial point of exploration for those curious about the lifestyle.

Key Terms

Asceticism: A lifestyle characterized by abstinence from various sorts of worldly pleasures (especially sexual activity and consumption of alcohol) often with the aim of pursuing morally or ethically informed goals. Ascetics often teach that personal salvation and collective social liberation involve a process of mind–body transformation brought about by exercising restraint with respect to actions of body, speech, and mind. Those who practice ascetic lifestyles do not consider their practices virtuous in themselves but pursue such a lifestyle in order to encourage self and others' mind–body transformations.

Habitus: A socially learned second nature that directs, but does not determine, one's tastes, preferences, or lifestyle choices. Habitus is internalized through socialization processes one experiences over the life-course, and helps to shape everything related to the individual, including one's body techniques for movement, speech patterns, clothing and fashion choices, career aspirations, sense of humour, and overall outlook on life.

Magical resolution: A supposed solution to a common social problem (such as inequality, oppression, or exploitation) that only symbolically resolves the issue. Resisting social inequality through flamboyant and resistant subcultural style, for example, may help to alleviate feelings of social impotence for youth, but this does not alter the conditions of inequality producing such alienation. So, magical resolutions are rather short-term solutions to deeply patterned conditions in a society.

Mimesis: A term with a full range of social and philosophical meanings, but generally refers to an act or representation of an act that 'stands in the place of' another. That which is mimetic resembles, or *mimics*, something 'real', but does so in a dramatic, fabricated, metaphorical, or socially controlled form. Sports violence is often considered mimetic of 'real' social violence on these grounds. Similarly, violence and the associated feelings accompanying it (such as anger, lust, greed, revenge) in movies is both 'real' (in that it involves human actors playing physical roles and doing stunts), but the showcased violence and emotionality is ultimately staged and carefully orchestrated to protect the actors from serious harm.

Straightedge: A style of life devoted to the total rejection of drugs and alcohol, promiscuity, and other vices that place the body at risk. Straightedgers believe through the intense and constant purification of the body, one achieves a sense of personal worth and control. Practitioners often see their ascetic lifestyles as morally and culturally superior to others. Straightedge originated as a predominantly youth subcultural musical scene in the United States, and is now a global social movement.

4 Male Femininities, Metrosexualities, and Liquid Ubersexualities

Chapter Objectives

This chapter introduces and critically explores the following:

⊛ The relationship between risk discourses and constructions of identity crisis among men
⊛ A deconstruction of the hybrid male-feminine identity
⊛ The cultural cross-fertilization between gay and straight male cultures in Canada
⊛ The rise in anti-crisis, anti-feminine, hyper-masculine media stars
⊛ How body modification practices are used by men in crisis as techniques for doing a form of plastic masculinity

In 1982 Bruce Feirstein penned an instantaneously iconic book, *Real Men Don't Eat Quiche*. The book lampooned and lauded traditional masculine habits and ethics in North America, and remained on the *New York Times* bestseller list for 53 weeks, selling 1.6 million copies worldwide. The title of the book referred to Feirstein's tongue-in-cheek reaction to the rise of yuppie, preppie, and other soft masculinities in the early 1980s, summarized as the crystallization of *quiche-eater* male cultures. The term 'quiche eater' quickly became assimilated in North American pop cultural lingo as a signifier of a man who is effeminate or one who lacks traditional masculine virtue (quiche, after all, is not the breakfast of champions). The book is overtly written as a nostalgic lament for the 'good old days' (i.e., pre-feminist America) when men were allowed to be men and gendered social roles were neatly cleaved and uncontested. Across the pages, men were told to engage and celebrate quintessentially hyper-masculine habits. They were encouraged, for instance, to look for two main attributes in a potential marriage partner: big breasts and trust funds.

To other readers, though, *Real Men Don't Eat Quiche* cleverly underlined the ridiculous, exploitive nature and cultural offensiveness of traditional patriarchal logic and practice. These people read the book as they might have watched the American sitcom, and brainchild of Norman Lear, *All in the Family*; with an understanding that Archie Bunker's character, while lovable, fallible, and vulnerable, represented the worst in American racism and hegemonic White masculinity. But Feirstein wrote the book and inserted it into public discourse at a time when masculinity was increasingly perceived as under attack from feminist academics, activists, and everyday people. As such, the book became part of a seemingly harmless backlash against American feminism, equal rights movements, and indeed, men who chose to stand outside of the hegemonic norm. I was 11 years old when the book surfaced, and I read it when my brother brought a copy home. I could not understand the depth or breadth of the satirical references and images painted across the pages at the time, but I do remember finding the book incredibly funny.

The danger of books like *Real Men Don't Eat Quiche* paralleled that of *All in the Family*, in that unless young men are aware of the multi-layered latticework of cultural critique and irony embedded in such texts, they can have a tendency to delegitimate, through seemingly innocuous humour, critiques from the outside. *Real Men Don't Eat Quiche* was followed in 1982 by a cookbook, *Real Men Don't Cook Quiche*, and an equally stereotyping and gender-traditionalist book by Joyce Jillson called *Real Women Don't Pump Gas*. Feirstein continued to write about the changing dynamics between the sexes in 1986, with his *Nice Guys Sleep Alone: Dating in the Difficult Eighties*. In 1992, another sequel, *Real Men Don't Bond* was released. The 'Real Men' series captured and exploited the collective and cultural existential angst of a continent wrestling with changing gender/sex codes and practices. The books use humour and (often misread) satire to document a growing trend in North American society: the changing nature of masculinity, men's roles, male identities, and forms of masculine representation. While the books are often read as celebrations of traditional masculinity or as a backlash to feminism, a closer reading of them might uncover how Feirstein and others were perhaps astutely aware of how the gender landscape had changed in North America. The books collectively poked fun at gender traditionalists. These books were often read as texts about women, and were co-opted into feminist discourses, But they were not about women. Different masculinities were creeping into public sight, new men had planted their flags in social space, and increased numbers of men preferred to opt out of the pursuit of traditional masculinities. The 'Real Men' series satirically attacked them and their presence in North America. The books created a witty and absurd 'us' versus 'them' mentality to illustrate the polarizing and oppressive nature of dominant masculine codes. I didn't get that when I was 11, and many people don't get that now.

We flash-forward 20 years to 2002, and Michael Flocker authors a book called *The Metrosexual Guide to Style: A Handbook for the Modern Man*. From a sociological perspective, the book might have been more accurately subtitled *A Handbook for the Late Modern Man*. Flocker's term *metrosexual* was quickly sucked up into pop culture discourse, and became a catchword for the styles of life shared among an entire generation of urban men. 'Metrosexual' refers to a man with an overt interest in liquidly masculine styles and tastes for diverse cultural (and quasi-feminine or queer forms); that is, a man who loves to shop and look good/stylish, and may be of ambiguous sexual orientation. According

PHOTOS 4.1 AND 4.2 The contrasting 'Bibles' of modern and late-modern masculinities

to the American journalist Mark Simpson, the metrosexual, 'might be officially gay, straight, or bisexual, but this is utterly immaterial because he has clearly taken himself as his own love object'. Flocker's guide did not encourage urban men to embrace or lament for traditional masculinity in a world struggling with gender roles and identities. By contrast, it advocated for the further loosening of gender codes and encouraged men to explore a range of male femininities. Flocker taught a generational class of 'new men' about the importance of non-traditional male music, film, art, home decorating, dating, fitness, and grooming styles at the same time that it taught them an updated version of Emily Post manners. What is particularly amazing is how many Canadian men extolled the virtues of metrosexuality in the early 2000s, and how metrosexual styles created an impact on the social politics of doing public masculinity. Such were the sorts of masculinity that were vilified and mocked only a short time ago in Feirstein's 'Real Men' series.

In this chapter, I examine the cultural time and space between and after the circulation of *Real Men Don't Eat Quiche* and *The Metrosexual Guide to Style*. Through the late 1980s and into the early 2000s, as crises of masculinity were increasingly internalized by a number of men, they explored the practice and representation of diverse masculinities. By direct contrast to the previous chapter, which illustrated how men seek to reclaim a flamboyantly hyperbolic hegemonic masculinity in many ways, this chapter examines the rise of a pair of non-traditional hegemonic masculinities in Canada. Attention is given to how and why a fuller range of heretofore stigmatized masculine body styles, aesthetic preferences, and *avant-garde* male identities became upheld by men. Among the masculinities discussed are male femininities, metrosexual masculinities, and ubersexual masculinities. A central argument across the chapter is that, late-modern social life is more tolerant of a range of masculinities', and yet, cadres of men 'in crisis' play with socially alternative masculinities in order to do pastiche hegemony and cleverly reaffirm old/traditional sources of masculine power.

Real Men Disappearing in a Risk Society

Every once in a while a social theorist breaks intellectual and public discourse ground with an incredibly novel and internationally relevant idea. Ulrich Beck did such a thing in 1992 with his book, *Risk Society: Towards a New Modernity*. Beck's thesis in *Risk Society* posits that people in technologically and capitalistically advanced Western nations transformed in the latter half of the twentieth century from industrial modern societies to so-called risk societies. In a risk-oriented society, social institutions are viewed less as collective producers of social goods like wealth, housing, safety, social bonds, employment, and health care, as they are producers of 'social bads'. (Beck, 1992: 48). The process of modern industrialization in nations like Canada has done more harm to people, argues Beck, than good in many respects. Think of the many 'bads' that now predominate in Canadian society. Violent crime, unemployment, disease, drug and alcohol abuse, energy shortages, banking and credit collapses, environmental change and decay, discrimination, and terrorism may each be extensively linked with the process of capitalist industrialization and the globalization of world economies. In a *risk society*, argues Beck (1992), people become acutely aware of, and preoccupied with, how the risks we produce as an overall capitalist culture now far outweigh the risks posed to us by nature, as a species. The net result is that Canadians, like members of other Western societies, are far more fear-oriented and disillusioned with traditional institutional logics (e.g., government, economy, higher education, etc.) and their practices. There is a spectacular presence of risks and an absence of solutions.

Beck (1992) argues that the real dilemma of living in a risk society is that, indeed, no one knows how to solve the majority of common, and most pressing, problems such as global warming, a dying economy, energy resource depletion, dwindling educational opportunities, and meaningful employment for all people. Modernist ways of managing risk, like drilling for oil in untapped places, sinking more money into employment insurance safety nets, going to war, or drastically raising the price of precious goods to quell the demand for them are recognized as antiquated and ineffective. From Beck's position, our systems and manners of problem-solving are buckling. We know little (or can do little) to affect change while we cling to solutions that reflect those systems that actually created the problems. Using the language of this book,

the proliferation of social risks/bads stimulates the growth of many social identity crises, and the generational development of crisis cultures. But why do I
mention Beck's assessment of risk society in the study of masculinities?

We must remember who are among the captains of modernity and capitalist
industrialism as well as institutions like the justice system, the government,
schools, health-care systems, and others, which were supposed to make our
lives better over the course of modern industrialization. Easy one. Any feminist
scholar will remind you that the authors of industrialization and the architects
of modern social institutions were, and perhaps still are, men. To this end,
White masculine hegemony has been maintained in Canada for quite some
time through the complex interplay between male-dominated capitalist power,
institutional authority, social position, and common ideology across the social
landscape (see chapter 1). The relative hegemony of men is only maintained,
though, as long as social institutions are able to produce institutional 'goods' for
people. Further still, Seidler (1994) argues that one of the best techniques for
maintaining this sort of social power also involves blaming those under the rule
of power (i.e., women, or non-hegemonic men) for the inevitable shortcomings
or failures of the rulers and their institutions. So, when teenage pregnancy or
drug use rates skyrocketed in the 1990s, Canadian conservatives and Members
of Parliament including Jacques Parizeau were often quick to point the finger
of blame at working mothers or single-parent families headed by women.

But in a risk society, the trustworthiness of male-dominated institutions
and the social relationships of power supporting them have come into serious
question. Those who were traditionally ruled asked very important questions
about the ability of the social engineers to rule effectively. The imploding trust
Canadians share toward our, still male-dominated, social institutions can be
evidenced everywhere. In the 2008 Canadian federal election voter turnout
dropped to 59 per cent, the lowest turnout for a national election since Confed-
eration. Belief in the effectiveness of the Canadian criminal justice system drops
almost yearly; health scares and epidemics in the last 10 years such H1N1, SARS
in British Columbia and Ontario, 'foot and mouth' and 'mad cow' diseases
in Alberta, and listeriosis and E. coli in Ontario, have amplified the Canadian
public's general frustration with the country's overburdened, underfunded,
and failing national health-care systems. Further evidence: participation in
traditional religious groups and their churches continues to wane; national
belief in or support for militarized responses to international problems such as
'terrorism' continues to dwindle; and, the globally mediated business scandals
and failures of transnational corporations such as Bre-X and (Conrad Black's)
Hollinger International have punctuated how male-dictated understandings of
how economic institutions should operate might not work anymore.

Over a decade ago, Robert Dunn (1998) noted that one of the defining
features of late-modern society is that traditional ideas about community and
the ordering of social life have shifted, blurred, or been erased following the

breakdown in our public trust of modernist social institutions (except, perhaps, in the example of hockey—which Canadians use more than ever as the one enduring institutional marker of our identity!). For Dunn, the ongoing dismantling of our collective trust in institutions as providers of *social goods* has led to a general reconsideration of how our communities are organized at every level: from the roles we play, the statuses we hold, and the identities we share. Quite simply, with the progression from modernity to late modernity, we move away from traditionalist ways of 'doing' and organizing social life. If we link what Beck (1992) suggests about social bads and their institutional locus with Dunn's (1998) ideas that late modernism is a period where traditionalist codes and practices are challenged or supplanted, two very important social contexts for a masculinity crisis are identified.

First, an era where risk discourses and ideologies are promoted is a fertile time for the proliferation of crisis. Such is the nature of a risk-oriented society. A society that considers, debates, and strives to control risks (whether these are real or imagined) is one inherently poised toward hyper-reflection about the sources of that risk (i.e., who creates the most risk), and the destablization of 'traditional' ways of organizing social life. If there is any enduring legacy of Durkheim's (1956) sociology to me, it is his recognition of how, when social life is destabilized rapidly, collective fear, crisis, and worry ensues.

Second, when collective belief in traditionalism fails, the norms, values, identities, and roles associated with those in charge of traditional life are subject to ongoing threat. I don't think it takes too much anticipation to predict where I am headed here; is the imagination too stretched if one is asked to consider what social group might experience tremendous identity crisis in a vast cultural and socio-structural movement away from traditionalist societies and their logics of order? But middle-class men in crisis have not withered away and died in a risk society that often points the finger at patriarchy as the source of many institutional bads. Quite to the contrary.

The practice of doing pastiche hegemony among middle-class men in Canada doesn't struggle against risk discourses. It embraces them. Why is this the case? The sociological thought of Anthony Giddens helps us understand why. When traditional identities and practices dominate in a society, argues Giddens (1991, 2001), individual actions do not have to be analyzed and thought about so much, because they are tightly constrained by cultural precedent and habit. But in post-traditional times, we are not as bound by historical codes and identities that constrain our choices for action and self-expression. Society becomes much more *reflexive,* that is, aware of its own precariously constructed state; the arbitrary linking of things like power and authority to particular genders, classes, races, or religions is challenged. We are encouraged to be ourselves, strive for anything, and most importantly, not to allow anyone to discriminate against us on the basis of historical stereotype and expectation. There is a growing freedom ,therefore, in Giddens's (2001) opinion, to narrate the self in new and novel ways; to create one's own individuality and to abandon historical frameworks of identity that control the individual. Such is a cultural mindset that smashes the codes and orders of hyper-masculine patriarchy and hegemony, and the categories of inequality it creates. Well . . . think again.

If Giddens is right, late modernity is a time when people are free to narrate their selves, rather than simply inherit them within a complex and heavily cleaved or stratified social-cultural hierarchy. In this consumer-oriented, self-serving, identity-rights, *me*-preoccupied culture, we often forget that more men than ever before are cut loose from traditional codes of dominant masculinities that actually served to render them powerless as non-hegemonic men. Quite simply, in a post-traditional society where individualism and the narration of individual identity reign supreme, men who have been historically out of the masculine power loop, or those who have been cast out of Eden in late modernity, now have the opportunity to locate and exercise pastiche hegemony in novel ways. They can tap and exploit the freedom to write one's own masculinity as an important technique of power. As discussed in this chapter, the rise of 'new masculinities' in Canada over the past two decades illustrates how risk culture and the breakdown of modernity's institutions, codes, and practices have opened the door for some men to become locally hegemonic in their lives; literally, to narrate power in their lives as 'new men' through embodied performances. Hegemonic masculinity had to die in our risk society, so that hegemonic men could survive.

Rosalind Gill (2005) points out that the 'new man' and new masculinities ostensibly symbolize the death of the stereotypical (that is *singular*) hegemonic male. A newly masculine man may be emotionally and domestically involved, and may be nurturing and profeminist in his orientation. He realizes that much can be personally gained (i.e., sex, money, love, children, harmony) by becoming overtly feminized. For other sociologists, new masculinities are the embodiments of highly narcissistic men who are preoccupied with writing their own masculinities in everyday life through the myriad social products they consume (see Luciano, 2001; Malossi, 2001; and Weltzien, 2005). For sociologists of sexuality, new masculinities represent groups of men who were brutally shunned, and in some cases criminalized, in historical societies. Whatever the focus, Gill teaches us something important about the rise of new masculinities. Not only did they emerge across social settings replete with risk and crisis discourses, they emerged at a time when media and commercial body industries were calling 'new men' to stand up and be counted.

In the 'greed is good' culture of the late 1980s, perhaps most convincingly embodied in Gordon Gekko from *Wall Street,* a dramatic decline in manufacturing and boom in the service sector and retailing markets encouraged more people to consume self-image and body-oriented products in order to keep the economy flowing (remember, again, Giddens's ideas about reflexive societies).

As the official North American recreational pastime, shopping culture targeted both men and women as primary consumers, and huge shopping multiplexes like the Eaton Centre in Toronto and West Edmonton Mall, along with smaller strip malls, outlet compounds, boutique arcades, and later big-box and online stores were created to facilitate the growing public interest in 'me' products. In realizing and tapping into the era's zeitgeist of self-indulgence and obsession, marketing companies began aggressively promoting new 'self-care', fashion, and identity products to men, heretofore a hugely untapped retail market. One no longer had to visit a Shoppers Drug Mart for Blue Stratos or English Leather cologne, as you could go to one of the many emergent men's fashion retailers and purchase your favourite haute couture brand from Calvin Klein, Ralph Lauren, or Hugo Boss (in the case of the latter, I am always reminded of a scene from the movie *Rocky IV*, when Sylvester Stallone wears a Hugo Boss branded hoodie into the ring before a boxing match—a far cry from the representation of masculinity Rocky espoused in the first, or indeed final, installment of the series!). Gill (2005) calls the late 1980s a 'quiet revolution' in men's self-obsession with consuming/narrating their masculinity through a huge range of styles.

Important, though largely dismissed or undervalued in examinations of the changing masculinities in the 1980s, is the influence of new wave, new romantic, and glam rock representations of men in music videos. Certainly the MTV and MuchMusic revolution in North America placed a litany of subtly (and sometimes not so subtly) queer and feminine men on stage. Groups including Bronski Beat, Platinum Blonde, Loverboy, The Smiths, A Flock of Seagulls, Duran Duran, The Cure, and even later heavy metal bands like Mötley Crüe, Quiet Riot, Twisted Sister, and Poison, built on the gender-bending traditions established by 1970s music vanguards like David Bowie and Iggy Pop, and showcased completely non-traditional representations of masculinity. I remember scads of kids my age (and teenagers over the entire course of the 1980s) who rushed out to stores like Le Château to try and assemble outfits representing these decisively non-traditional masculine personas. My brother, and of course my dad, used to shake their heads at me, and would say I looked queer. That was the point, though, as the fashions—just like the Teddy Boy and Mod fashions of the 1960s in the UK—turned traditional forms of masculinity (which many of us did not identify with) on their heads.

At pop clubs in Toronto, Montreal, and Vancouver, 'club kid' scenes that emerged from New York gay and lesbian bar cultures were more prominent. The rise of the gay movement in and of itself has been absolutely central to our understanding of representational practices for depicting new masculinities. A proliferation of North American magazines aimed at gay men like *Out* or *Outlook* showcased gay masculinities. Interestingly, they are no longer just targeted at a gay political activist audience, but they specifically offer new pleasurable representations of diverse masculinities. This reflects the increasing confidence of the gay community, at least in metropolitan areas, as well as the increasing corporate recognition of the power of the 'pink dollar'. And these magazines, together with gay porn, pin-ups, and particular subcultural styles within the club scene, have had a profound effect on representations of masculinity. Most notably they have cracked apart the association of masculinity with heterosexuality and the elision of masculinity with activity by showing men not simply as active sexual subjects, but as objects of desire.

The late 1980s and early 1990s also witnessed an unprecedented explosion in the representation of Black masculinities in magazines, films, and perhaps most importantly, in popular music genres like rap and hip-hop. While alternative, edgy, and historically soft representations of gender-bending or gay masculinities crept into pop culture in the 1980s and created new spaces for marginalized masculinities, Black masculinities jumped front and centre into pop culture during the 1990s. The 'Blaxploitation' films of the 1970s like *Sweet Sweetback's Baadasssss Song, Shaft, Super Fly, Cleopatra Jones, Blacula, Foxy Brown, Three the Hard Way, Dolemite*, and *Mandingo* certainly created a widespread White fascination with Black masculine 'cool', but it would not be until the emergence of rap and hip-hop pioneers such as Grandmaster Flash, Parliament, George Clinton, the Sugarhill Gang, Public Enemy, Run DMC, and a host of others that radical Black masculinities would encourage young (White) middle-class boys and men to see masculinity in different terms. Even though civil rights and liberties movements dating back to the turn of the twentieth century had lobbied North Americans to reconsider what a Black man 'is' or can be, as Lusane (1993), Keyes (2002), and Krims (2004) argue, no other system of Black masculine representation (save for professional sport) has similarly impacted cultural constructions of masculinity like rap.

I vividly remember the emergence of landmark albums across the tenure of my adolescence that every kid scrambled to get and then hid from their parents. How can I forget the insane popularity of Michael Jackson's *Thriller*, or in Grade 9 the release of Joy Division's *Substance* or Depeche Mode's *101*? But practically nothing matched the release of NWA's *Straight Outta Compton*. The high school boys of my generation all had bootleg tapes of the album. The graphic, explicit, violent, hyper-sexualized, radically political, and unapologetic lyrics delivered by Ice Cube, Dr. Dre, and Eazy-E brought us into another world of urban reality and masculinity. It woke up many of the kids in my generation and pointed us to rough, aggressive, poetic, and frustrated masculinities we had only seen caricatured in movies or whispered about on television. The songs did not resemble the whitewashed *Cosby Show* and Air Jordan Black lifestyle that had been mass-mediated to us for nearly a decade. These Black men were angry, determined, and present, and they hated everything about the kind of kids we were; and we loved them for it. Their disenfranchised and alienated rap masculinities replaced the decade-long love affair kids like me had with progressively 'soft' emo masculinities. We went from getting in touch with our feminine sides to exploring our angry, hyper-masculine sides. As I reflect now, rap songs like NWA's 'Fuck tha Police' or Public Enemy's 'Welcome to the Terrordome' appealed to many of us because, while we could never share empathy with the artists' experiences of racial discrimination, exploitation, and structural dislocation, we understood their frustration as males in a culture of risk and crisis. Critics may not understand that rap appealed to scores of young men in my generation because these Black men articulated a sense of frustration and anxiety our own fathers and brothers were feeling but never mentioned.

So, while growing up as young men in the 1980s and into the 1990s, the economic, political, and pop cultural world shifted beneath our feet. As more men with a range of masculinities fought to win a cultural presence and as our risk society fully blossomed, the boys of my generation were increasingly taught to poach, mix, match, experiment with, and find comfort in a host of masculinities. These were the seeds of pastiche hegemony in late modernity. Gay men, black men, soft men, and hard traditional men each became masculine models to different degrees and depths. The ironic outcome is that boys in my age group quickly jumped on the diffuse cultural movement to tolerate, nurture, and accept many of the historically marginalized masculinities in our own ways and for our own self-privileging purposes. In the true spirit of cultural co-option and appropriation we adopted the signifying and symbolic practices of these new men to find new places and statuses of power in Canadian society. We ate up, colonized, and deployed gay, emo, and Black masculine cool in very, very stereotypical ways. By doing so, we were liberal, hip, reflexive, and invested in the contemporary. We were not our fathers and would not emulate their out-of-touch power masculinities; and, the consumption of these new masculinities became our grand gesture of Oedipal defiance. Maybe my generation will go down in history as the one that struck the final blow against the sanctity of traditional masculinity. We became an army of ornamental men who had discovered liquid modern, pastiche hegemony. By adopting the roles, statuses, and identities of all social groups (particularly those who were challenging from the outside in our culture of risk), popular masculinity transformed from a relatively monolithic thing to everything. The pastiche hegemonic man became a cultural chameleon who could find power by adopting the guise of the other and incorporating it, seemingly harmlessly and appreciatively, into his noticeably muted masculine identity.

In what follows, I unpack two chameleon masculine forms of the late 1990s and 2000s. Both of these emerging masculinities are predicated on men's quest for power and status through the use of feminine, queer, and radically mixed masculine forms. By taking and rearranging competing gender identities (i.e., to traditional masculine identities in the culture of risk and crisis) these new men have wrestled considerable power away from 'outside' contenders to the masculine throne.

Male Femininity

Theorists of contemporary masculinity often make the general claim that men in crisis have a tendency to define themselves (i.e., their social personas and achieved identities) through their bodies and innovative gender-bending practices (Cregan, 2006). This tendency makes sense given the late-modern movement toward self-reflexive, risk-oriented, and hyper-consumer society, but it is also linked to more general sociological and economic arguments about what has happened to men's work and the end of the meaningful masculine careers in late modernity. The cultural separation between men, masculinity, and dominant workplace identities we have witnessed in risk societies has led theorists to assert that men—especially in the middle class—actively search for new sources of identity that allow them to appear as new, powerful, and decisively contemporary. Being a contemporary man, as Flocker (2002) instructs, is at once about embodying a masculine confidence, self-assuredness, self-control, and determination, but also about incorporating more reflexive, sensitive, self-monitoring, and aesthetically feminine traits. Through the consumption of historically feminized body practices, physical concern (like fashion) and forms of self-representation, these men have created new modes of metrosexuality or *male femininity* in Canada; these are hybrid masculinities that retain some of the more salient and power-producing qualities of traditional masculinities while simultaneously poaching select physical cultural practices of women. Using the terms of Michel Foucault, some men in the Canadian middle class play around and experiment with male feminine body practices as powerful *techniques of the self*. Techniques of the self are embodied 'arts of existence' according to Foucault (1987), by which men not only set their own rules of self-representation and masculine care, but also create new sensibilities about gender itself. Let's examine the case study of cosmetic surgery as a quintessential example of male feminine techniques of the self in action.

I started my study of cosmetic surgery on the heels of a study on tattooing in Canada (Atkinson, 2003a). Over the course of the latter, the massive groundswell I documented of women's involvement in tattooing over the last two decades shocked me. The dismantling of many of the masculine stereotypes and boundaries surrounding the culture of Canadian tattooing is emblematic of how women are progressively challenging how gender is embodied—just watch the TV show *Miami Ink* if you don't believe me. At the end of the study, I remember questioning whether there is a conceptual equivalent for men. I found that equivalent in the case study of cosmetic surgery.

Since 2000, men's involvement in cosmetic surgery in Canada has mushroomed. Estimates suggest that over 10,000 Canadian men have received aesthetic surgery in the past 10 years, with participation rates rising sharply in the past three years alone—a 25 per cent increase in participation (Medicard, 2006). Although there exists a rather full literature on women's experiences with cosmetic surgery in North America and elsewhere (Sarwer and Crerand, 2004), incredibly few body theorists have empirically addressed men's embodied interpretations of the cosmetic surgery process (Atkinson, 2008a; Davis, 2002). My own involvement with cosmetically altered men commenced when I first encountered a surgery patient named Les in southern Ontario. Following a brief conversation at the gym one day, he disclosed his experiences with three cosmetic procedures: Botox injections, liposuction, and an eye lift procedure. Over the course of time I pondered Les's confession to me, and considered the viability of a study of men and cosmetic surgery. By the autumn of 2004, I sought out and interviewed additional patients in the southern Ontario area (including Toronto, Hamilton, Mississauga, London, and Burlington).

With a population in excess of 4,000,000 and a booming cosmetic surgery industry, the number of cosmetic surgery patients in the southern Ontario region is increasing exponentially. Patients normally range in age from 19 to 65, are largely middle-class, with a mean income of approximately CDN$120,000, and predominantly of Anglo-Saxon heritage (Medicard, 2006). Most of the men I know who have experienced cosmetic surgery have undergone one or two treatments, while a small minority of others has received extensive bodywork. The most common procedures Canadian men request includes nose jobs (rhinoplasty), Botox, microdermabrasion, and liposuction (lipectomy). However, other men undergo hair replacements, breast reductions or reshapings (gynecomastia or mastopexy), eye lifts (blepharoplasty), skin smoothing or reductions and 'tummy tucks' (abdominoplasty), face lifts (rhytidectomy), and in rare cases, muscular implantations in the chest, biceps, or calves.

What I have come to learn about men who engage in cosmetic surgery is that they represent what Baudrillard (1986) called, 'the authentic [gender] fake'. These men are classic simulations of traditional masculine and feminine realities and personas. The metrosexual or otherwise male feminine man is outwardly concerned with his appearance to stereotypically feminine degrees, but is not a woman. He is a man who often aligns himself with flamboyantly caricatured ideas regarding gay men's preoccupations with slim, smooth, fit, style-conscious, and highly self-referential bodies, but whose sexuality never bends. He is, therefore, a man who seeks power through corporeal displays of modern sensibilities about being a non-traditional man, and relishes the symbolic practices and identities of the Other. He is, in Baudrillard's now classic terms, the simulation of a true gender reality. A metrosexual is neither male nor female in totality, but nor is 'metrosexual' a recognized and distinct gender either. He blends and reassembles the best of both gender worlds in a clever technique of power. As a form of simulacrum (which means 'likeness, similarity'; a reproduced image without the substance or qualities of the original), the metrosexual, male feminine character is not a copy of the real (male/female), but becomes a truth in its own right: the *hyper-real*. Like a plastic Christmas tree that looks better than a real Christmas tree ever could, the metrosexual is one who can appear to embodying the 'best' of both genders without any of the historical socio-cultural problems or baggage associated with either. It is a pornographic style of gender; a gender which is sexier than actual sex itself. But why do the men do this?

In a poignant analysis of the gendering of power in Western figurations, Brinkgreve (2004) comments that men's social control has been challenged along a number of lines, especially men's ability to wield unfettered dominance and social aggression as public practice. This is the nature of a post-traditional, late-modern society. Yet some men, contends Godenzi (1999), interpret the ongoing and unfinished attack on male dominance as a challenge to the very foundation of established masculinity. Labre (2002) examines how groups of men perceive the (external) restraint of men or male bodies as a critical condemnation of and control effort on the very basis of the male psyche and/or the male social order. In perceiving masculinity as threatened through diffuse anti-authoritarian (read *anti-male*) social doctrines and politically correct sensitivity policies, some Canadian men feel encouraged to reflexively engage in forms of bodywork to shore up their traditionally masculine images in socially 'non-threatening', gender hybrid manners; a clever trick, eh? The cosmetic surgery patient Allan (age 41) explains:

> I'd never looked like a handsome guy until I underwent the hair transplantation, you know . . . I'm like every other man who's lived with teasing about being bald so young. Women find the look totally unsexy and not very strong (looking). If I ever became angry about being teased for my baldness, I would be called hothead or the Alpha male trying to vent his anger . . . You catch more flies with honey than vinegar in today's society, and so I thought that I could do what women have done and use beauty and looking youthful as a way of achieving status. It worked like a charm.

As Allan and like-minded peers explain, these men in self-perceived crisis may find novel forms of social power by reclaiming their threatened identities and bodies and repackaging them as aesthetically desirable (i.e., as emotionally pacified). They tactically align with new images of male femininity and metrosexuality through cosmetic surgery as a technique for illustrating their consent to late-modern social codes about being a new man (Atkinson, 2006). By drawing on current cultural preferences in Canada for the fit, toned, groomed, and non-aggressive body (Niedzviecki, 2004), the men, at least from their interpretive standpoints, negotiate their way through the contemporary crisis of masculinity.

The late-modern male feminine Canadian gives his body to a corporeal professional such as a surgeon to be reworked in stereotypically feminine ways; in the process, he acknowledges a central deficiency with his male body and sense of self. It is both an admission of weakness (i.e., of being in crisis and at risk) and a moral gesture of the desire for self-improvement. Such a confessional practice finds grounding not only in one's desire to explore masculinity in novel but power-building ways, but also in a traditional Canadian middle-class aesthetic (see White, Young, and Gillett, 1995) that targets bodies as sites of strict monitoring and disciplining.

Although marked gaps continue to exist between the genders in relation to power chances within most institutions, the men I have spoken with about cosmetic surgeries believe their position as established (male) authority figures has been dislodged by women's participation in Canadian economic and political spheres. When telling stories about motivations underpinning cosmetic procedures, nearly three-quarters (74%) of the men I have interviewed to date talk about feeling threatened at work by younger, smarter, and healthier women—especially in image-oriented business environments that equate outward appeal with intellectual competency and moral worth. Peter (age 54) taught me:

> Our company hired three new managers last year, and two of them didn't look any older than 25. What makes it worse is that they are well-spoken, bright, charming women who are gorgeous. So there's me, an aging guy in a changing business environment who appears as if he's missed more nights of sleep than he should have. The superficiality of that realization kind of makes you sick . . . but these people won't want me around unless I adapt, unless I change. You either evolve or die off like a dinosaur.

Important is that Peter's fear-orientation encourages him to consider cosmetic bodywork as a rational solution to his incompetence anxieties. Peter's masculinity is partly anchored in his ability to appear physically as competent in the workplace. His masculinity is reconciled through radical, male feminine physical intervention. He, not accidentally, has adopted the physical practices of those who challenge him—in part because he, like other men I have interviewed, stereotypically and discriminatingly believe that women have attained power in late-modern Canada through their physical attributes and wiles.

Other men who describe risk or threat at work as a motivator for cosmetic surgery strategically employ classic 'techniques of neutralisation' (Sykes and Matza, 1956) to account for their male feminine body projects. When challenged about the source of their concerns at work or feeling at risk, and the perceived lack of control experienced in the workplace, the men typically argued with me that cosmetic bodywork is neither morally problematic nor physically dangerous to them as men. Derrick, a 52-year-old marketing expert who regularly receives Botox and microdermabrasion says:

> I can't wait another 20 years to take action. I need to be a man who walks into the room and no one says, damn he looks tired. If that continues to happen, I'll

be out the door. I could have experimented with herbal remedies, creams, or lotions to erase the years from my face, but it might take years, if it even works. Why wait when I can have better results from a doctor in only one day? That's not feminine, that's just plain smart.

For Derrick (whose words, in a Freudian slip, remind us that being feminine to him is not about being smart!!), any risk in or potential long-term effects of the procedures is secondary to the immediate gains received from medical intervention. This means-to-an-end, here-and-now mentality is directly reflective of the commodified and highly rationalized manner by which people come to approach bodies (and body problems) in late-modern, ornamental societies. Any service able to cure his problems of masculinity is thus justified as worthwhile, particularly when the service may be purchased from a qualified medical professional with celerity and precision. What the above narratives underscore is the process by which men come to frame and reframe their bodies/identities as innovatively male feminine through surgical intervention. For the men, actively responding to a perceived control threat through traditionally feminine bodywork is a newly and progressively masculine endeavour, a manoeuvre designed to make them appear culturally invested in burgeoning and widely mediated images of the new man. Surgery is configured as a technique of bio-power and control as it helps men respond to the fear of the masculinity crisis head-on (Sargent, 2000).

Compounding the threat some men perceive to exist regarding their masculinity in the workplace and across institutional settings is the type of work men are performing and the lack of spare-time exercise in which they partake. With more men than ever in service or information-processing industries, the current generation of middle-class Canadian men are perhaps the most stationary workforce in the country's history. With decreasing amounts of spare time, dietary habits revolving around high-calorie fast-food choices, and leisure time dominated by consumption and inactivity, the physical tolls on their bodies are evident (Critser, 2002). The late-modern risk economy and associated lifestyles, it seems, are not easily reconciled with traditional images of the powerful, performing, and dominant male (Faludi, 1999). The men with whom I spoke about surgery express a sense of frustration with the form and content of their work responsibilities. Ritually performing disembodied or virtual work (i.e., computer-facilitated) every day encourages a mind–body separation and neglect (Potts, 2002). Roger's (age 45) words are emblematic of the disaffection some men experience with their work:

Sitting at a desk for 10 hours a day, then a car for two, and then on your couch for three more wears your body down. Not to mention that my skin barely ever sees the light of day. At times, I can feel my face literally sagging because of my posture . . . Looking in the mirror when you're 40 and having a road map for a face shouldn't be surprising. That's not who I am, that's not the image of my inside I want to project.

Men like Roger refuse to link marginalized external bodies with inner selves. Roger's body is further objectified and instrumentalized in the cosmetic surgery process, as he views his physical form as a site of much-needed management. Cosmetic surgery provides a fast, efficient, and highly rational way of alleviating these psychological strains and social discomforts. For men like Leo (age 37), a graphics designer living in Sarnia, Ontario, his need for facial surgeries results from a social pressure to work in support of his extended family:

> It's not like I can quit my job, or be there for less than 12 hours a day if I want to earn a living. No one pays me for sitting on my ass and doing nothing, they pay me for sitting on my ass and designing! If I choose not to work, I'm choosing not to feed my family . . . We come from a very traditional Italian background, and it's not questioned that I'm the sole provider . . . There's an unspoken rule that a man who cannot provide [for his family] isn't really a man.

For nearly 10 years, Leo's work habits have, in his terms, 'weathered' his body. The three facial surgeries he has received temporarily remove the unwanted marks of an aged masculinity from his appearance. Like other men, Leo configures his surgical preferences as a symbol of his dedication to looking his best, even in the context of incredible social/work pressure. Surgery, for Leo, is a decisively calculated male feminine response to the social problems of 'men's work' inherent in everyday life. Still, when confronted about such constructions of cosmetic surgery, the men employ yet another set of neutralization techniques. For the most part, these include classic 'condemning the condemners' narratives. Steve (age 48) said to me one day, 'Why should anyone else care if I did this [Botox]? I'm not hurting anyone, or even myself, so whose business is it? No one should even try to tell me what to do with my own body!' While Steve engages in male feminine body projects in order to reframe himself as progressively masculine, the defensive posturing he adopts throughout his narrative might be described as quintessentially, or at least stereotypically, masculine. Steve refuses to have his body preferences interrogated, and responds to such challenges from an overtly powerful interpretive position of control.

Ironically, while men frequently position themselves as victims of work structures and expectations through their cosmetic surgery storytelling, they vehemently deny possessing an inferior masculine status or losing agency through the cosmetic surgery process. Quite predictably, as Davis (2002) mentions, these men never pathologize invasive body interventions as self-victimizing. Instead, they reframe surgical intervention as a clever form of contemporary masculine character building. The re-established powerful male feminine body, is, then one that is firm, fit, flexible, and fat-free, and open to exploring non-traditional (feminized) forms of bodywork in order to appear as innovatively male. But most importantly, as Frank (2004a) notes, it is a body that exudes a cultural awareness and acceptance of crisis, risk, and the need to adapt; it is a form that articulates a deep sensibility toward changing roles, statuses, and identities of the 'new man'. The male's cosmetically altered body is one that is economically invested in the established cultural brand of masculinity (Scmitt, 2001). At the same time, it is an aesthetically contoured body validated by muted social recognition and kudos from admiring others. The cosmetically altered body is interdependent with shifting constructions of masculinity, and derives social meaning from extended social interaction across social settings.

Liquid Ubersexuality

It seems as if the metrosexual had just arrived in Canada when the *ubersexual* threatened to dislodge him from the throne of contemporary, hip, crisis masculinity. After having read and been profoundly influenced by Faludi's construction of the ornamental late-modern man in *Stiffed*, I was personally not surprised. Ubersexuals are the most attractive (not just physically), most dynamic, and most compelling men of their generations. They are confident, masculine, stylish, and committed to uncompromising quality in all areas of life. Ubersexuals, unlike their metrosexual counterparts, are also recognized as having a personal depth of character. The ubersexual knows the difference between right and wrong and will make the right decision regardless of what others around him may think. The ubersexual is outwardly similar to a male feminine metrosexual in certain ways (i.e., flair for fashion, personal care, and a degree of consumer self-indulgence), but he is also a man who embodies traditional manly qualities such as confidence, strength, and class. He is yet another Frankenstein's monster, a hybrid, pastiche masculine invention in the crisis era. His is a masculinity that strangely poaches new (metro) masculinity and adds traditional hegemonic masculinity 'lite' to the gender recipe.

An ubersexual is in some ways a 'manly man' who displays all the good qualities associated with traditional and contemporary masculinities, without the associated masculine 'bads' such as chauvinism, emotional unavailability, and a brain only filled with sports stats, beer, and burgers. He does not, however, cross 'too far' over into the terrain of the feminine. Compared with the metrosexual, the ubersexual is more into relationships than self. His is a masculinity that combines the best of traditional manliness (strength, honour, character) with positive traits traditionally associated with females, such as nurturance, communicativeness, and co-operation. He is a gentleman in all manners of the definition: passionate about causes and contemporary politics; an intellectual and a thinker; a profeminist; confident and sensual; broadly interested in art, fashion, and culture; and confident about his own morals and ethics. U2's lead man Bono has been heralded as the archetypical ubersexual.

In terms used by social theorist Zygmunt Bauman (2000), the ubersexual is a 'liquid' gender category. It is a masculinity without solid form, boundaries, certainties, or referents. The liquid masculinity is one that is all-encompassing and sometimes impossibly contradictory; it is traditional but progressive, vain but aloof, independent but socially responsible, and morally committed but tolerant. I have met dozens, if not hundreds, of Canadian men who attempt to emulate the style and form of the ubersexual, whether in discourse or embodiment. The call to *ubersexuality* from and among them stems from their perceived crisis, as the men react to the softening of masculinity from male feminine cultural trends in the 1990s. Ubersexual preferences shared among them reflect a commonly held belief in their need to adopt the guise of the modern man, while resurrecting and reinventing the traditional man as a late-modern technique of power.

In what follows, I illustrate how ubersexuality may be constructed and played out by men as a response to crisis, using a case study of bodybuilding and exercise 'supplementation' (i.e., the use of over-the-counter sports nutrition products to help build svelte and toned male bodies) I began conducting in the early 2000s. As you read the case study, think about why so many Canadian men fill their bodies with pills, drinks, potions, and other 'sports nutritional supplements' to build and embody a particular kind of ubersexuality.

Ubersexuality and Body Supplementation

The sports nutrition or 'supplementation' industry is booming in Canada. Estimated annual sales of sports supplements, according to Agriculture and Agri-Food Canada, exceeded $1 billion in 2007 (**www.agr.gc.ca**). Legal, over-the-counter body-building or slimming products like creatine, whey protein, thermogenic fat burners, and human growth hormone enhancers are ubiquitous across Canadian marketplaces—sold anywhere from grocery stores to school cafeterias to gas stations. While some 'ready to eat' products like protein bars are rather inexpensive (ranging from $2–$5 for a single serving—very similar to price points of other fast foods), others are considerably more expensive (ranging in price from $75–$100 for a weekly or monthly dosage).

The ostensible link between supplementation and the desire to appear outwardly healthy is understandable given contemporary risk and masculinity crisis discourses in Canada. The boom in supplementation sales is occurring at a time when more Canadian men than in any other historical era are called obese, believed to be confronting health crises, and afraid of disease; in other words, they are being told to fear many, many institutionally produced 'bads' (Pronger, 2002). Pronger (2002) noted the recent promulgation of physical regimes of control (such as bodybuilding) have emerged among middle-class men as a response to a fear of these epidemics. White, Young, and Gillett (1995) similarly outlined the current moral imperative for men to appear fit and healthy within

a crisis of physical decay in Western cultures. Indeed, the dramaturgical performance of identity remains closely tied to physical discipline, especially as that
work pertains to food consumption and the display of healthy, fit, toned bodies.

But in truth, the public use of sports supplements has been scarcely understood by anyone other then the male consumers themselves. A series of media
scares and moral panics regarding the presence of high doses of ephedrine (a
stimulant similar to caffeine) in certain sports supplement products during the
early 2000s—particularly following the mysterious on-field deaths of American
football player Korey Stringer and American baseball player Steve Belcher—
called popular cultural attention to the dangers of using sports supplements.
But despite a momentary concern over the contents of sports-related weight-
gain or -loss supplements, the supplement production and distribution industries are still relatively unfettered in Canada. Further still, very few people
have ever questioned how and why scores of young and old Canadian men are
gobbling supplements and crafting lean bodies with increased gusto.

The primary consumers of sports supplements are indeed men; especially
young men aged 16–30 in the middle class (estimated as consumers of 80 per
cent of supplements sold in North America, see Atkinson, 2007). The most
popular over-the-counter legal supplements are creatine (an amino acid taken
with the belief that it will increase speed of muscle recovery) and whey protein,
and that supplementation cuts across class, ethnic, religious, and sexual preference categories. Still, as clinical psychologists argued, the primary consumers
are young, White males in the middle class (Pope et al., 2000). The extant literature on the medical use of sports supplements reveals an over-representation
of White, middle-class, and urban males as the primary consumers of legal
supplements; they are precisely the men in crisis I have studied.

Simpson (1994) predicted that alongside fear discourses, which encouraged men to become hyper-worried and protectionist about their bodies, the
queering of urban male body styles and aesthetics would equally pressure
young affluent men to 'pretty' their bodies through forms of supplementation;
but they are doing so in quasi-traditional male manners—and what better a
manner than to bodybuild, and use supplements to supposedly hasten the
process? Bauman's (2000) statement on the rise of individuality and cultural
fragmentation in the West underscores how dominant clusters of consumers
(such as White, middle-class, heterosexual males) respond to social trends of
traditional identity implosion through radical embodiment projects. Campos
(2004) added that men in the middle class are the primary interpreters and
definers of contemporary body problems like obesity, and further maintained that weight-loss strategies among the group reflect a common anxiety
or perceived crisis about their lifestyles of conspicuous consumption. The
increased amount of sports supplement products sold, one could argue, is an
indirect measure of such bourgeois guilt. Sociologists of masculinity including
Connell (2005) also cited blurring definitions of sexually acceptable male

body style as a precursor to the recent explosion in commercially sold men's products in the fitness sector.

I encountered a regular supplement user named Jimmy in 2003. Jimmy divulged his own experimentation with both creatine and whey protein powders to me one day. Following an extended conversation with him regarding supplement use, he disclosed a history of consistent sports supplementation of nearly ten years. I had been studying the representation of sports supplements in men's health magazines at the time of our conversation, and started to consider an ethnography on supplementation among gym members. Jimmy offered a dozen names of friends in the city of Hamilton at the time of his interview. The men I eventually interviewed range in age from 19 to 45 (with a mean age of 26), a majority were single (51%), middle-class (75%), with a mean income of approximately CDN$61,000. They share Anglo-Saxon heritages (90%) and heterosexual preferences (80%). Their levels of education varied, with some still in university (46%), but most were completely out of the educational system (54%) at the time of interview. Experience with sports supplementation varied, with most of the men using one or two supplements on a weekly basis (70%), while the others' volume of consumption ranged from 5–10 supplements daily (30%). The most frequently consumed supplements included creatine, whey protein, thermogenics (fat burners), human growth hormone stimulators, and testosterone enhancers.

From the narratives about supplementation I collected over time, it is evident that the men engage a series of calculated risks with their bodies through sports supplementation in order to achieve an ideal-type ubersexual body image. While they admit to finding it difficult to be a full-fledged ubersexual, they like the idea of appearing as one (perhaps typical in a liquid, ornamental, and hyper-consumer society where it only matters if you *look* the part!). The men described a desirable ubersexual masculine body as one that is lean, muscular but thin, groomed, free from blemish yet rugged, and sexually attractive but not threatening. The supplement users take dietary risks—the ingestion of chemical/natural products intended to radically alter the body's fat or muscular composition—as one step in the pursuit of the ideal. When explaining why they consume supplements, the men I studied described a sense of physical and social deficiency about their 'dated' and powerless masculine identities; and so they sought body modification through supplementation as a remedy. The men regularly express doubt, insecurity, and a lack of perceived social power and control: a fear of being small and unfit, of not having the right look, or not working hard enough to be attractive to women. Alan told me:

> Sure there's an attack on men in our culture. Are you kidding me? Have you paid attention at all to life in the past 30 or so years? Everywhere you go there are guys in anger management or sensitivity training classes at work who're being fucking emasculated . . . The only thing touchy-feely corporate culture can't take

away from me is my body. I'm not stupid though and understand that the 'new' guy is one who tones it down a bit and is put together but not ridiculously so. I take supplements that help with building lean muscle and maintaining lower water weight. (Alan, age 31)

As Alan and like-minded peers explained, they locate substantial social power by 'reclaiming' their threatened social roles as 'ubermen' through bodybuilding and weight management. They clearly accept and promote culture preferences for the fit, toned, groomed, and non-aggressive body, as a technique of empowerment in a time of anxiety.

The use of sports supplements and the pursuit of an ubersexual masculine physique as a cure for masculine anxiety clearly has something to do with what sociologists call the medicalization of everyday life in our risk society. More pharmaceutical products than ever before are taken by people in Western cultures. Critser (2002) decoded the contemporary push to medicalize social eating problems, sources of social stratification, and political anxieties as just one instance of how individuals are encouraged to seek scientific solutions to collective cultural problems (such as doubt about what constitutes acceptable masculinity):

Nowadays, you hear many conflicting opinions about what being a man means. Some women want you to be tough, others want sensitive and shy. My boss wants me to be [an office] leader, but my parents want me to follow their lead. When I pick up a magazine there's a new article about what a guy is supposed to look or talk like. But then, it's like, you have to watch out what you say because you don't want to sound sexist . . . We can't agree and men are frustrated with not knowing how to act.(Sid, age 35)

Consuming pills, drugs, or medicinal remedies has become part of daily routines in the West. For males in the present study, consuming sports supplements have certainly become a standard form of nutrition in their athletic and social bodybuilding endeavours. The men feel as if they are under an intense cultural pressure to perform as 'new men', and come to trust the advice of their doctors and trainers about how to medically build a better male body.

But clearly, anxious men in the middle class who are worried about their collective emasculation by women and/or the rise of male femininities in Canadian culture might revert to a more direct method of gaining social status by literally building stronger bodies. This is what, in the end, the ubersexual man really is: a man who conforms to contemporary cultural gender trends and styles, but who asserts an essentialist, physical, masculine dominance in subtly civilized ways. A sales associate named Ken (age 36) told me, 'I never thought it would be important to have six-pack abs so I could sit at a desk all day in a suit.' Men like Ken feel a new gender war, or at least a general feminizing, is happening at work; for Ken, bodybuilding and the pursuit of ubersexuality via supplementation is a new moral imperative. The supplemented and moderately bulked male body is for all intents and purposes, an embodied return to a very basic site of social control (i.e., the command of an outwardly strong, dominant, powerful, controlling body) in a context of cultural uncertainty.

Men like Ken seize control over their bodies in order to 'reframe' (White, Young, and McTeer, 1994) their masculinity as empowered (i.e., reflexive and invested) and vibrant (i.e., muscularly different and healthy) via rather essentialist masculine images. These men draw on and recalibrate widely disseminated images of the healthy, youthful, progressive, self-caring, and affluent urban male through the supplementation process, and they present themselves as powerful in social settings wherein their power has been ostensibly dislodged. Chris, a 27-year-old teacher who uses thermogenics and diuretics to shed weight, articulated:

> Women can say whatever they want about slim being 'in' for men, but a guy who invests in his body and his muscles will always be an attractive and rewarded man. I work in a very feminine environment, right, and the women at our school are very smart and politically aware people. So it's the last place where old school guy crap is tolerated, and that's fine with me. I don't sell my image and my strength that way, you know, I want people to see me as healthy and strong. Body-wise, that puts me at the head of the class in front of everyone in the school and people still respond to the dominant shape in a group as the leader.

Chris's narrative alludes to a generational shift in the mindset of a group of middle-class Canadian men. Donald (age 24), who uses more than a dozen supplements, described:

> Everyone who said that only women feel pressure to look a certain ideal way never spoke to a man in their life! Pick up any fitness magazine and you'll see. Why would I not want a body like one of those guys, it's the shape most women want, for sure. It's a powerful thing, to be built nowadays, people pay attention to you, and want to listen. It's a like a drug to them. People who are fit and healthy-looking get the attention, no question. It's more persuasive than a corporate title you hold. And today, being very thin, very fit, and not too boastful about it says you have principles and self-ethics.

When men like Donald, Ken, and Chris perceive a crisis of established masculinity, no matter the source, they respond through a basic form of social (self) control: body management and health-image modification. Sports supplementation is, to them, part of a process of self-medication and inoculation against perceived cultural ills and the fragmentation and perceived loss of masculine hegemony. Brad (age 25) argues:

It's not like I'm intimidated or threatened by the girls who work out in my gym, but I don't know, I don't want to have a girlfriend with bigger muscles than me. Women today are much smarter and fitter and in control, and guys have to step it up [get bigger] . . . that's nature; it's the law of the jungle. Guys should be bigger, even if we have to work together and share just about every other social role in the world.

Comments like Brad's also point to a fear I found to be common among the men in my sample, regarding women as colonizers in their gyms and in the social realm of athletics. Nearly two-thirds of the men in the study expressed a work-like and competitive desire to stay ahead of women in the gym. Ryan, a 26-year-old auto sales manager, said:

Women have stepped it up and aren't afraid to be big and strong. As a guy you have to respond, right, and stay on pace. If anything, it's one of the best motivations for me, because what fit woman wants an out of shape guy? We'll always have the biological advantage because guys are born with better genes for working out and athletics. We'll go the extra mile too by playing around with drugs to give us that other secret edge.

Men like Brad and Ryan supplement alongside weight training as a curious gesture of gendered empowerment. When cleverly rationalized as part of personal health rejuvenation in a culture replete with discourses about disease and obesity, the men in the sample believed their physical training and supplementation would be lauded as corporeally self-aware and responsible. Strange (and shallow) as it seems, this is where their ubersexual sense of civic responsibility comes in! Tony (age 44) told me:

I take supplements as strictly health aides. I can control my macronutrients perfectly and my body benefits. I don't want to look like one of those men walking around the park with their goddamn bellies hanging to the floor and the 'shit tits' poking out of their shirts. Who's going to respect that, especially when we know so much about what causes obesity and heart disease? I'm never going to be a burden on the health care system in this country.

Tony's construction of athletic body training and supplementation rings both with a Foucauldian (1981) description of bodywork as a *technology of the self* and with the ethics of ubersexual self-care. Foucault described technologies of the self as ascetic and ethical practices of personal transformation. 'Ascetic' in this context means an, 'exercise of self upon the self by which one attempts to develop and transform oneself, and to attain a certain mode of being' (Foucault, 1987, p. 282). Foucault insisted that technologies of the self could be liberating processes of moral self-realization, in which ethical self-care practices of the body constitute power for the individual, and have a transformative capacity in one's life. The process of self-liberation, in Foucault's model, emancipates the self from its bondage within conditions of dominant bio-power (i.e., the subjugated self-surveillance that is demanded by dominant social discourses). The self/body is ready to 'become' through a process of unfettered corporeal exploration and representation. If bodybuilding and supplementation is a technology of the self, as Foucault described one, the men in the sample might be considered conscious social resisters practicing and embodied and creative form of self-care.

Troublingly, though, in the narratives gathered the men alluded to varying degrees of *psychological* dependence on the supplements for everyday living and body satisfaction. Their stories also suggested how men's interpretations of moral worth, social recognition, and general self-image as males can be deeply affected by their commitment to sports supplementation as part of an overall 'healthy' lifestyle. The consumption of sports supplements therefore can indicate how some Canadian men in the middle class feel doubt, confusion, and anxiety with regard to the constitution of acceptable masculinity, as well as how healthy bodies 'should' be built to represent the pursuit of ubersexual masculinity. For these men, sports supplements are, at least partially, predictable solutions to ambiguous cultural problems like the changing roles and statuses of men. They use scientifically designed sports supplements to solve social psychological (psychogenic) anxieties, believing they can consume a full range of products to achieve their masculine physical goals. The strict control over their bodies, as well as their social identities as male, enacts a perceived sense of control they do not feel in other social spheres. The speed of the process is especially appealing for them, as they believe supplements tend to work in a matter of a few weeks. Furthermore, since the products are easily accessible and widely promoted/discussed as part of the new *ethnopharmacology* in fitness cultures, it is not surprising why these men experiment with one supplement or another.

Summary

The widening use of cosmetic surgery among men is an incredibly clever technique of masculine power attainment via collective image work. In a beauty/image-saturated and obsessed culture, male feminine men glean significant attention and social accolade for their secretly improved physical forms. The beautification of men's bodies through cosmetic surgery might be considered as the poaching of a traditionally feminine technique of power attainment through the body; inasmuch, men are colonizing a site of social power traditionally dominated by women. As Sarwer and Crerand (2004) suggest, the movement of men into cosmetic surgery could be simply a 'liquid' extension of the male gaze in Western cultures like Canada.

By contrast, the ubersexual man may be, despite first appearances, more solid than liquid. The guise and myth of the ubersexual man is one that seems to be at once progressive and nostalgic. But the ubersexual male is clearly more of the latter than the former. Ubersexuality is underpinned in principle with rather reactionary or backlash tones toward the socio-economic advancement of women in countries like Canada. Building a slim, ethical, and risk-free ubersexual body through supplementation, for example, is based on a very traditional masculine power play that involves using the essential, physical man to achieve social power and distinction. While the image of the ubersexual is wrapped nicely in discourses about being 'in touch' with one's feminine desire to look good and appear attractive, the men become attractive in decisively old masculine ways.

Discussion Questions

1. Can you identify and describe another male feminine category in Canadian society? Who are some of the most popular or mass-mediated male feminine figures in Canada?
2. Identify one metrosexual and one ubersexual you know. Define and interpret their differences and potential similarities.
3. Do you think metrosexuality or ubersexuality are here to stay? Or are these just passing trends in Canadian society?
4. How might sociological theory about gender need to change when we take into account how polymorphous gender identities might be in societies like Canada?
5. Are there any truly outsider masculinities in contemporary Canadian society? If so, why are they outsider masculinities?

Key Readings

Baudrillard, J. (1983). *Simulations*. London: Semiotext(e). The significance of *Simulations* cuts across most social scientific disciplines, making Baudrillard one of the most important contemporary thinkers of the twentieth century. Baudrillard's notion that Western cultures have moved toward a stage of hyper-simulation (where referents to hard realities dissolve into nothingness) has changed the ways in which media scholars and others understand how definitions of cultural truth often find basis in popular fiction.

Bauman, Z. (2000). *Liquid Modernity*. Cambridge: Basil Blackwell. Bauman's thoughts on the nature of contemporary Western cultures are foundational for students interested in the social construction of individuality and neo-liberalism. In this book,

Bauman outlines the shift from traditionalist societies bound by historic codes and statuses to societies categorized by flux and destabilization. Bauman's collective works are now primary reading for anyone interested in the sociology of identity, globalization, economics, and nationalism.

Beck, U. (1992). *Risk Society: Towards a New Modernity*. London: Sage. Beck's *Risk Society* is a watershed moment in theory regarding the macro-structural organization of society, and the micro-interaction experiences associated with living in late modernity. Beck deftly uncovers how social relations have been increasingly organized around a series of preventive and precautionary ideologies that encourage people to manage all aspects of their lives around the risks we regularly encounter. What are important to Beck, then, are the multi-institutional policies and practices developed to manage risks, and the ways in which risk cultures encourage people to think about the future rather than the present.

Faludi, S. (1999) *Stiffed: The Betrayal of the American Man*. New York: William Morrow & Company. Faludi's book dropped like a bombshell on North American society, as one of the first critically acclaimed books about the 'hard luck' many men in America have experienced in late modernity. As a lauded feminist thinker, Faludi surprised many gender scholars by publishing a book that partially unpacks why so many men in North America feel as if they have been culturally left behind in contemporary life. Among the important realizations offered in the book is that gender is far less static and unproblematic for men than typically considered by sociologists.

Giddens, A. (1991). *Modernity and Self-Identity: Self and Society in the Late Modern Age*. Cambridge: Polity. This book underscores what many sociologists of identity have written about over the last 20 years: the movement to hyper-reflexive and self-oriented cultural ways of living wherein people are obsessed with narrating their own, unique identities. Giddens partially makes a case for his theory of structuration through the text, discusses the implications of living in a consumer society, and underscores a primary theoretical idea that all of social life is interdependent and interactionally related.

Web Links

Cosmetic Surgery Magazine (www.cosmeticsurgerymagazine.com/). Among the first of mass-distributed trade magazines promoting the practice of cosmetic surgery. Once a taboo subject and untouched by mass marketers, the availability of such magazines signifies something important about the rising acceptance of cosmetic surgery in our society.

Hasting's Center (www.thehastingscenter.org/). A non-partisan American centre for the study of bioethics in medicine and elsewhere. Among the key areas of interest for academics at the Center are questions relating to the ethics of physical enhancement and the socio-cultural politics involved in aesthetically oriented surgeries.

Medicard Finance (www.medicard.com/). A Canadian financing company offering funds to individuals who are pursuing non-essential surgical interventions such as cosmetic ('plastic') surgeries. The company keeps demographic data on the most common procedures financed in Canada and who receives surgery.

Key Terms

Ethnopharmacology: A commonly held belief among athletes and bodybuilders that they, better than medical experts, have expert knowledge about ergogenic drugs and their effects. Such beliefs are generally based on first-hand experience with performance-enhancing drugs and exercise supplements, and tend to directly oppose medical knowledge regarding the long-term effects of the products.

Liquid modernity: A time of social life when (as a result of globalization and the increased mixing and matching of cultural norms and forms of representation around the world), people are not as anchored to traditional modes of living or even thinking. Some theorists believe that with the breakdown of cultural tradition and space between people, a new cult of hyper-individualism has arisen. Individuals are still involved in modernist institutions but social life is less governed by rigid absolutes, particularly as they relate to individual and collective identity.

Male femininity: An ambiguous and playful gender category in which aspects of proto-typical femininity and masculinity are blended together in, typically, non-queer ways. The male-feminine person seeks to poach and represent the most socially attractive or kudos-producing aspects of each stereotypical gender category without jeopardizing one's status as a 'legitimate' male. In many ways, it is synonymous with metrosexuality.

Risk society: A term made famous by the theorist Ulrich Beck. A risk society is one preoccupied with crises, epidemics, and the institutionally uncontrolled harms or 'bads' that face citizens. The development-of-risk ways of thinking and socially managing populations emerged quite closely with declining public faith in modernist social institutions and ideologies. Living in a risk society encourages people to be hyper-reflexive about their bodies and identities, and what they can do to protect themselves as a matter of everyday ritual.

Techniques of neutralization: Rhetorical devices people use when their thoughts or behaviours are called into question as illegitimate or deviant by another. The techniques (such as denial of responsibility or denial of injury) distance the person away from the acts or thoughts under question, and assert the individual's moral or ethical conformity with accepted cultural modes of behaviour.

Ubersexuality: A category of 'ultimate' or culturally exaggerated (near perfect) gender/sexuality. The ubersexual male is, for example, blessed with the body of a hegemonic man, is handsome, wealthy, socially respected by all men and women, cool under pressure, compassionate and politically minded, astute in the arts and sciences, and in touch with, but in total control of, his emotions.

5 | Sporting Masculinities

Chapter Objectives

This chapter introduces and critically explores the following:

- The link between traditional hegemonic masculinity and sport
- How masculinity codes in sport remain culturally protected, even when they lead to serious injury among participants, spectators, or others in and around the sport fields
- How the performance of dangerous masculinities in sport are often celebrated by men in crisis
- How social problems in sport may be linked to the performance of dominant masculinities
- How athletes experience anxiety, frustration, and doubt about their achieved masculinities as they do not feel they live up to inflexible hegemonic standards in sports cultures

As a socio-cultural researcher of male bodies, I often reflect on the logics and practices of a sport I grew up playing; ice hockey. The winters of my childhood were identical. Every weekday from mid-November to late March, I hurtled through the school doors every afternoon at 3:15, raced home to change attire, bolted from my house and joined a small crew of friends at a local tennis court, paved playground, or cul-de-sac for a game of street hockey. If there is anything I remember about Canadian winters during my childhood it is the smell, taste, sounds, and feeling of playing the game with my friends. Armed with sticks with blades worn down to toothpick thickness, frozen, 'no bounce' orange balls bought at Canadian Tire, aluminium goals with nets partially torn and fluttering in the wind, and wearing replica Montreal, Toronto, and other team jerseys on top of our winter coats, we played far past our curfews, and often until one of our parents physically interrupted the game. The sound of a blade dragging across the pavement or the rusty hinges of a goal carried temporarily across the street after the shout of 'CAR!', the sight of heat wafting from my friends' toques, the rankness of sweat mixed with polyester uniforms and leather hockey gloves, and the feel of my feet numbed from the snowy ground are etched into my understanding of Canadian boyhood. Dinner tasted better after two or three hours of street hockey, homework much more palatable, and sleep far deeper. We played other sports in the winter, and to be sure loved them all, but nothing was as regular, inclusive, creative, or just 'ours' like street hockey.

My experiences with street hockey do not mirror other athletic experiences of my youth, or even today. At times our games could get heated, we would argue, and we would even push and shove each other over petty disagreements. But they never progressed into violence; the streets were relatively free from the institutional codes and practices common at the rink. The games were, day in and day out, contexts in which we were allowed to be boys, safe, happy, and growing boys playing a simple game. Laughter, joking, camaraderie, and collective cohesion filled the air. Our sense of generational identity was as thick in the damp, frosty air as the billowing clouds above us. The afternoon's games were private spaces where teachers, parents, siblings, coaches, or any other authoritarian figures had no presence, no shadow lurking over or directing us. To me and many of my friends, street hockey meant escape.

Six years ago I found myself driving home from work in the late after-noon and noticed something peculiar. On this spectacular winter afternoon, I suddenly thought to myself, where are all the street hockey games? It dawned on me that I had not seen a street game anywhere in Hamilton for a long, long time. Weird. Curious about the observation, I asked friends and co-workers if their children played. 'Oh no,' my friend Carl said, 'most towns or cities in Ontario are trying to ban it. And, well, Mike, I don't feel safe letting my kids play unsupervised outside.' What?!?! Befuddled by this claim, I grabbed my proverbial researcher's hat from the closet and started on out on the trail. Sure enough, Carl's first account of the disappearance of the game had legitimacy. Beginning in the early 2000s, local residents across the country separately lobbied town councils in a range of regions to ban the playing of hockey on streets as a matter of public nuisance. Areas in Vancouver, Winnipeg, Toronto, Ottawa, and Halifax have all introduced public bans at one time or another. No catastrophic incidents involving the health and safety of a citizen were cited as precursors of the bans, merely the inconvenience of waiting for kids to move when cars want to pass. Some of the bans were repealed following public outcry, while a handful remain to date. I couldn't help thinking, yet another space for youthful freedom has been taken away at a time when we are asking youth in Canada to grow so very quickly.

But street hockey has not disappeared entirely in this country. Like other organic youth sports, the game has been co-opted, organized, institutionalized, and massively commercialized into a thoroughly late-modern phenomenon. There are leagues such as the Canadian Ball Hockey Association with official rulebooks for the game, tournaments including the Play On 4x4 Tournament and USA Cup, lines of equipment from Nike and Easton, indoor rinks and spaces designated for play, and a host of other innovations to transform the game into a heavily structured, monitored, and financial zone. The game now looks, feels, smells, and operates like a mainstream sport. Most of the young boys I know hate the game's modern form. While they may play sporadically within the narrow parameters of their tarmacked driveways on occasion, the game is increasingly removed from the life script of a typical young boy in this country.

And what about Carl's claims regarding safety? One simply cannot discount that the withdrawal of the game from our streets is happening at a time when moral panics about the presence of roaming pedophiles, drug dealers, gangs, and other 'risk persons' abound in Canada. While street hockey made me feel safe and warm in my young masculine skin, it seems as if young boys are now more likely, according to popular discourse and sentiment, to be unsafe while playing on the street in front of their own houses or in parking lots only a few metres from home. My investigation into Carl's claims about being safe as a boy in the street game would further dovetail with a study Kevin Young and I were conducting on violence in the ice version of the game in 2004 and 2005. Kevin and I were studying rates and cultures of violence in the sport, and were subsequently led to inspect (as but one facet of the study) why so many young boys are leaving the sport. Pascall and White's (2000) report on violence and attrition in the game had sparked our sociological curiosities about the contexts of attrition and (sub)cultures of intense masculinity in the sport; each of these seem to be alienating for growing numbers of youth in the country. What we found amazed us both. Young boys described hockey culture as unappealing, tedious, violent, bossy, and generally unpleasant. We asked, is this a crisis, and if so, what are its social roots? Could it have something to do with the overtly aggressive style of play solidified deep within the cultural bedrock of the sport? Does this now, perhaps more than ever, alienate young boys who just don't 'live up'?

Consider the following example of risk, violence, and ice hockey. Tim Gmeinweser, a volunteer hockey coach of the Knights of Columbus Sabres (Edmonton), removed his 13- and 14-year-old players from the ice during a game against a team from New Sarepta, Alberta. Gmeinweser's team was losing by a score of 7 to 1 during the second period of the game. Several of his players, including his own son, had been injured during the match, and he feared for the safety of the rest of his team. From his perspective, the violence in the game had escalated without effective intervention from the officials. Anticipating the injury of even more players, Gmeinweser called his players off the ice and forfeited the contest. In response, Gmeinweser received a one-year suspension from the Edmonton Minor Hockey Association (CBC News, 2003). Charlene Davis, the president of the association, remarked that 'coaches, who are volunteers, can't be made responsible for players' safety' (CBC News, 2003). Several weeks later, Kent Willert, head coach of the Knights of Columbus Thunder peewee ice hockey team (players aged 11–12), also received a one-year suspension from the Edmonton Minor Hockey Association for taking players off the ice for safety reasons.

Gmeinweser's and Willert's actions of protest are more meaningful if we further contextualize them within both the aggressively masculine character of the sport, and of policy initiatives within the Canadian Hockey Association (CHA) that place more young boys at risk of injury. Just prior to the start of the 2002–2003 minor hockey season across Canada, the Canadian Hockey Association decided to permit bodychecking at the Atom level. Also effective for the same hockey season was CHA's decision to lower the age for the Midget, Bantam, Peewee, and Atom Divisions by one year. In effect, by permitting bodychecking at the Atom level, the age at which bodychecking was permitted dropped from 14 to 9. Such a decision was made despite reams of research illustrating that there are four times as many reported injuries in body-checking versus non-bodychecking leagues across all age categories; the studies of Peewee players (then 12 and 13) that found that players in a league with bodychecking had a bone fracture rate 12 times higher than the players in the league without bodychecking; and, the studies of youth hockey in the United States (players ages 9–15) that found that 86 per cent of injuries were sustained due to bodychecking—and, that 72 per cent of the injuries caused by body-checking were from rule-sanctioned bodychecks (Weed, Brooks, and Blanaru, 2003). While hockey pundits and fans across the country were quick to weigh in with support for the move, many in the academic community warned the CHA and its provincial and municipal affiliates about the documented risks of such a move. Audiences were quick to admonish bodychecking naysayers as out of touch with the reality of the sport's aggressive culture.

The popular CBC program *Disclosure* aired a documentary episode that added further fuel to the fire. The CHA publicly defended its position on lowering the age of violence in the sport by suggesting that by doing so, players would learn at a young (and physiologically less differentiated age) to properly hit without seriously injuring each others' bodies. It ignored basic logic that most players did not venture into the elite junior or professional tiers of the game, and therefore would not be exposed to serious bodychecking at a later age anyway. Discourses from hockey insiders and proponents of violence in the sport added that by introducing checking at a young age (prepubescent), the novelty effect of hitting would wear off long before the boys were physically big and aggressive enough (i.e., 13–14 years old) to inflict serious damage on one another. What became known as the 'Atom Decision' in the sport stood firmly on these grounds. The *Disclosure* episode, however, exposed a chilling fact about the academic data used to justify their policy. *Disclosure* reported that the CHA's decision to permit bodychecking at the Atom level was prompted by a fundamentally flawed and statistically misleading study completed by Dr Bill Montelpare of Lakehead University. This study originally stood for support of the notion that the early introduction of bodychecking (in Atom) would reduce injuries. Montelpare's conclusions have now been established as being in error. A further review of his reported statistics showed that children involved in bodychecking at the Atom level are at least four times more likely to be injured than children who do not bodycheck. The program further showcased narratives from young boys who expressed fear over the move, highlighted their injuries, and pointed to the potential for the rule change to prompt mass attrition. Coaches like Gmeinweser and Willert clearly knew of, and witnessed, the dangers first-hand and would not allow the crisis context to continue; they paid the price within a sport culture that routinely castigates dissenters. The CHA did not budge despite burgeoning requests from across the country to raise the age to the Bantam (13–14) level of the sport; skyrocketing concussion and other injury rates in the game; growing attrition; or mass public criticism of the Alberta coaches' suspensions.

Sadly, the real-life consequences of ignoring the institutional logics and hyper-masculine codes of aggression and violence in this crisis sport are made plain from time to time. In this regard, NHL players provide the bulk of evidence. For example, Marty McSorley's slash to the back of Donald Brashear's head in 2000, and Todd Bertuzzi sucker-punching Steve Moore in 2005 are prime case studies. But none illustrate the consequences of dangerous codes of masculinity as well as the death of the Ontario Major League Hockey player Don Sanderson.

On 2 January 2009, Don Sanderson succumbed to his injury. He died only 20 days after banging his head on the ice after a hockey fight during a game that pitted his Whitby Dunlops against rival Brantford Blast. Three weeks after his death, the Whitby Dunlops hosted a tribute to the 21-year-old before a scheduled game. The pre-game ceremony climaxed on the ice, when at the end of a 35-minute video montage and public eulogizing of Don Sanderson's young life, his mother Dahna fell, sobbing, onto her ex-husband's shoulder. As a symbolic number '40' jersey was slowly raised to the ceiling, a children's choir sang 'You Raise Me Up'. Friends and family members remarked that Don Sanderson's fire for hockey and life led him to work harder than any of his teammates. In training camp, they said, he ran up and down the steps of the rink before the others had begun stretching. He earned high grades at York University while coaching girls' youth hockey with his father. His life plan was to become a high-school teacher and eventually a professional hockey coach. Yet people, including the patriarch of the Sanderson family, Mike Sanderson, suggested his son's 'fire' also made him an aggressive defenseman who earned four ejections for fighting in 11 games in the 2008 season alone.

His fateful last fight began as a mild scuffle next to the Dunlops' goal with the Brantford Blast player Corey Fulton. By all accounts it developed as a run-of-the-mill hockey fight, replete with inconsequential punches thrown by both players. Sanderson's teammates described the altercation as nothing special, adding that they thought Fulton had done nothing dirty or dangerous that may have placed Sanderson at risk of injury. Toward the end of the struggle, Sanderson's helmet slipped off and he stumbled from Fulton's grip and plummeted to the ice; his exposed head crashed against the ice and Don immediately slipped into unconsciousness. The tragedy of Don Sanderson almost instantly reverberated across Canada, instigating a prolonged debate about the role of fighting in the national sport. Print media, television, and the Internet were predictably abuzz with the issue. A poll reported by Sun Media (4 January 2009) shortly after Sanderson's death revealed that 59 per cent of respondents felt that fighting should be banned in minor and amateur hockey. Yet, National Hockey League Commissioner Gary Bettman routinely expressed a league reluctance to change the subcultural codes or official rules regulating fighting. Bettman, like other elite rulers in the world of hockey, is clearly mindful of the risk involved in alienating hockey's remaining 'passionate fans'. To many of the sport's devotees, hockey equals fighting, and they are unwilling to reconsider, and in some cases, even discuss, the violence in their sport as uncontrolled (Atkinson and Young, 2008). That group includes iconic commentator Don Cherry, who declared at Sanderson's funeral: 'I can't believe that some people in the anti-fighting group would take advantage of something like this to make their point.' Author Ross Bernstein, a pro-fighting advocate whose many books on hockey include *The Code: The Unwritten Rules of Fighting and Retaliation in the NHL*, publicly commented that hockey needs fighting for two reasons: revenue and holding dirty players accountable. 'The paying customers like it, so it serves a purpose,' Bernstein says. 'Plus, if you're doing something dirty, that's like whacking a guy in the mob. You have to take your medicine, and it's war' (Associated Press, 2009).

Still, the national hand-wringing over Sanderson's death led many, both inside and outside the hockey world, to lobby against prohibited forms of aggression that are still subculturally tolerated. Among these people were close friends of Don Sanderson including Rick Scragg. Scragg was Sanderson's youth basketball coach in nearby Port Perry, and Sanderson remained close with Scragg, his wife Cathy, and their 7-year-old son Nathan. The Scraggs remember Don as an advocate of fighting who was willing to engage in respectful debates with Rick, who is decisively anti-fighting. 'He said, "Fighting is part of the game." He was a very big defenseman. His role was to be that tough guy.' Rick grew up playing hockey and didn't back down from a fight, but fatherhood caused him to reconsider his actions on the ice. 'But if we don't want our kids fighting anywhere else, why would we want them fighting in the rink?' he says. 'Your kid says, "Daddy why are my heroes on TV fighting," and you have no answer' (Jones, 2009).

Sociologists of sport have offered many answers to questions regarding the logics and consequences of hockey violence for well over three decades. For as long as sociologists have inspected the cultural settings that give rise to, and provide meaning for, sporting practices, particular codes of masculinity have been linked to the performance of a full range of violent behaviours in athletics. Indeed, there are few other social institutions that have been as extensively probed for the link between gender and violence (Messner, Hunt, and Dunbar, 1999). Across empirical research on masculinity in sport, and how codes of aggression become second nature for many young men in sport, Erving Goffman's concept of a *total institution* potentially explains why and how such is the case.

Goffman (1961) contends that in most societies, certain groups exist that may be categorized as all-encompassing socializing agents. Each member is bound by a code of behaviour, socializes mainly with other members of the group, and is subject to constant monitoring and ideological training by authority figures and group leaders. Groups such as the military, religious sects, psychiatric hospitals, or private schools are all examples of social settings in which, upon entry, individuals are re-socialized to adopt master statuses of, respectively, soldier, convert, patient, or student. In his landmark text, *Asylums*, Goffman (1961) describes such institutions in the following way:

> Every institution captures something of the time and interest of its members and provides something of a world for them; in brief, every institution has encompassing tendencies. When we review the different institutions in our Western society, we find some that are encompassing to a degree discontinuously greater than the ones next in line. Their encompassing or total character is symbolized by the barrier to social intercourse with the outside and to departure that is often built right into the physical plant, such as locked doors, high walls, barbed wire, cliffs, water, forests, or moors. These establishments I am calling *total institutions*. (p. 15)

Goffman (1961, pp. 15–16) identifies five conceptual types of total institutions in his classification: i) those established to *care for incapable and 'harmless' persons* (e.g., an orphanage); ii) those established to *care for incapable but dangerous persons* (e.g., psychiatric institutions); iii) those organized to *protect the community* against what are felt to be intentional dangers to it (e.g., prisons); iv) those established to *pursue some work-like tasks*, and justifying themselves only on these instrumental grounds (e.g., the military); and, v) those established as *retreats from the world* (e.g., monasteries).

Goffman's fourth and fifth types of total institution reflect life within sports, and how crisis-producing codes of violence are generationally taught as normative within these particular subcultures. The application of Goffman's fourth category is easy to see because learning and playing the role of an athlete is obviously related to work-tasks, pay, and reputation. Although Goffman intended his fifth category to represent an ascetically oriented refuge such as a monastery, it might be argued that sports allow for a certain type of retreat from the banality of modern life. Figurational sociologists such as Elias and Dunning (1986) would argue that sport, as a social institution, serves to de-routinize social life. As such, sports organizations like the NHL possess a taken-for-granted license to create, through the showcasing of violence as part of sport, a retreat from the mundane or predictable world of everyday life where acts of physical aggression and harm are normally prohibited.

A closer inspection of power and performance sports like hockey reveals the power of sports organizations as total institutions. Thinking sociologically about how definitions of acceptable, wanted, unwanted, and even criminal violence in the sport of ice hockey are created, I would encourage sociologists to consider how ice hockey (and other) sports organizations manufacture consent to their ideologies of, and expectations for, traditional hegemonic male violence in the following way. *First*, as a total institution, ice hockey creates a culture of ideological insularity regarding violence in the sport (think of the case study noted above on the Atom Decision), underpinned by an historical ethos of traditional masculinity and aggression. *Second*, discursive strategies are deployed within the sport in order to publicly frame violence in the game as non-crisis-producing and socially unthreatening; in other words, tolerable.

Sport sociologists are rather unique in their empirical investigations of the residues of unfettered patriarchy and hegemonic masculinity, and its relationship to violence within the total institution of sport. Most of this research, either explicitly or implicitly, dialogically engages feminist and profeminist understandings of hegemonic masculinity and violence. Feminist and profeminist research on gender illustrates how interrogations of masculinity begin by acknowledging that traditionally hegemonic forms of masculinity characterize most sport institutions (McKay, Messner, and Sabo, 2000). Hegemonic masculinity is a conceptually idealized gender status across most institutionalized, power, and performance sports cultures like ice hockey. Through complex ideological and discursive frames that produce systems of socialization and institutional support within sport, the hegemonic brand of masculinity establishes, enforces, and legitimates the ascribed authority of a particular kind of male figure. Donaldson's account of hegemonic masculinity is particularly relevant to the study of sport:

> It is the common sense about breadwinning and manhood. It is exclusive, anxiety-provoking, internally and hierarchically differentiated, brutal, and violent. It is pseudo-natural, tough, contradictory, crisis-prone, rich, and socially sustained. While centrally connected with the institutions of male dominance, not all men practice it, though most men benefit from it. . . . It is a lived experience, and an economic and cultural force, and dependent on social arrangements. It is constructed through difficult negotiation over a lifetime. Fragile it may be, but it constructs the most dangerous things we live with. (1993, pp. 645–6)

Being an overly hegemonic male across sports cultures consistently proves to be a privileging cultural status for many athletic men, as it constructs the normative male identity as one exuding strength, courage, dominance, emotional detachment, social power, and authority. Indeed, sport is a sphere rife with the trappings of residual hegemonic authority and patriarchy. Sociological research on men in sport highlights the constitutive social processes involved in intextuating (de Certeau, 1984)—literally, embedding—hegemonic masculinity into cultural practice (see McKay, Messner, and Sabo, 2000). As Burstyn (1999) notes, possessing hegemonic masculinity in sport is not only rationalized as integral for winning contests but is also used as a signifier of men's ability to exert social dominance in life. In plain terms, the stark lesson derived from sport—which is often labelled *character building* (Miracle and Rees, 1994)—is that to be the acceptably masculine man is to be the successful and socially revered man. However, increasing numbers of sociologists of sport, including Burstyn (1999) and Whannel (2002), recognize that not all men can attain or maintain the ideal masculine status within the total institution of sport—that is, most men, including many hockey players, are gender deviants when it comes to living up to hegemonic standards. According to writers such as Colburn (1985) and Robidoux (2001), this fact is nowhere more socially obvious than it is in ice hockey cultures, where masculinity in its hegemonic form is both subculturally valued and commercially showcased.

Building on these concerns, White and Young (1997, 1999) describe hegemonic masculinity as a dangerous (or, one might suggest, *crisis*) cultural ideal in sports. They argue that a majority of the player violence and aggression in contact sports is attributable to athletes' overindulgence in hegemonic ideologies of masculinity, which are learned as part of socialization processes. Using extended case examples of the physical, emotional, and psychological risks to athletes created by the link between sport and masculinity, White and Young (1999) expose how many male athletes, especially in violent or contact sports, are regularly victimized. Rather than privileging male athletes, the acceptance and performance of the hegemonic ideal of masculinity endangers them, as it places men in contexts where physical injury and social marginalization are common.

Ehrenreich (1997) contends that the link between dangerous masculinities and player violence is at its strongest in sport. Although there are clearly other factors pertinent to the emergence of unsanctioned player violence, research on football, soccer, basketball, and boxing demonstrates how subcultural constructions of masculinity are among the major causes of player violence (Dunning, 1999; Young, 2000). The pursuit of dangerous masculinities leads athletes to treat their bodies as weapons, to utilize aggressive and illegal tactics in competition, and to ostracize others who fail to respect the norms of violence and risk-taking, which are tacitly embedded in sports cultures (Messner, 1990; Messner and Sabo, 1994; Young and White, 1995).

Weinstein, Smith, and Weisenthal (1995) argue that a gender code of masculinity teaches both young and veteran men in many different sports a set of normative standards that excuse even the most excessive player violence. The masculine ethos underpinning the sport is all encompassing, teaching young hockey players to frame most sport experiences along hyperbolic, and somewhat archaic, gender lines. Using Goffman's total institution metaphor, we can appreciate how ideologies of masculinity in sports like ice hockey frame violence as an instrumental work-task and a gender-appropriate behaviour. Violence is also reconcilable in relation to the mythic, hegemonic, and dangerous masculine ideologies underpinning the sport's culture (Gruneau and Whitson, 1993). Thus, men who exude this ideal of dangerous masculinity are in crisis of being injured, hurt, and victimized; those who reject its tenets are at risk of ostracism and alienation.

Victimological perspectives on sport (Faulkner, 1973; Young, 1991, 1993, 2002a; Young and Reasons, 1989) indicate that since most forms of vicious player violence are subculturally accepted by players, tolerated by fans, and commercially lucrative for leagues, little concern has been given to athletes who are emotionally, psychologically, or physically harmed by violence. Case after case of spectacular and tragic injury in youth, amateur, and professional sport suggest that while, as in the case of Don Sanderson, concern and moral panic may follow widely mediated cases of victimization, a status quo inevitably results. Yet, in taking a workers' advocacy perspective, Young (1991, 2002a) challenges the status quo by building on Smith's (1983) typology of violence in sport and arguing that athletes do not relinquish their civil rights while on the field, regardless of their acquiescence to dangerous masculine ideologies of hyperviolent play. Young suggests that as members of teams, leagues, and workplaces, many male athletes are not only asked but are instructionally encouraged to participate in contra-normative player–player violence. As such, young boys and men are constantly enmeshed in cultures of sporting crisis and risk, and have been taught to accept such crisis contexts as normative, laudable, and status-filled. Therefore we must be attentive to the ways in which dangerous masculinities become institutionally regulated doctrines, and the degrees to which they may do little to build positive masculine character (Pascall and White, 2000).

To this end, many of the men involved in junior professional sports like ice hockey disavow the *victim* as a potential masculine identity within the game. The stereotypical male athlete lives in a context of hyper-masculinity, consenting to self-vicitmization, and unfortunately learning to victimize others as part of 'doing' the culture of sport; one might argue that the very nature of the sport (i.e., including fist fights, brutal bodychecks, and other violence in sports like ice hockey) is chiselled out of hyperbolic masculine stereotypes. Among these stereotypes is the notion that a man does not cry, whine, wince, complain, or back down in the face of a physical challenge. The dangerous masculine culture of professional ice hockey flatly eschews discourses of victimization, preferring to reframe on-ice physicality as character-building, toughening, sacrificial, or as an act of dedication (as noted by Faulkner, 1973, Smith, 1983, and Barnes, 1988). Since ice hockey players and their fans often view players as warriors or iron men, the image of the professional ice hockey player as a victim of (criminal) violence is simply incongruent with cultural interpretations of the game (Gruneau and Whitson, 1993).

Explanations of player violence offered by coaches, league executives, and broadcasters equally support dangerous masculine practices in ice hockey, and restrict the possibility of players being considered victims of violence (Young, 2000). As part of framing ice hockey as an entertainment spectacle worthy of audience consumption, the exaltation of dangerous masculinity establishes a cultural condition in which players are valorized for their consent to physically harm or be victimized by one another. Players are viewed as heroes or weaklings, superstars or wimps, aggressors or losers, and men or sissies, depending on their ability to be a ruggedly masculine player. Conforming to the codes of dangerous masculinity can be informally rewarded within teams through salary and contract incentives, praise, and other forms of preferential treatment (Weinstein, Smith, and Wiesenthal, 1995). Similarly, fans and media broadcasters draw attention to the toughness and durability of the masculine or violent player and his ability to withstand ongoing victimization, often mythologizing tough players of the past as masculine legends. Such legends include Gordie Howe, Bobby Orr, Maurice Richard, and Dave 'Tiger' Williams (Young, 1993). Legal and illegal bodychecks, fist fights, and injuries are showcased on sport shows—often in segments dedicated to Plays of the Day. At the same time, social reaction to and support for violence in the game creates significant barriers for those athletes who hold alternative views on tolerating violence and risk within the game (Young, 1993; Young and White, 1995).

While there is a discernible shift in public opinion about violence in sports like ice hockey toward skepticism and review (Atkinson and Young, 2008), the continued mass support for, tolerance of, or lack of concern for egregious violence in the game illustrates something incredibly important regarding the way sporting spectacles remain culturally valued among generations of men in crisis as a form of 'social mimesis' (Dunning, 1999). Sociologists of sport violence have routinely argued that one of the main allures of watching athletes engage in aggressive and violent acts is that it becomes vehicle for indirectly participating in that which is regularly taboo in everyday life; and, because it may help to release, in a controlled and predicted manner, frustrations and aggressions male audiences carry with them resulting from family, work, peer, or general cultural conditions and contexts. In the midst of a supposed masculinity crisis, wherein some men feel they are attacked from all sides, the ability to cheer for hyperbolic displays of hegemonic masculinity in a culturally protected space can be incredibly exciting and satisfying. Players are the sacrificial lambs of a culture of spectators whose nostalgia for 'better' masculine times partially supports the crisis context for men in sport.

The context of crisis within many sports cultures for Canadian boys and men is a classic double bind. On the one hand, there are inherent (and often unwanted) risks posed to the body and mind in contact sports like ice hockey, which become symbolic of one's achieved male status in the sports world due to player tolerance and outward acceptance. Hughes and Coakley (1991) explain how (male) athletes in competitive amateur and professional sports learn such interpretive frames and use these frames to gauge commitment to the group and sport. The authors describe how athletes are taught to strive for distinction, accept no limits as players, make sacrifices for their sport, and play through pain and injury as part of an overarching sport ethic; each are stereotypically masculine characteristics required to be a social authority figure both on and away from the field. Such logics are apparent in old North American clichés that success in the culture of sport will translate into success in life (Miracle and Rees, 1994). While not all athletes are socialized quite so completely or assess all social interactions and athletic performances in relation to this masculinized sport ethic; this ethic is so ubiquitous and effective that most athletes must encounter it and reconcile themselves to it at some point in their sport careers.

On the other hand, there is the hazard of non-participation and non-compliance to the codes of masculinity and risk underpinning the sport. Indeed, mainstream sports cultures in Canada remain one of the last bastions for overtly extolling the virtues of hegemonic masculinity. Sports like hockey, football, rugby, baseball, and others remain a culturally protected social space replete with an unapologetic appeal to nostalgic notions of being manly in a hyper-traditionalist North American sense. Though not in all cases, sport spheres tend to prefer representations of an *emphasized masculinity* among its participants; here, the residual elements of patriarchy both subtly and blatantly colour the culture of amateur and professional sport. Sociologists of sport have long argued that the micro pockets of the world of athletics are among the most pronounced and confrontational battlegrounds about gender, power, and ideology (Atkinson, 2008c).

Although rarely thought of, or studied as such, I argue in the remainder of this chapter that where there is *residual patriarchy* in sport—enduring structures of practice and power, dominant ideologies, cultural statuses, and interpersonal roles still based upon hegemonic notions of masculinity and femininity that survive through clever reinvention and disguise—a full spate of masculine crises will exist for participants. As long as sporting practices and ideologies are constructed around and through dangerous, hyperbolized, and emphasized masculine doctrines, certain crises follow. For example, organized sport becomes a site of crisis production for many young boys, men, and others because it is inherently exclusionary along performance lines; almost immediately when boys enter the sport, winner and loser identities are linked to participants. There is of course a politics of exclusion—fitting nicely into the much mythologized 'sport as (male) war' cultural metaphor—that moulds experience and reaffirms divisions between popular/strong and deviant/weak boys and men. As Farr (1988) wrote, there is a palpable air of dominance bonding among successful boys in sports cultures. Such is often tolerated or ignored because, after all, participation in sport is voluntary and simply not for everyone. From this perspective, the residual patriarchy is excusable from the outside, since 'it's only sport'. Dismissals of residual patriarchy in sport tend to overlook how young girls, women, ethnic or religious minority boys and men, or anyone who deviates from culturally heteronormative sexual preferences in sport are often targeted as unwanted Others in the clubhouse and systematically excused from participation (Atkinson, 2008c).

Case Studies in Residual Patriarchy

A common finding across research on male privilege in sport is that especially dominant men in athletics are regularly granted a cultural license to participate in a range of rule-violating behaviours that others would not. As time passes, these athletes come to see themselves as untouchable (both on the playing field and in the culture of sport), and often develop a social psychological trait called *hubris*, a form of pride-driven arrogance (Benedict, 1997). Coakley and Donnelly (2005) describe how hubris germinates within athletes who feel as if their actions are beyond reproach. Why does hubris manifest? Athletes engaged in highly visible and culturally revered sports, even at young ages and amateur levels, may become celebrities in their communities, and are held up as quintessential male role models (Miracle and Rees, 1994). Athletes, especially young males participating in power-and-performance sports, are further socialized into believing that they are special and powerful men, whose social transgressions in and around the playing field will be handled by parents, coaches, teachers, and even police (Benedict, 1997). Over time, public accolade, attention, and special treatments encourages expectation, demand, and indifference to others within these special athlete cultures.

Hubris is, as a state of mind and behavioural trait, a crisis condition. Two case studies follow that illustrate the links between residual patriarchy, emphasized masculinity, and crisis. The first articulates how the internalization of hyper-masculine identities in sport creates sexual assault crises in particular sport settings. The second outlines and discusses the masculinized roots of *hazing* practices in sport.

I. Sexual Assault

Relationships involving sexual interaction between people in sports cultures are complicated and vastly under-studied. Until quite recently, consensual and non-consensual sexual practices between players, coaches, and other sports insiders have not been discussed publicly. . What we do know is that most forms of sexual contact or relationships are strictly prohibited in the majority of sports cultures (such as those between coaches and athletes). Nevertheless, athletes, coaches, and others frequently violate social and institutional taboos regarding sex in sport through abusive and exploitive means, and often without overt concern for being caught (such is the nature of hubris). Stories emerging from sports cultures in the past ten years have called attention to particularly troubling cases of sexual abuse, exploitation, and domination involving coaches and athletes from a full range of sports settings and levels.

Celia Brackenridge (1997) suggests that athletes encounter a continuum of sexual discrimination and abuse in sport. The types included 'sex discrimination' (i.e., a differential treatment regarding access, pay, and other structural aspects of sport), 'sexual harassment' (i.e., sexually offensive and/or intimidating behaviour), and 'sexual abuse' (i.e., rape, assault, groping, and other forms of sexually coercive behaviour). Aspects of sex discrimination have been well debated in the North American sports world, but our social understanding of the patterns of sexual harassment and sexual abuse in sports cultures remains critically fragmented and empirically disjointed. Particularly in the case of the latter, there is a lack of systematic research on the processes involved, extent of, and possibilities for reducing the sexual abuse of young athletes at the hands of coaches and other sports insiders. A working knowledge of sports cultures dictates that the increased number of reported cases of sexual abuse in sport involving athletes and their (predominantly male) coaches is neither a recent phenomenon, nor entirely accurate in its portrayal of sexual exploitation in sport. Still, Brackenridge (1997) estimates that roughly one in four female and one in nine male athletes have been sexually victimized in sport. Brackenridge (1997, 2001) notes that athletes are overwhelmingly reluctant to whistleblow on a male figure of power in the sporting community; this is partly because athletes are taught to be deferential to them as part of elite sport development, and partly in fear that no one will believe the allegations. This may be especially true as it pertains to male victims 'telling' on a male father figure in their sport.

The predominant explanation of why the sexual abuse of athletes occurs by coaches, administrators, or senior players, pertains to how hyper-masculine power and authority work in sports cultures. In brief, sexual abuse tends to occur between players and coaches due to the combination of a series of critical factors related to motivation and power. When a powerful, authoritative coach, who is sexually motivated to offend, is placed in a context of low social surveillance and easily exploitable targets, victimization will frequently occur. The typical sexual abuser is an older, highly-accredited, ostensibly trustworthy, male coach who is able to spend long periods of time alone with one or several athletes. Sports involving close contact between players and coaches as part of instruction; frequent travel for competitions; and that have weak or non-existent systems for monitoring coach behaviours are especially dangerous contexts for abuse. Victims of abuse tend to be young males, small in stature, plagued with low self-esteem, exhibiting intense commitment to their sport and their coach, and with strained relations at home. The work of crime theorists like Cohen and Felson (1979) may help to explain these trends. The heart of their *routine activities theory* is that we can explain rates of victimization in a given social setting by analyzing if three factors are present: *motivated offenders, suitable targets,* and an *absence of guardianship* over the targets. The probability of sexual victimization in sport is therefore high when these three factors converge, or are consistently present over the course of time. In the language of Cohen and Felson's theory, the 'routine activities' of sport—such as being trained by a coach in an insular sports environment—expose individuals to potential offenders. Simply put, the routine activities of social life provide motivated offenders (who are presumed to be everywhere) with opportunities to engage in crime.

Grooming is another significant trend in the abuse of athletes at the hands of coaches. *Grooming* refers to the systematic sexual targeting, nurturing, and long-term dominance over particular athletes. Over the course of months, or in some cases years, male coaches become very close friends with their targets, developing a family-like bond with them. Through this process, physical, psychological, and emotional boundaries separating them are broken down by the coach. Important is that the boundary-crossing may seem at first to occur as an act of friendship or parental concern, but turns into a process of social psychological control where the coach coercively demands that the athlete reciprocates his/her physical (sexual) advances. A groomed athlete is one who fears the coach as a sexual abuser but feels a strong emotional loyalty to them, is constantly monitored and dominated by the coach, and feels shame for their involvement in the relationship (i.e., thinking it is one's own fault).

Journalist and former Canadian national athlete Laura Robinson has conducted long-term research on another pathological form of sexual relationships in sport: the culture of gang/group sex involving athletes (Robinson, 1998). A disturbing trend in high school, amateur, and university/college sport is the practice of male athletes engaging in group/public sex with one or more females, either with their consent, or by force. Group sex becomes culturally practiced by the athletes over time as a hyper-masculine rite of passage, a display of hubris, or a symbolic, albeit esoteric, celebration of male hegemony in particular sport subcultures or on certain teams. The abuse of young female participants through group sex with male athletes reflects a culture of privilege and a socialized sense of impunity. Violent or publicly lewd sexual relationships illustrate a desire to engage in a 'sneaky thrill' (Katz, 1988) or an excessively deviant practice to which they believe their high social status entitles them. But from a general perspective, while females who are asked or forced to participate are sexually exploited and abused, one must ask whether the existing culture of group sex in certain sports also coerces young male players to participate, lest they face ostracism, alienation, and outright discrimination on their teams (potentially interfering with their future aspirations in sport).

The last five years of the twentieth century, and first five of the twenty-first, produced landmark cases of sexually inappropriate behaviours between athletes, coaches, and others in sport. Among the cases that underscore the massively concealed problem of athlete sexual exploitation at the hands of

BOX 5.1 ❀ THE NOT-SO-DIRTY SECRET IN SPORT

Sociologists of sport like Jeffrey Benedict (1997) have linked participation at a young age in aggressively sexual cultures in sport to patterns of domestic violence among older male athletes. In the mid-1990s, a spate of domestic violence allegations against professional athletes in the United States prompted national attention on the issue. Between 1990 and 1996, 150 formal complaints were issued against Division I or professional athletes for domestic violence, with 77 of those complaints filed in 1995 and 1996. All but seven of the allegations involved football or basketball players. In seven of the cases, the victims were pregnant. Abusers were convicted in only 28 of the 150 cases, and many of those involved plea bargains. Jeff Benedict's (2004) *Out of Bounds: Inside the NBA's Culture of Rape, Violence & Crime* documents 33 complaints during the 2001–2002 season alone.

Unfortunately, domestic violence and sexual assault involving athletes occurs as patterned behaviour in sports cultures. Benedict argues that athletes may have a difficult time understanding how to behave at home when they are immersed daily in what is essentially a violent culture. Benedict lists scores of cases involving athletes who have allegedly abused. Former Portland Trail Blazer's guard Rod Strickland was arrested when he gave an ex-girlfriend a black eye. A day after scoring four touchdowns for the University of Nebraska, Lawrence Phillips was charged with assaulting his girlfriend. Former National Football League (NFL) quarterback Warren Moon publicly apologized for repeatedly assaulting his wife. Kansas City Chiefs running back Harvey Williams was arrested for domestic violence twice in 1993, then again in 1995 after he had been traded to the L.A. Raiders. In 1993, 310-pound Houston Oiler Doug Smith assaulted his wife, Rebecca, by choking, head-butting, and punching her in the eyes so hard she needed head surgery. Homerun king Barry Bonds was arrested in 1993 for threatening his wife, choking her, and allegedly throwing her against a car and kicking her while she was on the ground. In 1997, Wil Cordero of the Boston Red Sox was arrested for spousal abuse. On 28 January 2000, Colorado Rockies Pitcher Pedro Astacio pleaded guilty to third-degree assault for punching his wife. Barely a week later, Bobby Chouinard of the Arizona Diamondbacks was released from the team after admitting he choked, slapped, and held a gun to his wife Erica's head. In 2000, Colorado Avalanche goaltender Patrick Roy was arrested for domestic violence just days after he set the record for career victories by a National Hockey League (NHL) goalie. Roy admitted to police that he ripped two doors off their hinges during an argument in the couple's bedroom. In 2001, New Jersey Nets star Jason Kidd pleaded guilty to assaulting his wife. In 2007, Kidd shocked sports fans when he took out a restraining order against her, Joumana Kidd. He accused Joumana of extreme cruelty and alleged she physically and mentally abused him over the course of their ten-year marriage. In March 2003, former heavyweight champion Riddick Bowe was arrested on charges of second-degree assault against his wife. This was less than a week before Bowe was to begin serving prison time for abducting his first wife and their five children. The list goes on.

coaches was Sheldon Kennedy's. Kennedy was a young Canadian hockey player coached by Graham James, a highly respected and nationally recognized coach. Kennedy had first been coached by James as a junior-level hockey player in Winnipeg, and then during the late 1980s, on the Swift Current Broncos of Canada's Western Hockey League. Between the ages of 14 and 19, James sexually abused Kennedy on a repeated basis. Kennedy has said that James sexually assaulted him more than 350 times, beginning when Kennedy was 14. The Kennedy case represents, in many ways, a classic case of grooming a young athlete. Every Tuesday and Thursday for six years, Kennedy went to James's house, where James would sexually assault him. James told Kennedy that they were like husband and wife, and that no matter where Kennedy would go, James would follow him. Emotional and psychological pressure in Kennedy built up over time, and on several occasions the young player considered suicide as his only escape from James. Eventually, Kennedy left the Broncos after being drafted by the NHL's Calgary Flames.

In 1995, Kennedy broke his silence, and the story became the most internationally mediated case of abuse in decades. Hockey insiders, including some of Kennedy's own teammates, knew of the abuse, but the story only broke in Canada when Kennedy finally pressed criminal charges against James. In January 1997, Graham James was sentenced to three years in prison for sexually assaulting Kennedy and another unidentified player. As a result, the Canadian Hockey Association instituted new coach screening and monitoring policies, and developed a grassroots program called 'Speak Out', designed to encourage young players to report physical, emotional, or mental abuse they have suffered in the sport. The Kennedy case became a watershed moment in the reporting of abuse by athletes, encouraging athletes across North America to step forward. While many did, Mike Danton, a hockey player with the St Louis Blues was not among them. Nevertheless, his shocking story of sexual exploitation at the hands of a coach emerged in 2004.

In the late spring of 2004, Mike Danton (born Michael Jefferson) was arrested and prosecuted for hiring a hitman to murder his agent, David Frost. Danton was found guilty and sentenced to seven and a half years in jail. The trial exposed, however, another tragic tale of coach–athlete abuse and control. Danton had known Frost since he was 12 years old. Frost had been Danton's coach at an early age, and shepherded his career through Ontario minor and junior hockey leagues. Frost coached Danton on the Quinte Hawks Junior A team, but was suspended for sexual misconduct with a player, and for allowing his players to engage in sex acts with teenage girls while he watched. Stories started to surface about Frost's penchant for young boys, but their details were not pursued. Questions about his relationship with four young players he coached at Quinte (called his 'Brampton Boys' by insiders) surrounded Frost, with claims suggesting he had sexually assaulted and psychologically controlled them for years.

In the case of Danton, however, a 'special' relationship seemed to be in place. Danton spent most of his free time with Frost (who had actually relocated to Danton's Brampton, Ontario, neighbourhood to be near him) and called him repeatedly during the day to profess how he 'loved' him, while Danton's parents were not allowed (by Frost) to speak to their son in and around the hockey arena. Danton spent time with his younger brother Tom at Frost's cottage, and spent Christmases with Frost instead of his parents. Frost even helped to convince Mike Danton (who was legally named Mike Jefferson at the time) to change his name to distance himself from his family. When the New Jersey Devils drafted Danton in 2000, Frost actually became a legal player agent to maintain his contact with Danton. For the next four years, Frost retained his sexual and psychological control over Danton. But after years of abuse, control, and exploitation, Danton buckled under the pressure and attempted to hire the contract killer's services to terminate their relationship at last. A 2005 CBC investigation exposed Frost's legacy of abuse and sexual control. To date, however, while Frost lost his agent's licence, he has not been criminally charged for sexual assault because the boys he abused have refused to testify against him.

The Kennedy and Danton cases helped blow the metaphorical lid off the culture of sexual abuse and exploitation of athletes by coaches in American high school sports. Between 2004–8, an almost exponential increase in cases of alleged abuse involving coaches and high school athletes has been tracked. Crime-watch website www.Badjocks.com has collected data on filed or reported cases of coach-athlete sexual exploitation, reporting the mean number of 213 cases per year in that time period. For example, girls' high school basketball coach Rick Lopez faced 55 felony counts of alleged sexual assault on a child in 2004. According to three of his female players, Lopez, who coached the elite Colorado Hoopsters, had a standard operating procedure: he would choose a girl on his team, move into her basement, groom her over time, and have sex with her on a regular basis. Lopez admitted that his first alleged victim was 13 when he initiated sexual contact with her.

Critics of these case studies might suggest that instances of abuse and sexual exploitation are waning, that these particular events are atypical in sports cultures, or that leagues are showing a concerted effort to drum out cultures of overt masculine power in sports. To these readers, the suspension of NHL player Sean Avery for sexist comments he made is a prime example of how the culture of residual patriarchy and dangerous masculinity in sport is shifting. In early December 2008, the NHL indefinitely suspended Sean Avery from his team the Dallas Stars because he made untoward comments about

Calgary Flames defenceman Dion Phaneuf's girlfriend, actress Elisha Cuthbert (who was also Avery's ex-girlfriend). In a pre-match interview, Avery stated, 'I am really happy to be back in Calgary, I love Canada. But I just want to comment on how it's become like a common thing in the NHL for guys to fall in love with my *sloppy seconds*. I don't know what that's about. Enjoy the game tonight.' Public reaction to Avery's comments was swift and severe. The NHL immediately suspended the player, who happened to be someone with a long history of rule violations and behaviour that was publicly embarrassing to the league. While the league's move may indeed symbolize a progressive intolerance toward old codes of hegemonic masculinity and misogyny, others would question whether the league suspended Avery for sexist and humiliating descriptions of Cuthbert, or rather for the player's outright insult to the masculine identity of another player. Avery's own teammate, Mike Modano, commented, 'I think the words, the words and disrespect *for an opponent like that is something* . . . there's lots of trash talking that goes on, on the ice, but that to announce something like that for everybody to hear, to me that crosses the line and the league and our ownership felt that too' (emphasis added). Later asked about his comments and his reputation, as well as public perception that he is a villain, Avery responded with unabashed hubris to a *New York Times* reporter, saying, 'It's better than being known as soft.'

II. Hazing

Hazing is most commonly practiced in university fraternities and sports teams, but it also has a long history in the military, police forces, rescue services, and even some social service clubs in North America. Hazing may be defined as a coercive, and often physically dangerous, initiation activity undergone by someone joining a sports team. Hazing activities are designed and overseen by veteran members of a sports team, and generally carried out in front of the entire team as part of an 'initiation night'. Hazing rituals are intended to humiliate, degrade, and abuse young or new members of a team. On many sports teams at the university or college levels, a young player is not socially recognized as a legitimate team member until he or she has passed through one or more hazing rituals.

Knowledge of the history and contemporary pervasiveness of hazing in sport is limited. Hazing practices, because they are officially banned in most university- and professional-level sports teams, have become rather esoteric practices and thus tightly guarded by participants. From anecdotal evidence gathered in the last third of the twentieth century (Nuwer, 2002, 2004), until quite recently hazing has been found in male team sports at the high school, university/college, or semi-professional levels. Hazing rituals are common in contact sports like ice hockey, rugby, wrestling, and football. The rituals, either conducted throughout an initiation week or in one evening (known as

---

BOX 5.2 ❖ EXAMPLES OF HAZING RITUALS

The list of hazing rituals practiced on Canadian teams is lengthy. Here are a few typical rituals:

Running the gauntlet: The athlete is forced to run naked while being hit with a paddle.

Red rover: Two males are stripped, and one end of a rope is tied to each male's penis. They are then instructed to perform a tug-of-war.

Marshmallow races: Nude participants are made to pick up marshmallows with their buttocks, and then run a designated distance, competing with other rookies. Last person across the finish line is forced to eat their marshmallow.

The elephant walk: Nude participants bend over and walk in a straight line, taking turns tugging at each other's genitalia.

Kangaroo court: Athletes are stripped and blindfolded, and then accused of various 'crimes'. They are then forced to consume heavy amounts of alcohol within a short time frame.

The Holocaust: Rookies are stripped, blindfolded, and driven to a remote location during the night. Their clothes are soaked, balled up, taped together, and thrown into a ditch. The rookies are then let off the bus and told to find their clothes, untangle them, and make their own way back to town.

Scavenger hunt: Rookies are forced to dress in flamboyant and outdated clothing, and sent to a public location (like a bar or gymnasium) with a list of items to find and bring back (rarely any of which are actually present at the location). For any item the rookie does not recover, s/he is required to drink a predetermined amount of alcohol.

a 'Rookie Night' or 'Rookie Show'), frequently involve nudity, binge drinking, eating disgusting substances, shaving body hair, and certain levels of violence.

Despite the fact that most North American high schools, colleges, semi-professional, and professional teams have banned hazing outright, hazing cultures continue to flourish in sport. Teams with young participants (high school and university/college) tend to be the most vicious and unapologetic about their hazing rituals. At the professional sport level, hazing is still present, but may take on a less dangerous and publicly humiliating tone. For example, first-year members of a professional team will often be forced to pick up the

bill after the team goes out to an expensive restaurant. In professional baseball, a rookie player is often forced to field questions from reporters after a
game while dressed in women's clothing. In September 2004, a member of
the Cleveland Indians was dressed as a cheerleader on the team bus on the
way to the airport in Kansas City. In 2000, San Diego Chargers veterans tied
a rookie to a pole in the downtown area of San Diego and threw eggs at him
while onlookers laughed.

Regardless of the level of sport, or the seriousness of the outcome, the main
point of hazing rituals is clear. The acts are classic social degradation ceremonies that symbolize a young player's willingness to respect his or her elders'
statuses on a team. Hazing rituals are intended to lower the person's status in
the group while publicly illustrating this low status to others. The hazing ritual
reinforces the idea that as a group, a sports team is defined in part by a rigid
social hierarchy. At the same time, rookies receive great kudos from veteran
players for undergoing the rituals. For this reason, athletes familiar with hazing
rituals often value them as a key team bonding ceremonies. When challenged
about the appropriateness of hazing by outsiders, team members often aggressively defend their rights to haze, and claim that people outside of sport cannot
understand 'what it takes' to be a member of a sports team.

Not all athletes want or celebrate hazing practices. From the mid-1980s
onward, more players and their parents have been willing to come forward
and challenge the legitimacy of hazing rituals and the residual patriarchy they
perpetuate in sports cultures. These players have often been ostracized by
their teammates and coaches. Universities and agents of social control have
not, however, ignored player complaints. Players and coaches responsible for
the structure and culture of hyper-masculine hazing rituals in high school and
university/college sports have been fined, dismissed, sentenced to community
service, or ordered to participate in psychological counselling as a result. Still,
a chilly climate exists for players who choose to violate the code of silence
about hazing in sport.

The problem of hazing in sports cultures runs deeper than it might at first
seem. A young boy will face his first real experience with hazing not on an
organized adolescent sports team, but rather in a gym class. Hazing rituals are
common in locker rooms and might be tied to escalating rates of gym class
dropout among boys in Canada. In 2008, along with Michael Kehler and Kevin
Wamsley (both at the University of Western Ontario, Canada), I started an
investigation of the links between masculinity codes and boys' dropout rates.
In Ontario, all high school students are required to take at least one course in
health and physical education. Most boys choose to take the mandatory course
in Grade 9. Others postpone the physical education requirement until a later
year when the topic is related to health issues and does not include activities in the gymnasium or on the playing field; the translation is that growing
numbers of boys in Canada are avoiding gym class like the bubonic plague.

In speaking with boys about why they are choosing to drop out of gym, they routinely recount stories of being ostracized, stigmatized, and bullied by other boys in the locker room. They were snapped with towels, teased about their lack of muscles, had their abilities mocked, and in some cases were physically assaulted. In response to an article about our study that was circulated in the Canadian press, one man suggested in a public blog post:

> Unfortunately, this type of teasing is going to happen—it's a part of the process of growing up for most kids. Boys need to test out their strength, determine their social ranking, and physical prowess is one of the ways they do it. If my son was being teased that way, I might help him find a way to develop his own strength and sense of self, either through a sport or weight training (which any kid can do), or a martial art. If we instil in our kids a sense of self-worth, no amount of teasing will leave lasting scars. It might be tough while it is happening, but be there for your son, do things with him that provide a sense of competence. In the long run, it'll pay off in a better relationship with your boy, and with him being more successful in life. (http://masculineheart.blogspot.com/)

The anonymous man's comments draw into sharp relief how this form of hazing is still viewed by many as an instance of masculine character building. Despite an acceptance that gym class bullying is alienating and gut-wrenching for boys who do not measure up, it is for their own good in the long run.

A series of media-amplified cases of hazing in the United States during the early 1990s brought new light to the danger of hazing in sport cultures. Each of the cases showed, on the one hand, that schools and local police forces would not tolerate hazing as it had been in the past. But on the other hand, each case illustrated that the increased punishment of hazing by schools and other agents of social control had only a minimal deterrent effect. Other critics of hazing in North American sport have suggested that the increased media exposure of the practices would not help to eliminate them, but rather would force them further underground. Two infamous cases of sports-related hazing show these points quite clearly.

In 2005, the Ontario Hockey League (OHL) has levied fines totalling CDN$35,000 against the Windsor Spitfires, and suspended the team's coach and general manager, Moe Mantha, for 40 games. The fines, of $25,000 and $10,000 respectively, followed an investigation by the OHL into a hazing incident that occurred on 9 September 2005 on the team bus. The hazing incident occurred when the Spitfires were returning from an exhibition game in London, Ontario, against the London Knights. It involved four players being told by their teammates to strip and stand in the washroom (designed to fit one person) at the back of the bus. The ritual is known in the league as the 'hot box', and is common within the sport's culture. The players were told to enter the washroom at the beginning of the two-hour trip, and to remain there for

BOX 5.3 ❖ WE ARE NOT ALONE: NOTORIOUS HAZING CASES IN THE UNITED
STATES

1980, University of Michigan, Hockey

J.T. Todd, a freshman, reportedly was given large quantities of alcohol in a player's
off-campus house in what had become an annual initiation ritual. He allegedly was
stripped, shaved, covered with jam, eggs, and cologne and left outside in near-
freezing weather for 90 minutes.

1988, Lyndhurst High School, New Jersey, Football

At a football camp in Pennsylvania, one sophomore was allegedly forced to insert
his finger into the anus of another sophomore while 20 to 30 other teammates
looked on. Two upperclassmen were dismissed from the team, and two others were
demoted on the squad as a result of a school inquiry into the matter.

1988, Kent State University, Ohio, Hockey

The hockey season was cancelled after 12 players were charged with violating various
hazing and drinking laws during an off-campus initiation party, which resulted in the
shaving of heads and bodies of the students involved. One rookie nearly died after
veterans coerced him to chug liquor and beer through a bong.

1990, Western Illinois University, Illinois, Lacrosse

Nicholas Haben, a member of the school's lacrosse club, died in a dormitory after
being carried back to school following a drinking initiation in a wooded area near
campus. Twelve veteran participants were given community service.

1992, Sunnyside High School, Washington, Wrestling

In the school's wrestling room, a 15-year-old boy was allegedly sodomized with a
mop handle while teammates held him down and dozens of other wrestlers watched.
The attack sent the boy, bleeding and traumatized, to the hospital for a week. He
suffered internal injuries. Richard Melendrez, 18, pleaded guilty to second-degree
reckless endangerment and was given 60 days in a work-release program.

1996, Alexander High School, Ohio, Football

Travis Hawk, a team captain, pleaded no contest to a misdemeanour charge of
hazing involving several freshman teammates in the locker room showers. Parents
of the victims contended their sons were sodomized with shampoo bottles after
football practice on separate nights and suffered from mental anguish and continued
harassment in school. Hawk was given a suspended sentence, a $50 fine, and a
community service requirement.

1998, New Orleans Saints, NFL Football

In a hazing similar to a gang 'jump-in' ritual, rookie Cam Cleeland suffered an eye
injury when bashed with a bag of coins, and rookie Jeff Danish was sent through

a window and hospitalized for stitches. Danish sued the Saints, teammate Andre Royal, an assistant coach, and five other players, seeking damages from the team of more than $650,000.

1999, North Branch High School, Michigan, Basketball
One player was expelled and six players were suspended for a series of hazing acts at a summer camp. One freshman was allegedly hit in the genitals with a wooden coat hanger, another was sprayed with urine from a shampoo bottle, and a third player's face was forced onto another player's buttocks. Two coaches lost their jobs for failing to provide adequate supervision.

the duration. News of the incident was leaked by an unnamed source to the OHL, and the league initiated the investigation. What is not clear is the impact of the decision to suspend Mantha on the culture of hazing in the sport.

The case of hazing at McGill University in Montreal, Canada, in 2005, drew attention to one of sport's most victimizing hazing traditions. In this case, the player came forward to complain. An 18-year-old member of the university's 'football team, the Redmen, reported being sodomized by other members of the team as part of a hazing ritual. The player was taken to a darkened squash court on the last day of training camp in late August, and told to remove his pants. The player allegedly refused several times, but was reportedly coerced into compliance by fellow teammates. The player was then brought to his hands and knees, and other players prodded his rectum with a broomstick, referred to within the team subculture as 'Dr Broom'.

McGill University launched an investigation and found that despite its anti-hazing policies, despite the fact that all of its football players signed commitments that they would not engage in hazing, and despite warnings from the coach that inappropriate behaviour would not be tolerated, the hazing ritual was planned and carried out in clear violation of the rules. Cases of hazing in sport that so flagrantly violate league rules have been cited as prime examples of male athlete hubris. As a result of the football team's hazing, McGill University cancelled the remainder of the varsity football season, took disciplinary action against several individuals on the team (university suspensions), forced players to engage in community service, reviewed and renewed its policies and procedures regarding hazing, and launched a series of alternative educational and team-building initiatives. In addition, the University further challenged other sports programs, leagues, and federations to adopt several of their 'new' rules, including: to immediately suspend, for an entire season, anyone who engages in hazing; to revoke the athletic awards of any student who engages in hazing; to appoint special monitors of teams to police hazing/initiation week practices; and, to broaden the definition of hazing to include not only physical acts, but also emotionally and psychologically damaging acts such as verbal abuse. These cases illustrate that even in an era of widespread criticism and control of hazing, the practices continue within a cultural insularity often cherished on sports teams. Especially in the case of the McGill Redmen football team, it is most troubling that the players engaged in hazing despite having promised, in writing, that they would not. These cases similarly point to the pervasive problem: institutions might be policing the practice of hazing with harsh punishment, but they are not addressing the culture of hazing in sport, and its role therein. Without recognizing why hazing occurs, critics argue, no new policy aimed at punishment will be effective.

Hazing might only disappear if subcultural traditions, and cultures of masculine hubris, within sport is challenged and changed. Though at present the culture/practice is under threat from the outside, it can only be changed from within. A promising step, argues hazing critic Jay Johnson (2004), is to replace physically dangerous and psychologically damaging hazing rituals with other pro-social and positive experiences. Week-long retreats at wilderness camps, participation in 'Outward Bound' or adventure sports events, and involvement in collective public service programs such as Habitat for Humanity have all been recommended as group-cohesion-building exercises for athletes. Standing in the way of these innovative ideas is a generational payback mentality among athletes, in which they find comfort in the idea that they can haze other players in ways they experienced in the past; or, coaches who feel as if hazing, as long as it remains unseen by outsiders, serves a critical function in team sports.

Summary

In this chapter, we examined several case studies of masculine crisis in sport. In a few cases, the crises revolve around an overcommitment to or association with hyper-masculine identities and subcultural practices in sport; many young male athletes strive toward this type of attitude in order to attain a kind of pastiche hegemony. Other cases discussed draw attention to the ways young men are silenced or targeted as victims of exclusion or violence if they do not live up to the codes of emphasized masculinity in sport. But all of these cases reveal something important about the subtle, overt, and occasionally very dangerous ways 'traditional' ideas about masculinity are stitched into sport.

Discussion Questions

1. Do you think boys are often encouraged to link their male identities with successes and failures in sport and athletics?
2. Do you think that girls' and women's increased participation in sport has changed the culture of masculinity in sport?

3. It has been said that sport is one of the remaining social places where homophobia is tolerated. Do you agree or disagree?
4. Do research on what is called 'the code' in professional hockey. What are 'the code's' links to the construction of masculinity in the sport?

Key Readings

Anderson, E. (2005). *In the Game: Gay Athletes and the Cult of Masculinity*. Albany: SUNY. Anderson examines how homophobia is reproduced in sport, and how gay male athletes navigate this difficult social terrain. By detailing individual athlete experiences with homophobia, Anderson shows how athletes are emerging from their athletic closets and contesting the dominant norms of masculinity. From the locker rooms of high school sports, where a 'don't ask, don't tell' atmosphere often exists, to the unique circumstances that gay athletes encounter in professional team sports, this book analyzes the agency to change their enivronments that openly gay athletes possess.

Burstyn, V. (1999). *Rites of Men: Manhood, Politics, and the Culture of Sport*. Toronto: University of Toronto Press. Burstyn's book provides a systematic deconstruction of the hyper-masculine performance and identity expectations taught to young boys and men in sport zones. The book delves especially deep into logics of heteronormativity in sport, socialization of boys through coaching and subcultural affiliation, and the politics of masculine embodiment in sport.

Messner, M. (2002). *Taking the Field: Men, Women, and Sport*. Minneapolis: University of Minnesota Press. This widely cited text on the importance of gender in sport is written by perhaps the leading authority in the sociology of sport. The book serves as an important primer for students and researchers interested in the gendered structures and cultural dynamics that cut across most sporting practices in North America.

Robinson, L. (1998). *Crossing the Line: Violence and Sexual Assault in Canada's National Sport*. Toronto: McClelland and Stewart. Robinson's end-of-the-century exposé on rape and abuse cultures in Canadian minor hockey blew the lid off a social phenomenon that few, until that time, had the courage to acknowledge, let alone speak about, in public. The book paints a chilling portrait of how cultures of rape are justified and hidden by a full range of hockey insiders.

Young, K. (2004). *Sporting Bodies, Damaged Selves*. London: Elsevier. This edited collection of essays by leading authorities on the sociology of pain and injury provides case study analysis of the links between injury and gendered identity. Across the volume, readers are consistently exposed to the idea that playing while in pain is not only normalized within male sports cultures, but understood subculturally as a badge of honour.

Web Links

Badjocks (www.badjocks.com). An exposé-oriented website devoted to discovering and cataloguing cases of violence, abuse, sexual misconduct, and other crimes in amateur and professional sport in North America. The cases documented on the website are incredibly detailed and substantially diverse.

Hockey Canada Safety Program (www.hockeycanada.ca/index.php/ci_id/60967/la_ id/1.htm). This subsection of Hockey Canada's website is devoted to a series of policy initiatives and programs designed by the organization to curb a full range of unwanted behaviours in the sport, such as sexual victimization, violence, and bullying.

Stop Hazing (www.stophazing.org). An online resource for people searching for information related to common hazing practices, the frequency of hazing in a range of institutions, and stories about the consequences of hazing in groups like sports teams and fraternities.

Centre for Sports Policy Studies (www.sportspolicy.ca). The website of the Centre for Sports Policy Studies at the University of Toronto. Members of the Centre study, among other things, policies related to the protection of child and amateur athletes and how adherence to exaggerated gender codes are often prominent in athlete victimization processes.

Key Terms

Emphasized masculinity: A hyperbolic expression or embodiment of the hegemonic masculine myth. An 'emphasized man' is one who is excessively aggressive, dominant, controlling, muscular, authoritarian, or symbolically male. Emphasized masculinity is especially common in sports and military cultures, because both groups celebrate and reward stereotypically traditional constructions of masculinity and its performance.

Grooming: Actions (such as praise, counselling, and light physical contact) deliberately undertaken with the aim of befriending and establishing an emotional connection with a child or teenager in order to develop a intense relationship with them, and to lower their inhibitions in preparation for sexual abuse. Grooming is most commonly found in sport between coaches and young athletes, especially in contexts wherein coaches predisposed to sexual abuse spend long and unsupervised periods of time with the targeted youth.

Hazing: Rituals and other activities involving the harassment, abuse, or humiliation of neophyte members of a group. Hazing is used as a way of initiating (almost as a ritual baptism) a person into a tightly knit group. Hazing is often prohibited by law or institutional policy, because it involves physical, violent, and/or degrading practices. It may also include nudity or sexually oriented activities.

Hubris: A pride-driven arrogance common among high-profile people in a society. Hubris usually manifests as a personal sense that one is above the proverbial law in a society or an institution because s/he has widely accepted cultural significance therein.

Total institution: Certain groups exist that may be categorized as all-encompassing socializing agents. Each member is bound by a code of behaviour, socializes mainly with other members of the group, and is subject to constant monitoring and ideological training by authority figures and group leaders. Groups such as the military, religious sects, psychiatric hospitals, or private schools are all examples of social settings in which, upon entry, individuals are re-socialized to adopt master statuses of, respectively, soldier, convert, patient or student.

Victimology: The study of the victim or victims of a particular offender (or crime category in general). In other terms, it is the scientific/criminological study of victimization, including the relationships between victims and offenders, the interactions between victims and the criminal justice system (the police and courts, and corrections officials). Victimologists also often explore the connections between victims and other social groups and institutions, such as the media, businesses, and social movements.

6 | Mass-Mediating Risk Masculinities

Chapter Objectives

This chapter introduces and critically explores the following:

- How the media helps to shape public discourse about masculinity and masculinity crises
- The argument among crisis theorists that the media spreads misandry
- A review of the three main ways in which boys and men are portrayed on Canadian television
- Case analyses of popular Canadian television programs over the past 20 years

Writing this chapter is, and is not, easy for me. I am one of those people who drives up the average television hours watched per day among Canadians. I have been fascinated with television for as long as I can remember; from the moment I saw my first Rocket Robin Hood cartoon on the CBC as a lad. I watch anything and everything in which I find the smallest hint of cultural interest. Maybe my brain will one day turn into laundry detergent as my mother predicts, but I happily run that risk.

A central socio-cultural question in media/gender research is whether television represents cultural trends and patterns in a society, or whether it serves to create them (or, in the extreme argument, to create hyper-real images of people and practices with no empirical point of relevance). Students of popular culture often find themselves on either side of this theoretical polemic. Many sit on the fence, acknowledging how movies, shows, advertisements, and magazines at the same time produce and reproduce ideas, for example, regarding what it means to be a man in traditional or contemporary manners. The core concept in media studies on gender is, then, *representation*. Representation refers to the construction in any medium of aspects of 'reality' such as people, places, objects, events, and cultural identities. Such representations may be in speech or writing as well as still or moving pictures. The term refers to the processes involved as well as to its products. For instance, in relation to key markers of identity such as gender, representation involves not only how identities are represented (or constructed) within the text but also how and why they are produced and received by people whose identities are differentially marked (McRobbie, 2008). Critical media scholars note that when we deconstruct images of masculinity/

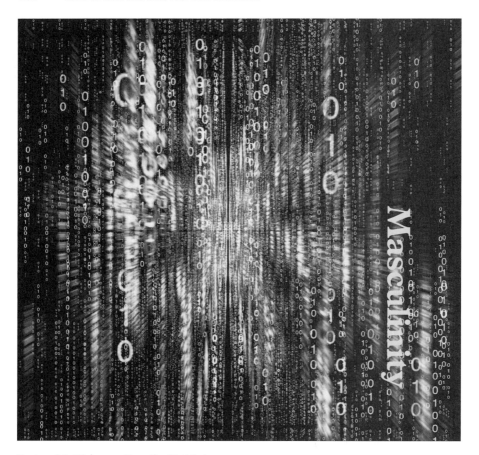

PHOTO 6.1 Wake up, Neo, the Matrix has you . . .

femininity in social texts, we are able to see how messages about social power, influence, and cultural worth are attributed to particular gender forms. Even the most haphazard or unsystematic review of the literature on gender and the media reveals how mass mediations of masculinity and femininity in films, art, television, novels, comic books, and advertisements tend to legitimate and re-inforce sex/gender stereotypes that have historically positioned men and women in powerful/powerless social positions.

Every media text containing a message about gender is standpoint representation by definition (Hall, 1980). All mass mediations of masculinity, as representations of what a man 'is', are intentionally written, framed, cropped, captioned, branded, targeted, and censored by their producers to portray a particular perspective on gendered reality; thus, they are carefully choreographed versions of gendered realities. When studying the representation of masculinities in the media, it is vital to remember this—every media form, from a home video to a glossy magazine, is a representation of an individual's or a group's concept of masculinity, codified into a series of *signs* (see Key Terms) and symbols that can be perceived and then 'read' by audiences. Representation is a fluid, two-way process because producers position a text somewhere in relation to a common, shared reality, and then audiences assess the text on its relationship to their own constructions of reality. I read and use mediated images of masculinity, for example, in reference to how I understand masculinity from my own cultural vantage point. What often makes my students scratch their heads is the idea that by giving audiences information about masculinity, media texts actually extend and shape the experience of the 'realities' of masculinity. Every time you watch a representation of boys or men, you are assessing (and potentially incorporating) something about masculinity and its embodiment in your worldview. Also important to remember is that because the producers of the media text have selected the information we receive, our readings of masculinity in any text are restricted: we only see selected cultural constructions of masculinity in any text featuring men (White and Gillett, 1997).

Here's a better example. I used to watch the American sitcom *Friends* with my university friends. Three of us would spend Thursday evenings glued to the television watching the simulation of New York life of six, twenty(thirty) something urbanites. Everyone I knew in my extended White, middle-class circle of friends could personally identify with a character on the show. As a guy with the goal of earning a Ph.D. in sociology, with a forward and outspoken sister, and with a less than successful history with women, I always saw myself in the representation of Ross. Not until late in my undergraduate career did I finally see the hugely stereotypical representation of gender roles on *Friends*. Ross the elite educator, Joey the sexual conqueror/actor, and Chandler the middle-manager/statistician perfectly countered Monica the chef, Rachel the waitress/fashion expert, and Phoebe the 'floopy' artist. Comfortable and safe media representations of gender like those in *Friends* tend to be popular on North American television; from *CSI* to *Sex and the City* to *The Royal Canadian Air Farce* to *Weeds* to *The Young and the Restless* to *The Price is Right* to *Dora the Explorer* to *Glee* to *House* to *Extreme Makeover* to *Two and a Half Men* to *Survivor* and hundreds of others. They strike warm and fuzzy nostalgic chords in many audiences and steer clear of the messy details about gender, inequality, opportunity, and ideology in our lives. Gender stereotypes wrap around us like warm, four-stripe Hudson's Bay blankets at a time when battles between the genders exhaust people in practically every sphere of life. But they only represent one of the many constructions of gender in our societies.

Within the field of gender studies, research on male/female representation tends to focus on the process of decoding the different layers of truth/fiction about gendered realities and experiences such as those on *Friends*. Crisis advocates have theoretically decoded how popular media representations of masculinity have become more varied since the early 1980s, and yet they are still underpinned by several offensive themes. For example, Malin (2005) notes that since the early 1990s, men/masculinity have been increasingly objectified and essentialized in the media. In a shocking cultural turnaround, men are now facing the same brand of physical scrutiny and ideal-typing that women have experienced for decades. Until the mid-1990s in North American culture, hyper-sexualized or provocative representations of the male body were rarely displayed in mainstream media (Davis, 2002; Lehman, 2007). Sexual objectification was historically restricted to representations of femininity, and linked to the hegemonic process of symbolically demonstrating women's general inferiority to men (Garovich-Szabo and Lueptow, 2001; Lehman, 2007; McRobbie, 2008). The naked, raw, vulnerable male body itself was practically invisible in popular visual *discourse*, and when portrayed in such ways within media advertisements or movies, the representations were often met with resistance and public complaints of overexposure (Bordo, 1999).

Jeffords (1993) notes how the male body, particularly muscular White men's bodies, in film has increasingly been used as a vehicle of commercialism and sexual display. Bordo's (1999) deconstruction of the 1995 Calvin Klein men's underwear advertisement campaign, for example, states how '[it was] the first time in my experience that I had encountered a commercial representation of the male body that seemed to deliberately invite me to linger over it' (p. 168). Bordo and other scholars of the gendered body document how the objectifying stare of the media is turning toward men. As such, more people than ever before are aware that the majority of men in Canada and elsewhere simply do not measure up to historical standards of hegemonic masculinity. Pope et al. (2000) claim that super-male images in the media have become commonplace over time, such that they are now rarely noticed as extraordinary. In a recent mega-analysis of boys and masculinity, Kimmel (2008) argues that boys often point to mass mediations of physically perfect masculinity as the source of poor body image, gender anxiety, and poor sense of self-worth.

Theoretical arguments addressing the genesis and impact of the more visible and oppressively sexual male body in the media focus on a number of factors including the gay movement; several waves of feminism in popular culture; the rise of the late-modern style press (see below) and self-reflexive industries; changing gender roles; and shifting occupational needs (Chapman and Rutherford, 1988; Featherstone, 1991; Gill, Henwood, and McLean, 2005; Moore, 1998; Simpson, 1994; Wells, 1994). Feminist and gay movements have largely influenced how masculinity is presented and understood, such that notions of conventional masculinity (e.g., distant, unemotional, and aggressive) were challenged. This led to the presentation of a new form of masculinity that crossed into the domain of traits and body styles previously considered feminine (e.g., being emotional, caring, and nurturing) (Chapman and Rutherford, 1988; Gill et al., 2005). Thus, new understandings of masculinity emerged in response to social changes based on feminism and gay liberation, and in the process these movements helped the male body to become more visible, acceptable, and commonplace in the media (Wykes, 2004). Specifically, it was within the gay media that men were first presented as openly and unapologetically erotic objects of desire (Gill et al., 2005), a trend that presaged images of men being presented for heterosexual women to desire too.

The rise of the late-modern *style press* has also clearly impacted the shift toward the visibility of male bodies in the media. The first North American self-described style magazine, *The Face,* targeted men—particularly male consumers with expendable income—and was created by Nick Logan in 1982 (Gill et al., 2005). The emergence of style magazines exclusively for men has ushered in a new era of masculine representation, placing what it is to be, and to look like, a man under an intense microscope of cultural scrutiny (Benwell, 2003). As masculinity is showcased as a plastic, commodity-based phenomenon, widespread feelings of inferiority and poor self-esteem among men have been documented (West, 2000). Male bodies are presented in the media as they have never been before: as open, imperfect, anxiety-filled, and frail entities in need of constant attention and reaffirmation through tactically organized physical regimes of self-care and identity-work (Shilling, 2008). For example, psychological studies reveal how exposure to mediations of athletic and muscular body-types can produce intense body dissatisfaction in men (Agliata and Tantleff-Dunn, 2004; Leit, Gray, and Pope, 2002). Furthermore, Pope et al. (2000) illustrated that because men are bombarded with supermale images in the media, and each image associated the male appearance with social, sexual, and financial success, increasing numbers of North American men are unhappy with their own appearance (Atkinson, 2007). Baglia's (2005) study of the mass mediation of the so-called wonder-drug Viagra illustrates how the image and discourse of male deficiency is more common than the image of strength and prowess in popular representations of masculinity. Edwards (1997) argued almost a decade earlier how a man's perceived deficiency with regard to his own masculinity has been used as a marketing tool in men's style magazines. Edwards notes that the representation of masculinity as an ongoing identity problem for men (rather than a way access to power) is a clever marketing technique at a time when social constructions of masculinity are in flux, while certain groups of men in the Canadian middle class feel as if masculinity is in crisis. Edwards explores how representations of masculinity in the popular media have been constructed to convey anything but uniform male hegemony in late-modern society.

Atkinson (2006) argues that the ways of representing masculinity have been opened up now symbolically strike at the heart of male power in countries like Canada. Bourdieu (2005) theorizes that men's (historical) symbolic domination 'is something you absorb like air . . . it is everywhere and nowhere, and to escape from that is very difficult', until, that is, it is visually vivisected in popular culture. Contemporary media depictions of imperfect and confused masculinities in film and advertisements have the potential to destabilize traditional constructions of men, masculinity, and social power (Alba, 2000; Bargh, 2002; Baurneister, 2002; Jacoby, Johar, and Morrin, 1999). Representations of the man who worries about what car he drives, face cream he uses, insurance company he purchases from, how his wife perceives his greying hair, and if he will be able to retire by the age of 55 are not images that connote hegemonic power. Media images of the traditional, hegemonic male do still abound in countries like Canada, but they share time with a litany of fractured representations of men and masculinity. True to form in late-modern Canadian society, there is no single definitive image of perfect manliness or blueprint for how to achieve such a gendered status.

Crisis advocates frequently decry the objectification/feminization of men in the popular media as part of selling 'fear based' products to men and women, as noted above. But crisis advocates more voraciously decry how the hegemonic ideal of a traditional man has been openly assaulted and vilified in mainstream media. Selling fear to men about their 'deficient' bodies and 'imperfect' selves might be one thing, but to crisis advocates, the open attack of men and masculinity is quite another. Like controversial men's rights activist Glenn Sacks, and men's rights theorist Warren Farrell (2007), Nathanson and Young (2001, 2006) describe contemporary Canadian life as essentially *gynocentric* (focusing on the rights and world views of women) and increasingly intolerant of men. This leads to a state of *misandry*. Misandry is the conceptual opposite of misogyny: a rejection, or outright hatred, of men, masculinity, and all things overtly male. Misandry is prevalent across Canadian culture and within institutional matrices of power according to Nathanson and Young (2001) and this is perhaps best evidenced in Canadian popular culture. Film, television, and magazines are rife with misandric messages, which most people rarely question or problematize. Misandry is excusable in popular culture because it seems harmless, humorous, and excusable as an offshoot of historical patriarchy. Misandry is in many ways *the* flashpoint crisis issue and discourse.

Nathanson and Young (2001, 2006) claim that misandry is spread in popular representations of men in six principal manners. In the first instance, we are encouraged to *laugh at men*: in this form of misandry, men are routinely made the objects of stereotypical ridicule in ways that would generate sustained outrage were the sexes reversed. Second, we are encouraged to *look down on men:* in these representations, men are portrayed as morally, intellectually, or socially inferior to women. Third, we are encouraged to *bypass men:* typical representations in this genre showcase men as useless lovers, husbands, fathers, and human beings. Fourth, misandric media representations *blame men:* where all social problems, inequalities, and sources of victimization are consequences of patriarchy. Fifth, the media routinely *dehumanizes men:* in this instance, men are shown as inherently evil while women are seen as inherently good or even heroic. Finally, men are not only dehumanized but *demonized:* where masculinity is linked to devilish or even alien personal qualities. When I read

Nathanson and Young's (2001) book in early 2005, I reflected on its contents with a wave of conflicting thoughts and emotions. I simultaneously understood and identified with their arguments, but as a profeminist gender researcher, I felt uncomfortable with the idea of gynocentrism in popular culture. I came to the personal and theoretical conclusion that studying misandry does not lead one down and anti-feminist road, and that one may understand crisis masculinities and misandry without rejecting feminist theory.

Misandry Is the Message

Many people might decode the advertisement below as a representation of docile, objectified femininity. But consider how Nathanson and Young (2001) might read the portrayal of masculinity in an advertisement for Dolce & Gabbana clothing (take a look at it online: www.adpunch.org/entry/dolce-gabbana-pulls-controversial-ad-from-spain).

I am personally fascinated by the the concept of misandry. I did not know it existed before reading about concept in 2005. Strange that—I have been studying gender since the early 1990s and had never come across the concept. There is not a tremendous amount of research on misandry in Canada (indeed, it is a highly contested political, social, cultural, and academic subject that is often rejected or denied), but I read backward chronologically into the spotted research on misandry and, of course, discovered one of the earliest misandric statements in popular culture offered by the American group SCUM (Society for Cutting Up Men). The *SCUM Manifesto* is a text written in 1968 by openly misandrist activist Valerie Solanas that calls for the 'gendercide' of men. After being put in the spotlight for shooting pop artist Andy Warhol, Solanas claimed that her writing was a satirical literary device to elicit debate about gender relations in North America. The *SCUM Manifesto* met with considerable public debate from men and women, as the essential statement in the separatist feminist movement of the twentieth century. A portion of the *Manifesto* reads:

> The male is completely egocentric, trapped inside himself, incapable of empathizing or identifying with others, or love, friendship, affection or tenderness. He is a completely isolated unit, incapable of rapport with anyone. His responses are entirely visceral, not cerebral; his intelligence is a mere tool in the services of his drives and needs; he is incapable of mental passion, mental interaction; he can't relate to anything other than his own physical sensations. He is a half-dead, unresponsive lump, incapable of giving or receiving pleasure or happiness; consequently, he is at best an utter bore, an inoffensive blob, since only those capable of absorption in others can be charming. He is trapped in a twilight zone halfway between humans and apes, and is far worse off than the apes because, unlike the apes, he is capable of a large array of negative feelings—hate, jealousy, contempt, disgust, guilt, shame, doubt—and moreover, he is *aware* of what he is and what he

isn't . . . Completely egocentric, unable to relate, empathize or identify, and filled with a vast, pervasive, diffuse sexuality, the male is psychically passive. He hates his passivity, so he projects it onto women, defines the male as active, then sets out to prove that he is ('prove that he is a Man'). His main means of attempting to prove it is screwing (Big Man with a Big Dick tearing off a Big Piece). Since he's attempting to prove an error, he must prove it again and again. Screwing, then, is a desperate compulsive, attempt to prove he's not passive, not a woman; but he *is* passive and *does* want to be a woman. (Valerie Solanas, AK Press, 1997)

Solanas's text faded out of cultural discourses by the late 1970s. However, Nathanson and Young (2001, 2006) note how anti-men discourses like those contained in the *SCUM Manifesto* did not disappear entirely from popular representations of men in the media. By the late 1970s and early 1980s, misandry seethed into a full spate of television programming and print advertisements. In *Spreading Misandry*, Nathanson and Young (2001) contend that popular culture is now rife with anti-male sentiment. Rather than being overtly politically charged and brutal like the *SCUM Manifesto*, it is far more subtle and comical. The authors examine everything from Hallmark cards, to popular movies, to sitcoms, and comment on how ongoing (post)industrialization, shifts in religious understanding/readings, and differences between moral values, emotions, and world views have lead to an acceptable mediation of male hatred in late-modern society. In these misandric popular cultural representations, men are most often aligned with the characteristics of stupidity, sexual obsession, self-promotion, gluttony, fraud, and death, while women are aligned with higher human attributes, such as intelligence, heroism, nature, emotionality, and spirituality. Quite simply, men are often portrayed as failures, morons, or just down-right evil. Nathanson and Young argue that misandry is one of the only openly allowed prejudices in Canadian and American societies. In what they believe to be a gynocentric world, signs of misogyny are watched for closely, and acts of misogyny are now morally and legally unallowable. Misandry is, however, allowable, excusable, and not seen as a problem—because after all, men still play the dominant economic and political role in society, right?

Like examples of sexism and the objectification of women, examples of misandry are not difficult to find in everyday television, films, music, and other media. In the early part of 2007 I started to review 45 Canadian television series from 1980 to 2007 to explore misandric themes. The remainder of this chapter examines three consistent thematic representations of masculinity in Canadian television. The representations are neither straightforwardly nostalgic appeals to a hegemonic past, nor are they decisively misandric. Each type of masculinity showcased must be, however, contextualized against a general backdrop of masculinity flux and debate in Canada. A review of selected Canadian programs suggests that masculinity is both simple and complex to read in Canadian television, in that while very stereotypical images of unapologetic

---

BOX 6.1 ❀ MEMBERS OF THE 'MISANDRY IN TELEVISION' HALL OF FAME

Consider each of the following television characters.

Kramer from *Seinfeld* [see www.sonypictures.com/tv/shows/seinfeld/about/?sl=cast_and_characters&tab=kramer]

Sam Malone from *Cheers* [see www.tvland.com/shows/cheers/characters/char1.jhtml]

Elvin Tibideaux from *The Cosby Show* [see http://www.virginmedia.com/tvradio/cult-tv/trivia/cosby-show-where-are-they-now.php?ssid=19]

Al Bundy from *Married with Children* [see www.marriedwithchildren.com/cast.html]

Homer from *The Simpsons* [see www.thesimpsons.com/characters/home.htm]

Tim Taylor from *Home Improvement* [see http://bventertainment.go.com/tv/touch-stone/homeimprovement/bios/allen.html]

Each is a representation of masculinity, and each character hyperbolizes traits of the atavist male, the lout, the boor, the playboy, the anti-feminist, and the socially backward. Sitcoms of the late 1980s and early 1990s drew millions of viewers for the seemingly satiric portrayal of men who just 'didn't get it'.

---

masculinity are represented on television, risk and crisis masculinities also feature prominently.

Three Faces of Televised Masculinity

The world of television masculinities in Canada and elsewhere is unquestion-ably more open and multi-dimensional than in any previous era. The lingering question pertains to why this is the case. No longer do stoic and rigidly tradi-tional male characters like Knowlton Nash or Alex Trebek dominate the televi-sual landscape. Media researchers like Stern (2003) classify at least nine main types of men/masculinity represented on television:

    I. *The superhero*: active and aggressive, invades and dominates
   II. *The male-bolder:* lacks emotional sensibility
  III. *The androgynous man*: passive, sensitive, neurotic, narcissistic, and feminized
  IV. *The phallocentric*: gay image associated with promiscuity and uncurbed lust

    V. *The bodybuilding*: focus on size and body perfection
   VI. *The Black male*: subversive who counters images of White men
  VII. *The family man*: protective and caring about his family
 VIII. *The authority figure*: man as source of evidence and information
   IX. *The executive*: successful modern man in business and corporation activities

Most of the categories listed by Stern are neither new representations of men in Canadian society nor are they empirically surprising. Without repeating arguments offered in the first three chapters of this book, of sociological interest is how the growing frequency of non-traditional representations of masculinity on Canadian television (like categories II, III, IV, and VI listed above) map almost perfectly with the emergence of late-modern modes of living, and masculinity crisis discourses. There is a curious empirical relationship between the emergence of multiple masculinities on television, late modernity, and perceived male crisis. The relationship leads us back to the hallmark question in media research: does art imitate life, or vice versa? Do shifting representations of men reflect shifting definitions of masculinity in Canadian society, or are televised depictions of men and masculinity only artistic or fictional interpretations of traditional, new, crisis, or at-risk men? I tend to believe the former rather than the latter. The Canadian *vertical mosaic* of social power has cracked, and television portrayals of gendered identities, roles, and statuses show this to varying degrees.

    References to the vertical mosaic in Canadian media/gender research are rare. But research on the mass mediation of social inequality and cultural contestation in Canada owes an enormous debt to John Porter and his concept of the vertical mosaic. I probably did not appreciate this in Rick Helmes-Hayes's undergraduate class on Canadian sociological theory I took in the early 1990s at the University of Waterloo, but I think it is true today. Porter's *The Vertical Mosaic* (1965) set the agenda for several major streams of Canadian sociological research, including studies of elites and the structure of power, social mobility and the role of education in the occupational attainment process, and immigrant integration and ethnic inequality. *The Vertical Mosaic* principally illustrates how Canadian society is organized hierarchically by (ethnic) groups; the British and the French comprise historical *charter groups* who have institutional and cultural access to capital, while others are slotted into a *great mass* of *entrance groups* with far less access to elite sources of social power (First Nations populations form a special group called a *treaty group*). Members of the charter group become, in other theoreticians' language, the social hegemony and their interests, identities, and values tend to become represented in the media.

    Helmes-Hayes and Curtis (1998) discuss the ongoing importance of the vertical mosaic in determining access to power and resources in Canada. They draw to our attention how political and economic struggles within the vertical mosaic relate predominantly to the distribution of scarce resources and rewards rather than on class relations. Porter (1965) himself largely eschewed class as the basis of social power, discussing the relative fragmentation and instability of class in Canada (quite a late-modern argument for someone in the 1960s!). Much recent scholarship in numerous countries pertaining to globalization, power, identity, and cultural studies supports Porter's assessment of class. Indeed, the preponderance of evidence suggests that the salience of class in late-modern societies is declining, and that many of the more developed countries can no longer be considered class societies. In my own analysis of the masculinity crisis, such is the basic understanding of 'male problems' in the 1990s, the death of class-based power for men.

Hamilton (1996) draws on the notion of the vertical mosaic in arguing that neither ethnicity nor class is the major source of hierarchical division in Canadian society. Hamilton presents a feminist reading of Canadian history in order to expose the historically gendered, patriarchal vertical mosaic. She argues that while class and ethnicity continue to have relevance in the division of social power in the country, a group's access to power must also be understood through their gendered status. Women have been positioned at the bottom rungs of the vertical mosaic until relatively recently. As patriarchy has been deconstructed as a social elite power structure in late modernity, and as demographic membership in the upper rungs of the mosaic slowly changes, resistance and change follows. Once again, such is the basis of popular arguments about the origin of the masculinity crisis. Building on Hamilton's argument, of what consequence is the ongoing de-gendering of the Canadian vertical mosaic on televised representations of men and masculinity? Has the first affected the second? I say yes, and let me convince you why.

Here is where we review a bit of what life is like in late modernity. The fracturing, the fragmentation, and redrawing of historical social structures (like the vertical mosaic), and the movement toward hyper-reflexive styles of living all foster an overarching sensitivity to *life politics* (Giddens, 1998) in Canadian culture. Think about it this way: whenever something in our lives breaks down—for example our car, our job, a computer, or our marriage—we almost always question the manner by which it was assembled and operated in the first place. When structure is broken, we examine its pieces and reflect on them intensely. Life politics, often called *sub-politics*, tackle moral and ethical questions in everyday life (how to live, what to think, how the self is understood) that modernist institutions failed to answer. Life politics has become an interesting topic in recent years, related to discussions about individualization, reflexivity, personal choice, ethics, minds and consciousnesses, the politics of recognition, and gendered/raced/sexed/classed identities. Theorists including Anthony Giddens, Ulrich Beck, Nikolas Rose, and Charles Taylor each outline how the media play a role in both reflecting individual and collective life political beliefs, and informing life politics themselves.

According to Giddens (1998) life politics consists of the following: political decisions flowing from freedom of choice in late modernity; creation of morally justifiable forms of life that will promote self-actualization in an era of hyper-reflexivity; and ethics concerning the issue of how we should live in a late-modern, fragmented social order. If the ordering systems of modernity have lapsed, and if people have far greater choice to 'be' in these social contexts, we are faced with a situation where people have new choices, resources, and risks posed to them in everyday life. As it pertains to gender, life political questions relate to the increased abilities of all of us to make educated choices about the enabling and constraining aspects of gender in our own lives, to reflect upon our situation as gendered actors and to understand more of the long-term consequences of our acceptance of gendered ideologies and actions. Other life political questions pertain to how we promote and encourage particularly gendered ways of thinking through mass mediations of stories, such as those found in television and in film. A world ordered by life politics is concerned, then, precisely with how people make and represent decisions that affect their own lives and how life politics are to be represented. As such, individuals and groups struggle for representational power in the media sphere, with groups seizing television, movie, Internet, magazine, and other spaces to communicate their life political experiences and values.

So, late-modern television is not the land of gender à la *Little House on the Prairie, Mr Dressup,* or *Father Knows Best.* Late-modern television is saturated with the life political debates (including those about gender) preoccupying our everyday lives. Such mediations of life politics also frame gendered issues, identities, and possibilities. They direct and inform as much as they reflect. Crisis advocates claim media representations of masculinity reflect the fracturing of the vertical mosaic in deeply misandric ways. My genealogical review of masculinity in Canadian television in a late-modern, identity crisis society reveals three main life political representations of boys, men, and masculinity: *the unapologetic men, men on the margins,* and *boys in crisis.* In what follows, each category is outlined and a core case is examined.

I. Unapologetic Men: Take Off, You Hoser

Growing up in Bedford, Nova Scotia, I knew dozens of male *hosers*. I was a hoser as a child, and probably still am a bit of a hoser today. If you ever go to a restaurant or pub with fake log cabin architecture (or one that has 'Moose' somewhere in its name), call your friend 'buddy', regularly cut the 'g' off verbs, know how to catch a black fly with two fingers, or have an inexplicable taste for peanut butter and bacon sandwiches, you just might be a hoser. The hoser is one of Canada's truly unique contributions to masculine social identity. Hosers are not a subculture of boys or men per se, but hosers have their own unique values, practices, and masculine identities. The representation of

---

Box 6.2 ❊ Hoser Manifesto: Joe's 'I am Canadian' Rant

'I am Canadian' was the slogan of Molson Canadian beer from 1994 until 2004. In one of Molson's television advertisements during the 'I am Canadian' campaign, a hoser simply named Joe proceeds to give a speech about what being a Canadian is and is not. Joe's speech is now simply referred to in Canadian popular culture as 'The Rant':

> Hey, I'm not a lumberjack, or a fur trader,
> I don't live in an igloo or eat blubber, or own a dogsled,
> and I don't know Jimmy, Sally or Suzy from Canada,
> although I'm certain they're really, really nice.
> I have a Prime Minister, not a president.
> I speak English and French, not American.
> I pronounce it 'about', not 'a boot'.
> I can proudly sew my country's flag on my backpack.
> I believe in peacekeeping, not policing, diversity, not assimilation,
> and that the beaver is a truly proud and noble animal.
> A toque is a hat.
> A chesterfield is a couch.
> And it is pronounced 'zed' not 'zee', 'zed'.
> Canada is the second largest land mass,
> the first nation of hockey,
> and the best part of North America.
> My name is Joe,
> and I am Canadian!

Canadian male hosers are both subtly and unabashedly woven into dominant discourses about men and masculinity in late modernity; it is the gold standard, the common, and the normal on television. Hoserdom is not a flattering portrait of masculinity, but it is truly and uniquely Canadian. The hoser is the everyman, the quasi-simpleton, the guy who will come over to your house in his 1980 Monte Carlo at 6:30 a.m. on a cold winter morning to help dig your car out of the snow so that you can get to work before he does. He is unaffected by modernity, late modernity, and masculinity crises. He has been attacked as a lout and as a primitive in the last 20 years, but his life politics do not change. The hoser is a nostalgic male who is a part of dozens and dozens of male characters on Canadian television. He is the last bastion of traditional working-class and lower middle-class masculinity, and from time to time, the hoser lifestyle is showcased in surreptitious ways as a means of bringing Canadian men in crisis together.

Like the very similar term *hosehead*, the term hoser has multiple meanings, but generally refers to someone who is backward, stupid, or merely hapless in one manner or another. In certain contexts, the verb 'to hose' refers to someone being cheated, conned, or taken advantage of by another (like, 'Shit, did I ever got hosed by the tax man this year!'). The most dominant use of the term in Canadian popular culture is in reference to a stereotypical White, Canadian, working-class male. This manual laborer is a 'good-time guy' in many respects. He drinks Canadian beer, smokes gratuitously, and would probably listen to Kim Mitchell, Rush, or the Tragically Hip over any other artists. He dons a Mark's Work Wearhouse black and red hunter's jacket, flannel shirts, ripped blue jeans from Zellers, a toque with a pom-pom, sports Kodiak boots year round, and eats most of his meals from a bag or a box. He is Red Green, he is Wayne Campbell, he is 'Mike from Canmore'. He is simply the average Canadian Joe, who became somewhat of a definitive Canadian icon in 2005, when his identity was immortalized in a Molson Canadian beer advertisement. Hoser culture ascended to unprecedented heights of global recognition in 2010 when Canada's Winter Olympic team was fully outfitted in hoserwear (e.g., plaid jackets, mock long underwear shirts, toques, and hunting hats) by the Hudson's Bay Company.

One of my first recollections of hoser culture on Canadian television is *The Beachcombers*. Filmed in Gibsons, BC, the Beachcombers followed the life of Nick Adonidas (Bruno Gerussi), a log salvager who earned a living travelling the British Columbian coastline tracking down logs that had broken away from logging barges.

Plausible and implausible at times, *Beachcombers,* like other Vancouver series of the era like *Danger Bay*, depicted Canadian men in very traditional social roles and statuses. Set against a stereotypical Canadian landscape of primary production and communion with nature, these men were manly men. From the 1980s to the early 2000s, hoser television shows like *King of Kensington, He Shoots, He Scores, North of 60, Due South, The Red Green Show, Open Mike with Mike Bullard, Corner Gas, The Tom Green Show, The Rez,* and *Chilly Beach* have been among the most popular series of all time in Canada; further, they tend to be those most in demand for international export to countries including Australia, the United States, the UK, France, and Germany. Canadian comedian Mike Myers drew heavily on the hoser model of masculinity in creating his Saturday Night Live character Wayne Campbell, whose community cable access show, *Wayne's World*—co-hosted with his sidekick Garth Algar (Dana Carvey)—pays definite homage to hoser culture. Representations of hoser masculinity featured front and centre in the critically acclaimed movie *fubar* (Fucked up Beyond all Recognition).

Two representations of hoser masculinity in Canada are perhaps the quintessential representations. *SCTV*'s Bob and Doug McKenzie characters (played by Rick Moranis and Dave Thomas) practically announced the arrival of hoser masculinity in Canadian media, while the 'Coach's Corner' segment of *Hockey*

Night in Canada (hosted by presenters Ron MacLean and Don Cherry) has been the keystone representation for well over two decades.

Brothers Bob and Doug McKenzie hosted a fictitious public service program called 'The Great White North'. The comedy sketch was introduced on the program *SCTV* (Second City Television) for the show's third season, when it moved in 1980 to the CBC. Originally known as 'Kanadian Korner' on SCTV, 'The Great White North' was staged as a panel show that played upon hoser stereotypes. Bob and Doug were featured as two dim-witted, beer-swilling brothers wearing heavy winter clothing and toques, and would comment on various elements of everyday life in working man's Canada. Among their topics of the day were snow routes, why disco sucks, the inappropriateness of bedtime stories about dogfights, flat tires, how to get a mouse in a beer bottle, and parking spaces at take-out donut shops. Each 'episode' was approximately three minutes long, and began with the now legendary introduction,

Bob: *I'm Bob McKenzie, and this is my brother Doug.*

Doug: *How's it goin', eh.*

The popularity of the show swelled, and discourses about Canadian life on the show both imitated male hoser culture, and influenced a generation of Canadians to embrace a stereotypical representation of masculinity in the country. The comedy bit inspired a movie, *Strange Brew*, and two comedy albums for Moranis and Thomas. The first album, *The Great White North,* is noted for the song 'Take Off', featuring fellow Canadian Geddy Lee of the rock group Rush chorusing between the McKenzies' lyrical banter. The record climbed into the Top 20 on the US record charts, a loftier perch than any of Rush's other singles. On the same album they sung their own improvised version of the 'Twelve Days of Christmas', which is still played on the radio around the holidays in Canada and the US. By the early 1990s, their popularity had faded, but the duo returned in 2009 in an animated television show called *Bob & Doug*, produced by Animax Entertainment (airing on the Global Television Network in Canada and on Fox in the United States).

Bob and Doug's representation of hoser masculinity is at once an irreverent refusal of any masculinity crisis, and a misandric representation of men in the Canadian working and middle classes. This is true of most representations of hoser masculinity in the Canadian media. Either hosers just do not worry about their gendered life politics, or they do not understand the masculinity frames they embody in everyday life. The representation of the free hoser spirit is particularly appealing in certain boyish ways. They are not politically correct, fearful of male statuses, or outwardly concerned with economic success. They drink beer, watch hockey, eat donuts, and are free to do as they please. Like other hosers, Bob and Doug show no sign of a present-centred fatalism about their statuses or concern for being at risk of anything, and they see the world through incredibly traditional eyes. A masculine utopia, no? Well, from another perspective, such mediation is similar to a trend in the 1980s and 1990s toward misandrically portraying men from their social positions as unenlightened, ignorant knuckle-draggers. They are not reflexive creatures, nor are their life politics sustainable. Hosers like Bob and Doug were embraced in popular culture precisely at a time when men like them were being cast off the vertical mosaic. Bob and Doug stood for an entire generation of men who were being called hoser and mocked in a spectacular fashion as part of the popular culture's misandry.

If Bob and Doug were the hapless, apolitical hosers of Canadian television, Don Cherry is certainly the four–maple leaf general of the radical political wing of Hoser Nation. Voted in 2004 as one of the ten 'greatest Canadians' in history (The CBC's 'Greatest Canadian' poll), Kingston, Ontario, native Cherry is the outspoken commentator on CBC's *Hockey Night in Canada*. A former NHL player and coach, Cherry co-hosts 'Coach's Corner' with Ron MacLean—a first period intermission segment tackling topical issues in professional and amateur hockey in Canada. In 1980 a chance appearance on *Hockey Night In Canada*, across from then-host Dave Hodge, impressed CBC officials enough for them to create a platform for the bombastic ex-player and coach. The new segment has since courted both controversy and high ratings, as hockey fans rushed to their televisions to take in his singular mix of game analysis, cultural commentary, and ideological parrying with MacLean. Cherry has parlayed his broadcast success into a line of popular 'Rock 'Em Sock 'Em' ice hockey videos, a chain of restaurants (Don Cherry's), a television show of his own (*Don Cherry's Grapevine*), a syndicated radio show, and lucrative endorsements. Cherry is a self-proclaimed simple guy and defender of Canadian hockey, heritage, and the life politics of the common man. He has been called the 'Prime Minister of Saturday Night' (Gillett, White, and Young, 1999), and attracts considerable ire from social rights groups who claim his rants on 'Coach's Corner' promote jingoism, anti-government views, xenophobia, misogyny, and violence toward others in sport.

Like other hosers, however, Cherry is popular because he is outspoken against many of the very sources of male crisis identified in the gender literature. Cherry hails from a lower-middle-class, Anglo-Saxon, conservative background and the political views he interweaves into his hockey analysis are neither disguised nor apologetic. His hoser masculinity is still very much a rugged, frontier masculinity, and his anti-feminist, anti-liberal, anti-government, pro-sport, pro-military, pro-Anglo ideologies are worn on his notoriously loud suit sleeves. Set against the far more liberal and rationalized MacLean, Cherry's voice is positioned in broadcasts as the commonsense hoser deconstruction of life in sport and society for the average man. He is a male who speaks in a language and with imagery that men in crisis are too afraid to vocalize. Repeated threats and attempts to fire Cherry from the show, or movements to curtail his speech, only fuel his legendary status as king of the hosers (Gillett, White, and Young, 1999).

Don Cherry, 'Coach's Corner', and *Hockey Night in Canada* itself present a decisively unapologetic image of traditional masculinity. The program is one of the most contested on the CBC, but the one that has changed the least ideologically in the past 20 years. Unlike Bob and Doug and other stereotypical hosers, Cherry does not lace his life politics with humour and self-deprecation in the process of defending or caricaturing his male hoserdom. Cherry is clearly aware that the world around hosers has changed, and that their signifying practices like hockey are not impervious from gendered critique emanating from the outside. His defense of violence in hockey, for example, is commentary not only about the game itself but the ways in which young boys are overly coddled, apologized for, or demonized in other settings (Atkinson and Young, 2008). Hosers like Cherry are modernists at heart who seek to draw attention to the perils and consequences of gendered politics in late modernity, through symbolic protest and crisis declaration in sport. But for hockey fans like me, Cherry is often far more entertaining than anything featured on the ice.

II. On the Margins: Boys and Men at Risk

I remember sitting on the couch in our basement family room in Bedford in late summer of 1984, eagerly awaiting the first day of MuchMusic's broadcasting. I was barely 13 years old and just getting into everything about popular culture. It's the stage in adolescence when young boys and girls look for pop cultural icons to help mould their budding social images and identities with poached styles and lingoes. My sister and I used to stay up late on Friday evenings to watch music video shows broadcasted from the ABC or NBC affiliates in Bangor, Maine, like *Friday Night Videos*. But MuchMusic created a popular culture platform we could access 24 hours a day, live from our own Canadian shores.

MuchMusic launched on 1 September 1984 and changed the face of masculinity in Canadian popular culture more than we might at first consider. The first permanent 'veejay' on the show was Christopher Ward, a musician and composer from Toronto. Ward did not represent the stereotypical man in any number of ways. His style and comportment reflected more of the new Romantic trend in early 1980s music, with artistic and effeminate tones. Other veejays included Steve Anthony, Kim Clarke Champniss, Michael Williams, and Terry David Mulligan. Each one embodied a non-standard brand of masculinity on television. Anthony represented a typical masculine heartthrob to a degree, but his long, bleached blonde hair and penchant for arm bangles distanced him from the mainstream. British veejay Champniss (former manager of New Wave band Images in Vogue) represented an 'emo' style alternative masculinity, eventually hosting Much's alternative rock segment 'City Limits'. Michael Williams would be the first African-Canadian veejay, hosting segments including 'Soul in the City' and 'Rap City'. Terry David Mulligan, former RCMP officer and then radio DJ (who I remember first watching on BCTV children's program *Zig Zag*), looked more like a friendly uncle from the west coast of Canada than a television personality.

Separately and together, the first generation of veejays on MuchMusic thrust viewers into a televisual space of liminal masculinity. These were images of masculinity relatively unseen on popular television. They did not embody a news presenter masculinity, but rather brought a critical assemblage of emerging masculinities to the fore in urban areas like Toronto, Montreal, and Vancouver. They were neither represented as men in crisis, nor as men worthy of misandry. They appeared not as superiors but as equals to their female veejay counterparts like Erica Ehm, Jeanne Beker, and Ziggy Lorenc. They were not hosers in any sense of the word (well, maybe J.D. Walsh came close—and he is now a news anchor for CNN). These were heretofore marginal masculinities in popular culture, but their presence on television in the 1980s represented a movement of marginal men into popular cultural discourses and identities.

A few years before Much transformed the masculine face of popular culture in Canada, a series of small budget after school specials produced in Toronto by the CBC, called *Kids of Degrassi Street*, had showcased young, struggling masculinities in the inner city. *Kids* ran between 1979–86 on the CBC, using local, untrained child actors to narrate common moral and ethical dilemmas in everyday kiddom. The show received considerable acclaim in Canada, and I recall watching episodes in my Grade 5 classroom (circa 1981) as part of social studies lessons. Embedded across the 26 episodes were broad illustrations of young masculinity. The boys were multi-dimensional characters who dealt with moral problems in a variety of ways. They struggled with their masculinities and the male role models in their lives. The character Chuck's male alienation and isolation resulting from his father's imprisonment is showcased. The proto-typical child brainiac Jeffery is displaced from his academic throne in the classroom by fellow student Connie. The character Martin deals with acute hearing loss and the subsequent need for a hearing aid. The character Griff (played by Neil Hope, who would be recast and renamed in later episodes as Wheels), transformed from a bully in the Pirates gang from Boulton Avenue, to a sensitive young boy with learning difficulties who regularly deals with a deadbeat father. Such are not mythic male representations of what boys endure in the classroom or in everyday life. They are, however, real representations of young masculinities. A substantial portion of its public acclaim came from the way the show opened a cultural dialogue about young, marginal masculinities at risk. As a small but interesting side note, MuchMusic veejay Christopher Ward actually appeared as a musician on one of the early *Kids of Degrassi Street* shows.

If *Kids* quietly circulated an important gender discourse about masculinities at risk, *Degrassi Junior High* (1987–9) trumpeted the discourse from the Canadian media rooftop. I would have personally moved heaven and earth so as not to miss an episode during its original airing. The show included a sizable ensemble cast, but predominantly revolved around three main male protagonists: Wheels (a.k.a. Derek), Joey, and Snake (a.k.a. Archie). Wheels represented a typical teenager in many respects, eager to express his sexuality, driven by hormones and generally indifferent to the rigours of school. Most likely a remnant from his *Kids* character Griff, Wheels embodied a working-class, mulleted, hoser persona. An air of failure and fatalism always hung over Wheels. His closest compatriot, Joey Jeremiah, embodied a smooth-talking, slick, but also doomed-to-fail masculinity. Joey's regular schemes to get girls, do well in school, or generally break a rule, would explode in his face. He chased, caught, and lost his main love interested Caitlin. A small boy in size and stature, his position on Degrassi teetered between class clown and reprobate. Meanwhile Snake embodied the awkward, insecure male. Too tall for his age, ginger haired, freckled, stigmatized by braces, and the academic achiever, Snake was neither a social winner nor a loser. Even the trio's garage band named 'Zit Remedy' (which only seemed to perform one song) represents a less than hegemonic image. Collectively, the boys were not positioned squarely among the hyper-popular boys like Simon or 'BLT', or lovable outcasts like the overweight Arthur or bookworm Yick (each of whom constantly deal with poor body image issues throughout the series). But they survive each risk-producing ordeal thrown their way. Other at-risk male characters include Rick, who is abused by his father, Shane, who takes drugs and eventually throws himself from a bridge (suffering brain trauma), and Snake's brother (and male role model) Glenn, who makes a special visit home from university to come out of the closet in front of the family.

Degrassi Junior High connected with male teenagers of generation X. Each of the central protagonists was a frail and imperfect guy outside hegemonically privileged cliques. Most dealt with being a young male and trying to maintain personal control in a socially confusing contexts. These themes were underlined in an even greater dramatic fashion in the series' next iteration, *Degrassi High* (1989–91). As the boys enter high school, they are submerged in an entirely new sea of risk, doubt, anxiety, and conflict. Viewers surprisingly learn that all strata of boys on the high school social hierarchy need to manage their own risk masculinities as a daily regimen. *Degrassi High* tackled nonconventional issues for boys (and girls) in a raw and open fashion. It dealt with issues including AIDS, abortion, physical abuse, alcoholism, cheating, teen sex and rape, pornography and masturbation, divorce, death and suicide, depression, bullying, women's rights, gay/lesbian rights and homophobia, racism, the environment, drugs, and eating disorders. Joey's learning disability is discovered, Wheels steals, drops out, and runs away from home, Scott abuses his girlfriend Kathleen, class bully and football icon Dwayne contracts HIV, and the misunderstood environmental activist and poet Claude kills himself in the school bathroom. Many hail the series as a cult classic for being a realistic and often unapologetic portrayal of teen life. The series finale, a two-hour CBC special called *Degrassi: School's Out* (1992), raises the representational game even further. Joey loses Caitlin after cheating on her all summer and after a graduation party, Wheels (now a part-time mechanic and alcoholic), has a drunk-driving accident and kills a small child. The newest iteration of the show, *Degrassi: The Next Generation* (2001–present) is far less edgy and innovative as its precursors, but retains a loyal audience.

The *Degrassi* genre's legacy, and the cultural space it opened for the critical analysis of youth masculinities, is not easy to summarize. At a time when Canadian comedy shows like *Kids in the Hall* were hyperbolically smashing stereotypical images of gay and transgender men on television with characters like Kathy (with a 'K') and Cathy (with a 'C'), the *Degrassi* series consistently placed a full range of young masculinities under the microscope. Rated among the most syndicated and internationally distributed CBC series of all time, *Degrassi* dragged young men on the social margins into the spotlight. The show's timing and keen sensitivity to the life politics of young masculinities in schools and elsewhere was nothing short of astounding. The writers and producers of the teen drama tapped very real shifts and fluctuations in crisis masculinities during the era.

III. Boys in Crisis: Atavism as Spectacle

For over seven years I have watched and re-watched episodes from this Show-case television series. Maybe it's a guilty pleasure for me, perhaps I identify with it because it is filmed so close to where I grew up, or maybe the hoser deep down in me truly understands how the characters' minds operate. *Trailer Park Boys* is a television and movie serial following the lives and times of three central protagonists/antagonists who live in the fictitious 'Sunnyvale Trailer Park', Ricky, Julian, and Bubbles. The first two characters are classic recidivists (repeat offenders) in every sense of the word, with a sustained involvement in drug (marijuana and hash) growing and distribution. Each season of the show follows the same basic pattern. Ricky, Julian, and Bubbles are nearly always trying to figure out new ways to get rich and get high while avoiding the law and the alcoholic, ex-cop trailer park supervisor Jim Lahey (and Jim's lover, sidekick, and assistant park supervisor, the cheeseburger-eating, former male prostitute Randy). Their get-rich-quick schemes are usually foiled by their own stupidity. Every season usually begins with the boys getting out of jail and usually ends with them going back into jail. The series is shot in a mockumentary style, creating an intimate connection between the characters and the audience. The language is raw, the characters openly drink and take drugs, sexuality is everywhere, and the satirical references to Canadiana are brilliant. What is incredible about the show and its connection with audiences is that since early on in the series, many of the actors (particularly Robb Wells, John Paul Tremblay, and Mike Smith—Ricky, Julian, and Bubbles respectively) often make public appearances at high-profile events such as the Canadian Juno Awards without breaking character.

The legacy of *Trailer Park Boys* began in 1998, when Canadian producer/ director Mike Clattenburg created a film short based loosely on the characters of Ricky and Julian. The 1998 short was critically acclaimed in Canadian film-making circles, prompting Clattenburg to produce a 72-minute movie called *Trailer Park Boys* which debuted at the Atlantic Film Festival in 1999. Clatten-burg was then approached by producer Barrie Dunn, who was passionate about creating a television series from the movie. Along with Wells and Tremblay they brainstormed outlines for 13 one-hour-long episodes. In November 1999 Dunn and Clattenburg traveled to Toronto and proposed the idea to the alternative and provocative Canadian programming network Showcase. Showcase agreed in principle to a deal to air the show if Wells and Tremblay would further consult with Canadian producer Michael Volpe. In late 2000, the first six half-hour episodes were made and aired on Showcase. The rest, as they say, is history.

Since 2002, *Trailer Park Boys* is the most popular series on Canadian cable television and the characters have made an indelible mark on Canadian popular culture. The show's lead trio, for example, toured with Canadian band Our Lady Peace, and with Guns N' Roses. The boys have also appeared in a music video with The Tragically Hip, and have been presenters at numerous Canadian award shows—always in character. The program, unlike any of its contemporaries, airs in Australia, the UK, the Republic of Ireland, Iceland, New Zealand, Israel, the Netherlands, Denmark, Portugal, Germany, Poland, Finland, Bulgaria, and the United States. In 2009, Clattenburg announced that after eight seasons, two one-hour stand-alone specials, and two feature-length movies, *Trailer Park Boys* voluntarily left the airwaves while still on top.

The representation of masculinity on the show is rife for analysis, and certainly worthy of falling under the category of misandry (perhaps uninten-tionally so, but quite misandric nevertheless). The main characters feature Ricky, who is a drug dealer and alcoholic chain-smoker who is Grade 6 educated and grammatically challenged (some of my favourite 'Ricky-isms' on the show include 'sweet and power chicken', 'hiposuction', 'Lahey is my mother's mating name', 'it doesn't take rocket appliances to realize', 'denial and error', 'The People's Freedom of Choices and Voices Act', 'gorilla see, gorilla do', 'horviculture', 'Saskatchewans' [for Sasquatches], 'let's get two birds stoned at once', 'it's basically peaches and cake', 'what Julian doesn't know won't burn him', and 'he passed that test with flying carpets'), abusive to his trailer park groupies Cory and Trevor, and hyper-violent. Ricky's sociopathic masculinity has no bounds. He is rude, violent, and cruel at times (except to his daughter Trinity, by estranged girlfriend Lucy), and generally unaware of his shortcomings. Julian plays the proverbial good cop to Ricky's bad cop. He is the social conscience of Sunnyvale, and while he is still complicit in the illegal wheelings and dealings (indeed, he shoots guns, smokes drugs, has a rum and Coke in his hand in every scene in the show, and actually masterminds most of their get-rich-quick schemes like 'Freedom 35' and 'Stay out of Jail and Let's Set Sail'), he represents the Canadian male who recognizes his own deficiencies but has no means to become a better man. Bubbles lives in a shed on Julian's trailer park lot and is played by Mike Smith almost as though he has Down's Syndrome, in a somewhat edgy and response-provoking fashion. However, Bubbles is the rational, clear-thinking, and essentially good character among the three who gets dragged into the boys' schemes after noted protest.

Other regular male characters on the show include: Cory and Trevor (two of the boys' out-of-work, drug-taking groupies); Jim and Randy (the two gay, alcoholic park supervisors); Ricky's father Ray (an alcoholic, worker's compensation scam artist); J-Roc and Tyrone (two wannabe rappers, pornography producers, and former fencers); Sam (a small-time criminal and veterinarian); and Cyrus (the boys' drug-dealing arch nemesis). The collective representation of men on the show is less than flattering. The boys represent the most primitive and *atavistic* characteristics of men; the brute, the hedonist, the exploiter, the deadbeat father, and the fatalist. Differences in male sexual orientation, physical ability, and ethnicity are mocked and caricatured. The women on the show, like Jim Lahey's ex-wife Barb, and the boys' girlfriends including Lucy and Sarah, are shown as the real brains of Sunnyvale, though their lives are routinely disturbed, disordered, or ruined by men. One of the most current themes running across the eight seasons is how Ricky's pathetic parenting will ruin Trinity's future by destroying her innocent femininity (simply through his presence in the park). The series consistently highlights a White, working-class masculinity as the ultimate source of social problems in a world far beyond, and in no need, of them. These men, while lovable and comical in many ways, are shown to be superfluous in late-modern Canada. When decontextualized from the park and situated in banks, corner stores, public parks, liquor stores, business offices, or other everyday settings, their alienation from mainstream society is palpable, as if Neanderthal man came alive and staggered into rush hour in downtown Halifax.

Trailer Park Boys emerged as a successful television venture in 2000s Canada not in spite of its misandry but in many ways because of it. This misandric spectacle is clearly marketable to middle-class hosers eager to voyeuristically transport themselves into a hyper-real world of working-class park life. Parts of the story and references to Canadian life clearly resonate with audiences (such as references to 'Crappy Tire', tabletop hockey, street hockey played with plastic blade sticks and hard orange balls, and Tim Horton's), and other moments are so insanely implausible that they become comical by any standard (such as when Bubbles befriends a mountain lion whom he calls Steve French, or the boys' plan to hide hashish from the police by paving their driveway with it). Still, *Trailer Park Boys* taps and profits from what Nathanson and Young (2001, 2006) claim to be the highly marketable image of atavistic men in a society that routinely derides men/males as biologically inferior to women and out of step with the late-modern world (i.e., emotionally incapable, aggressive, and physically rather than mentally oriented).

The brands of broken, pre-modern, throwback masculinities represented on *Trailer Park Boys* come to symbolize hoserdom to the extreme. Our interest in both them and the show's unmistakable motif that their animalism cannot be cured by any intervention resonates with current trends with psychology and criminology regarding the rebirth of somatotyping (i.e., the classification of people by body shape and size) and physiognomy (i.e., the study of facial shape and features as a technique of 'reading' one's personality) and other forms of biological/genetic typing (Rowe, 2002). Among other sociologists, Giddens (1989) notes how a turn to biological determinism in criminological sciences has infiltrated popular cultural discourses in silent yet prolific ways. The implication on *Trailer Park Boys* is that biologically inferior men will always be in crisis in late-modern society because their genes have not prepared them to thrive or adapt in the contemporary socio-cultural environment. They engage in risk-filled behaviours without foresight, care, or fear of reprisal. The show starkly reminds us how uncontrolled men and masculinities are the real source of problems in society, and that without incarceration or sterilization, their breed will continue to plague law-abiding others. They are the subjects of the *SCUM Manifesto*.

The representation of extreme hoser spectacles on *Trailer Park Boys* is the most exaggerated example, but certainly not the only one on Canadian television. The adult-oriented cartoon *Kevin Spencer* (which aired for eight seasons on The Comedy Network), is almost as spectacularly misandric as *TPB*. *Kevin Spencer* is set in Ottawa and revolves around the everyday happenings of the Spencer family (most frequently Kevin himself). Kevin's parents are Anastasia and Percy—both curious crosses between hosers and trailer park hicks. Kevin, aged 14, is described in the introductory jingle for the show as a 'chain-smoking, alcoholic, sociopathic juvenile delinquent'. Most of the adventures on the show revolve along illegal schemes committed by Kevin or all three of the lead characters. While other characters on the show speak, Kevin is never given a voice. The anonymous narrator articulates all of Kevin's thoughts and actions. Kevin responds to practically every situation he encounters with violence, and is often led to act by his imaginary friend, 'Allen the Magic Goose' (an anthropomorphic chain-smoking goose). The bird contributes to Kevin's sociopathic nature, usually asking him to do illegal, indecent, and dangerous things simply for the sake of a sneaky thrill. *Kevin Spencer* never reached the popularity of *Trailer Park Boys* but developed a cult following in Canada nonetheless. Misandric themes are prominent in the series, and its fear mongering about boys in crisis is evident.

Programs like *Trailer Park Boys* and *Kevin Spencer* cannot be decoupled from media representations of masculinity in crisis. While the programs represent the worst in masculinity and its representation, they also represent how boys and men are struggling to cope with their masculinity and accompanying role sets in a world seemingly against them at every turn. The misandry embedded in the shows is patently obvious and entertaining in a culture that regularly mocks masculinity in the media, but the shows do portray a concomitant awareness of how men like Kevin, Ricky, Julian, and Bubbles live in a world of crisis where they have no moral or appropriately gendered cultural scripts to guide them. Their masculinities are like crashed, mangled cars on the highway that we all slow down to steal a glance at while silently saying to ourselves, 'Oh, how horrible'. We move on toward our destination while they remain immovable and disfigured, waiting to be carted away to the wrecking lot.

Summary

The face of masculinity on Canadian television is complex and at times contradictory. Crisis advocates might predict a general tone of misandry on Canadian television, and to some extent they are correct. Most of the popular Canadian series tend to represent masculinity in patently unflattering, or at least traditional, manners. Masculine risk, misandry, doubt, and confusion have cut across popular television programming in the country for nearly three decades. But so does the loyalist brand of male hoserism that seems irreverent to widespread social change and cultural fragmentation. The degree to which any of these representations of masculinity reflect the life politics of wider groups of men (and women) is always the most relevant question. Crisis and misandry obviously sells 'good copy' and a critical awareness of how media create fabricated realities rather than represent lived experience goes a long way. Nevertheless, elements of the representations touch a common interpretive chord among Canadians (consider the sheer popularity of the shows I have reviewed), and as such there are realities that are definitely accessed by the programs. If the vertical mosaic has cracked, television is surely documenting and mockumenting its impact among men. The short- or long-term effects of such mediation remain to be studied.

Discussion Questions ··

1. Pick a television show you watch on a regular basis and identify the main male characters on the show. Describe their 'manliness' and the gendered attributes they embody.
2. Do you think misandry is either real or as pervasive as crisis advocates believe?
3. Are media representations of men on shows like *Trailer Park Boys* beyond reasonable, or do they have some important cultural messages about the status of masculinity in Canada?

4. Watch a sample of prime-time television shows on the CBC in any given week. Using the tripartite model of masculinity representation provided in this chapter, critically compare and contrast what you find with what I have presented.

5. Critics of media research might suggest that just because men are featured on a television program, nothing critical about their masculinity is being represented. Can you think of a case where this is true?

Key Readings

Beaty, B., and R. Sullivan. (2006). *Canadian Television Today.* Calgary, University of Calgary Press. *Canadian Television Today* takes an in-depth look at the formidable challenges facing the Canadian television industry, and the ways in which Canadian television represents aspects of Canadian culture. The current consensus within the industry alternates between a paternalistic model that promotes national culture and identity, and a laissez-faire approach that calls for a large-scale deregulation of the industry. To better understand why the industry is confronted with this difficult choice, the authors explore a number of key political decisions that have helped shape what parts of Canada are represented on television programming.

Ellis, T. (2005). *The Rantings of a Single Male: Losing Patience with Feminism, Political Correctness . . . and Basically Everything.* New York: Rannenburg. Unlike so many other publications that approach human sexuality, feminism, and political correctness from an academic vantage point, *The Rantings of a Single Male* is a personal narrative drawing on Ellis's encounters with both foreign and domestic women. Ellis offers up this collection of stories, satire, and social commentary about gender politics in late-modern America. His 'rants' employ dark humor to illuminate the many absurdities of our gendered life politics. Ellis is unapologetic and unrestrained in his handling of women's history, women's spirituality, gender norming, implants, affirmative action, rape hysteria, pornography, homophobia, and bad dates. It is principal masculinity crisis reading.

Hall, S. (1980). 'Encoding/Decoding'. In S. Hall, *Culture, Media, Language: Working Papers in Cultural Studies.* London: Hutchinson. Hall's seminal essay on the manners by which messages are produced, circulated, and then read by audiences should be primary reading for anyone interested in media studies. Among the central contributions of the statement is Hall's discussion of how the meanings of media texts are decoded/read by audiences in a range of preferred, negotiated, and resistive ways. The basic translation of his message is that while dominant themes or life politics may be structurally embedded in and communicated through texts, there is ultimately no guarantee that a media text will not be poached and reused in a pastiche manner by any number of interpretive communities of people.

Hamilton, R. (1996). *Gendering the Vertical Mosaic: Feminist Perspectives on Canadian Society.* Toronto: Copp Clark Ltd. *Gendering the Vertical Mosaic* is an excellent introduction to the analysis of Canadian society from a feminist perspective. Hamilton effectively argues for a fundamental integration of a gendered perspective in our understanding of social processes. After reading the book, it is difficult to contemplate omitting this perspective from consideration of social behaviour. She builds on both macro and micro analyses of gendered life in Canada to illustrate how Canadian society is still structured along lines of gender inequality.

Nathanson, P., and K. Young. (2001). *Spreading Misandry: The Teaching of Contempt for Men in Popular Culture*. Montreal: McGill-Queen's University Press. The first of a three-part series on masculinity by the authors, *Spreading Misandry* offers an impressive critique of popular culture to identify a phenomenon that is just now being recognized as a serious cultural problem: the sexist counterpart of misogyny. Nathanson and Young urge us to rethink prevalent assumptions about men that result in profoundly disturbing stereotypes, which in turn foster contempt. The book breaks new ground by discussing misandry in moral terms rather than purely psychological or sociological ones, and by criticizing not only ideological feminism per se, but other ideologies on both the political left and the right.

Web Links

Trailer Park Boys (www.trailerparkboys.com). The home site of the iconic Canadian show. Across the pages are accounts of the show's genesis, the bases its production, and season by season summaries of each episode.

Adbusters (www.adbusters.org). A website devoted to the critical analysis of media, and the manners by which normality is constructed in the media. The site is a great resource for encouraging students of the media to think critically about its ideological content.

Misandry Review (www.misandryreview.com). A blog-based website devoted to the review of anti-misandric thought and writing in popular culture.

Key Terms

Atavism: A tendency to reproduce ancestral type in plants and in animals; to resemble one's grandparents or great-grandparents more than parents. In popular speech, a biological 'throw back'. This concept was used by Cesare Lombroso (1835-1909) to describe a type of criminal he called the born criminal. The atavistic criminal was one representing an earlier stage of human evolution (thus representing the ancestral type more than the parental type).

Charter group: A founding or organizing member group of a society holding considerable institutional and cultural power to govern. In the development of what is now known as Canada, the English and the French are regarded as historical charter groups.

Discourse: Referring to a system or structure of language containing rules and orders of symbolic representation. Discourses are regarded by contemporary sociologists as vessels of meaning construction, conduits of power, and central forces in shaping social identities.

Gynocentric: A system of thought or a set of social practices dominated by or emphasizing feminine interests or a hyper-feminine point of view (or gaze).

Representation: The construction in any medium (especially the mass media) of aspects of 'reality'. Such aspects might include people, places, objects, events, or cultural identities and other abstract concepts. Such representations may be in speech or writing as well as still or moving pictures. The term refers to the processes involved as well as to its products.

Sign: An entity that symbolizes another entity. In the study of representation, signs can be pictures, bodies, words, commodities, animals, or events that symbolize something more abstract. For example, the proliferation of anti-male music in North America could be read as a signifier of the masculinity crisis.

Vertical mosaic: John Porter's (1965) idea that in societies like Canada, social and ethnic groups exist in a 'vertical' hierarchy based on their relative entrance (i.e., timing, numbers) into the social milieu. The vertical mosaic is Porter's metaphor for describing a structure of social stratification in Canada, and how group access to material resources, power, and collective representation is influenced by long-term historical processes of inclusion and exclusion.

7 The Unbearable Whiteness of Being

Chapter Objectives

This chapter introduces and critically explores the following:

- ⊛ The field of whiteness studies in North America
- ⊛ What bio-politics means, and its relationship to whiteness
- ⊛ Physical cultural studies as a basis for conceiving whiteness in society
- ⊛ The link between transhumanism and the masculinity crisis
- ⊛ Notions of extropianism and their implications on raced relations in Canada and elsewhere

This chapter is, let's just say, a bit 'different' from the rest of the book. I developed an interest in race and ethnicity studies only quite recently, and this chapter is one of my first attempts to theorize race in an imaginative sociological manner. The chapter ties together how 'whiteness' is salient within accounts of masculinity crises in Canada, and toward its end, presents a partial rereading of several physical cultural practices emblematic of the masculinity crisis I offered in the previous six chapters. At the substantive heart of the present chapter, and this is where my analysis may slip across the border into the unconventional, I couple whiteness and masculinity crises with a new social movement in North America called *transhumanism*.

I read Vallières's (1971) controversial text *White Niggers of America* as an undergraduate student in sociology at the University of Waterloo. The book is a stinging class-based analysis of French Canadien settlement and social, political, and economic life in pre- and post-Confederation Canada. Vallières lambastes French Canadien exploitation by English upper-class entrepreneurs of the late nineteenth and early twentieth century, ultimately arguing that modern industrial Canada was built on the backs of les Canadiens. To create an emotionally charged metaphor in the narrative, he draws parallels between the cultural position of the French in Canada and Black slaves in the United States. Vallières suggests further how French whiteness in many respects embodied a historically inferior social status for much of Canadia(e)n history. Vallières employs the racial epithet 'nigger' not only as a cultural or racial indicator, but as a concept encompassing social class and power. He states that the liberation movements of Black people in America have provided inspiration for French

Canadiens in the modern era. The book serves as Vallières's call to arms for the exploited masses of French Canadiens, encouraging the development of a class consciousness among them through which they become cognizant of their position as oppressed. Reading his book as a young student of the social sciences exposed me to a central problematic beyond French-English relations; the concept of whiteness as a contested term.

This is not a revelation that sits easily in the mind of a young man in the Canadian middle class. The historical luxury of being socially recognized as White allowed a guy like me, immersed in an undergraduate program in 1993 within a sleepy, very White university town in central Canada, to think about his whiteness at times when race actually mattered very little, such as when watching a music video or sports contest. Young, White, middle-class men of my generation rarely encountered problems with being White, learning White history, embodying White styles, speaking in White tongues, aspiring to White (collar) careers, or living White lives, and borrowing from the culture of racialized others when the occasion arose. But after reading *White Niggers of America* and listening to lectures on race and ethnicity as a sociology major, I *had* to face my own whiteness, its historical production, and the extensive manners by which White guys 'like me' were enmeshed in radically different ethnic and racial milieus as young adults than we might have first imagined. I read intently and reflected on comments about whiteness like those offered by Canadian race and education scholar George Sefa Dei (2005, p. 43):

> To my reading and experience, whiteness is never invisible to those who daily live the effects of white dominance. Many whites may see their whiteness, and yet they are able to deny the dominance associated with it. This denial is not unconscious, nor is it accidental; I believe it is deliberate. Critical anti-racism maintains that we will only do away with racism when whiteness no longer infers dominance and whites acknowledge and work towards this end. In noting this I also agree that there are contradictory (and sometimes competing) meanings of whiteness, as in the way whites and subordinate groups understand contemporary whiteness.

Sefa Dei is partly right, but most likely overestimates how homogenous White Canadians' understanding is of the parameters of their own whiteness. Like other young Canadian men of my generation, I had to forcibly encounter the privilege and trappings of my whiteness in school, popular culture, on the street, or elsewhere. As an academic, I see how class-based challenge to codes and practices of hegemonic masculinity through the 1990s and early 2000s recalibrated power balances for Whites in Canada, where it intersects with an ongoing historical deconstruction of whiteness in Canadian society. Although the notion of white privilege crops up in any class- or sexuality-based examination of the masculinity crisis, the degrees to which the public debates about whiteness fuels perceived crisis for some Canadian men is difficult to over-emphasize.

As a sub-field of critical race theory, *whiteness studies* are surprisingly under-developed within the social sciences. Major areas of research include the nature of White identity and of White privilege; the historical process by which a White racial identity is created; the relation of culture to White identity and possible processes of social change as they affect White identities. Keystone texts including Allen's (1994) *The Invention of the White Race*, Berger's *White Lies: Race and the Myths of Whiteness* (1999), Bonnett's *White Identities: Historical and International Perspectives* (2000), Dyer's *White* (1997), Hill's *After Whiteness: Unmaking an American Majority* (2004), Jensen's *The Heart of Whiteness: Confronting Race, Racism and White Privilege* (2005), Lipsitz's *The Possessive Investment in Whiteness: How White People Profit from Identity Politics* (2006), Roediger's *The Wages of Whiteness: Race and the Making of the American Working Class* (1991), and Young's *White Mythologies: Writing History and the West* (1990) vivisect race relations in North America and how whiteness is structurally, culturally, and ideologically embedded in dominant social practices and relationships in North America. If a White student of the social sciences is being truly honest and self-reflexive, the revelations about whiteness contained within these books should ring true. But by and large, what is striking about whiteness studies is how *white subjects* are rarely the centre of analysis in the pursuit of understanding how whiteness impacts the lived realities of Others. Whiteness studies, as an outgrowth of the critical race theory movement of the late 1970s, is predominantly contoured by accounts of how whiteness serves to marginalize and exclude racialized Others. There are a few notable exceptions.

Tim Wise is a leading whiteness studies scholar, and his text *White Like Me* (2007) differs radically from the majority of books or readers in the field. Wise's tome is a penetrating and self-critical narrative of White privilege in the United States. (For similar studies, see Landsmaen's *Growing Up White* [2008], McKinney's *Being White* [2004], and Rivel's *Uprooting Racism* [2002].) Wise discusses how White Americans (especially White American *men*) must recognize the arbitrary and victim-producing power lines drawn by racial categorization and hierarchies. *White Like Me* convinced and startled me without rhetoric or dogma, while passionately calling me to analyze the dimensions of my own whiteness. Wise highlights reactionary tendencies among White men in the United States and elsewhere; he interprets the deconstruction of racial privilege and the White mainstreaming of American culture as an overt attack on White masculinities.

A thorough review of whiteness studies research suggests empirical and theoretical accounts of the importance of White masculinity fall into three main (and often overlapping) camps. Theorists in the first camp stress the importance of male whiteness at the level of *social structure*. These theorists in this camp ask how White males as a group come to enjoy and maintain privileged (dare we say hegemonic) access to tangible goods—everyday benefits such as well-paying jobs, health protection, safe neighbourhoods, access to education, and basic civil liberties (see chapters 1 and 2 of this book). These male whiteness studies are concerned with entire systems of privilege producing clear material consequences because they are part of the organization of institutions like banks, schools, universities, and hospitals.

Second, *discursive studies* of male whiteness analyze how White male systems of representation, mass media, discourses, and symbols tend to organize cultural meaning so that male whiteness is framed as both the normal and the preferred state of being/existence/identity. Discursive theories identify culturally diffuse binaries (eg. Black/White, rich/poor) portraying male/female blackness or brownness as the antithesis of whiteness, allowing dominant male whiteness to emerge as special and desirable. The overarching focus of discursive theories is that taken-for-granted cultural perceptions and ideologies are organized by the manipulation of symbols and intersecting binaries (e.g., male+White=light=good vs. male/female+Black=dark=evil) in popular culture.

Third, whiteness research accounts for the ways in which dominant White male *institutional and discursive practices become intertwined and encoded* in cultural relations and embodied in practice. Such studies of whiteness address the ways in which mechanisms that male whiteness historically build up in a number of ways, including in vast socio-cultural relationships, an individual's sense of self, culturally dominant physical gestures and tastes for body comportment, codes of etiquette, common beauty preferences, and diffuse assumptions about personal growth, morality, and decency. These are classic examples, as I eventually describe below, of physical cultural studies research. At this point, each camp's emphasis on the role of male whiteness in organizing social life and marginalizing others has produced *backlash* by masculinity crisis advocates.

Not so subtly embedded in crisis discourses is an implicit lament of the death of White masculine society, and associated reactions against Other men claiming victimization. Crisis advocates including Clare (*On Men: Masculinity in Crisis*, 2000) assail whiteness and blackness research as polarizing and ideologically naïve, silencing men in the White middle classes. Examinations of Black masculinity, for example, like bell hooks's *We Real Cool* (2003) and Anthony Neal's *New Black Man* (2005) nevertheless point to the multi-layered methods by which Black masculinity is far more of a measurable crisis category for young men than whiteness. hooks asserts that Black men have been so dehumanized by White (male) America that they are in crisis emotionally and at risk within society (i.e., through drugs, crime, gangs, chronic unemployment, and disease). She posits the greatest threat to Black life in America is the institutional residue of White male patriarchal thinking and practices. hooks further contracts improved employment opportunities for Black women with the instability of Black male employment, something many Black men have

trouble accepting because of the cultural often dictates that men should dominate women. Too many Black men face a host of troubling social dynamics—
including alienation from their fathers and their children—and in degrees
unmatched for White men supposedly in crisis. hooks, like other critical race
scholars, indicates that men on the racial margins are therefore far more likely
to be in crisis than Whites anywhere in the social hierarchy; these men, in short,
are the ones with a legitimate claim to crisis.

Once more, White men in the middle end up feeling socially attacked on the
basis of their whiteness (not only from all women, critical race and whiteness
theorists, and from Othered men), and are told they do not have legitimate
cultural access to crisis feelings, discourses, or experiences (Wise, 2007). Poor
guys, eh? Well, not entirely.

Physical Cultural [Whiteness] Studies

As an artefact of a residual (White) patriarchy in Canada, Canadian men
in crisis can invent their own contexts and practices of power via pastiche
hegemony. To explore the notions of pastiche hegemony and residual White
patriarchy in Canada I detour slightly before rereading how White men in the
middle are fabricating fascinating responses to perceived crisis. I introduced the
idea of *physical cultural studies* (PCS) in the first chapter of this book and we will
examine this concept first. PCS is not an entirely new concept in the academy,
but has received scant exploration or application to date as a viable disciplinary
organizer (Andrews, 2008; Ingham, 1997). To the best of my knowledge, no
academic to date has used the concept in the process of exploring either whiteness or the masculinity crisis. David Andrews's (2008, p. 54) definition of PCS
is worth quoting at length:

> Physical cultural studies advances the critical and theoretical analysis of physical
> culture, in all its myriad forms. These include sport, exercise, health, dance and
> movement related practices, which PCS research locates and analyzes within the
> broader social, political, economic and technological contexts in which they are
> situated. More specifically, *PCS is dedicated to the contextually based understanding
> of the corporeal practices, discourses and subjectivities through which active bodies
> become organized, represented and experienced in relation to the operations of social
> power. PCS identifies the role played by physical culture in reproducing, and some-
> times challenging, particular class, ethnic, gender, ability, generational, national, racial
> and/or sexual norms and differences* . . . PCS advances an equally fluid theoretical
> vocabulary, utilizing concepts and theories from a variety of disciplines (including
> cultural studies, economics, history, media studies, philosophy, sociology and
> urban studies) in engaging and interpreting the particular aspect of physical
> culture under scrutiny. [emphasis added]

I increasingly define myself as a fervent PCS researcher instead of a traditional, boundary-protecting, and theoretically precious sociologist. The promise of PCS is the disciplinary meta-theme of this book on (let's be fair and honest by saying 'White') masculinity. A physical cultural studies examination of (White) masculinity focuses on the manners by which identity crises are ultimately embodied and articulated within contexts of discursive, structural, and ideological power. The politics of the masculinity crisis plainly illustrate the potential of physical cultural studies for laying bare how ideology, structures, identities, and embodied practices intersect in everyday life. I have examined the masculinity crisis and the experiences of living in a post-crisis Canadian society through case studies of physical culture, and argued how physical practices signify and allow inspectors to come to terms with how men in situated contexts manage, negotiate, represent, and struggle to transform relations of social power (including perceived inequality) through ritual and common physical practices. Chapters in this book on masculinity reveal how politics of power in the (middle-class White) masculinity crisis will, in the end, almost always manifest at the level of the body.

Another point worth reconsidering is how crisis emerges within conditions characterized by *presence or absence* in a society. If anything, the perceived masculinity crisis in Canada emerged in a context of a spectacular gender–race power vacuum. What vacuum? Doesn't the socio-demographic data outlining conditions of structural inequality in Canada plainly evidence a residual patriarchy for White men? Well, not entirely. Several decades' worth of challenges to the ontological stability of masculinity and neatly defined men's roles in Canada have chipped away at upper- and middle-class white men's structural and ideological ownership of power. As a related consequence, there is no publicly lauded White masculinity in the singular sense in Canada any longer, nor is there an outright connection between any male gender categories and exclusive ownership of power. I sincerely hope the previous chapters of this book emphasize such a point. So, there is a vacuum, an absence of a dominant and racialized gender master at the head of the social table of power. How is this related to physical cultural studies and theorizing whiteness in crisis-sensitive research? I would encourage readers to remember arguments offered in the Introduction of this book and in chapter 1 regarding the implosion of socio-cultural meta-narratives over the past 40 or so years. From here, let's add to our understanding of how identity-power vacuums are created (leading to crisis) in relation to a few other social trends.

Post-colonialism and Whiteness Studies

Post-colonial studies provide insight as to why growing numbers of White men in the middle class feel, let's say, frustrated by contemporary identity politics and localized power vacuums. Post-colonial theories and research extend across a full range of academic disciplines and generally seek to challenge modernist (White, masculinist) ways of thinking, therefore creating space for the *subaltern* (socially marginalized) to speak and produce alternative discourses and knowledge (Gilroy, 2006). Edward Said's (1978) book *Orientalism* is heralded as the pioneering text in post-colonial studies, and it emphasizes the degree to which scientific knowledge of the world tends to be framed around White, Western notions of reality. For Said, the ability to 'name' or objectively define social processes, identities, laws, and scientific facts through academic documention and discourses in the world is power; that power has been held by White Westerners through modernity until quite recently. Another prominent post-colonial theorist, Gayatri Spivak (1994) contends that the public must engage a sort of *epistemic violence* (literally, a mental and ideological debate regarding what is knowledge) against colonial ways of seeing and defining the world in order to 'let the subaltern speak'. Spivak principally refers to dismantling White, hegemonically male (Said's 'colonial') ways of defining the world. As a post-colonialist, Homi Bhabha (1994) argues for cultural pluralism and hybridization, where socially disintegrative boundaries such as Western/Eastern, White/Other, or male/female are smashed and mixed back together as progressive cultural politics. In short, post-colonialists struggle against historically pervasive identity boundaries and forms of essentialism that serve to maintain power imbalances between cultural groups.

The accelerating interest in post-colonial studies is a signifier in certain respects of what legions of men in the Canadian White middle class irrationally fear and struggle to come to terms with in everyday life. The destabilization of modernist knowledge bases involves a destabilization of people in those bases (see chapters 1 and 2 of this book!). In the process of destabilization, the lament from male Whites in the middle class about post-colonial ways of thinking in the news, at work, in school, on television, in religion, and elsewhere tends to revolve around the notion of 'reverse discrimination' (Hill, 2004). The multicultural, post-colonial reality of Canada (one *becoming* multicultural rather than one that has *arrived* as multicultural) is reacted to emotionally by particular men in the privileged middle class as an attack on some mythological *imagined community* (Anderson, 1991) of Whites. These men feel as if Whites are collectively victimized by racial, ethnic, and others forms of identity politics that give voice to the subaltern and grant them access to social power. Roger Hewitt's *White Backlash and the Politics of Multiculturalism* (2005) documents how a host of White male backlash movements cropped up in the past 50 years as responses to perceived reverse discrimination in countries like the United States, Great Britain, and Canada.

But for certain innovative men in the middle classes, the movement toward an increasingly post-colonial, non-White dominant society poses little crisis at all (Gilroy, 2006). In fact, it poses a pastiche hegemonic opportunity for power.

Critical race scholars and post-colonial theorists rightly discuss how 'White' is an historical construction, and is embodied as a set of physical cultural practices with no inherent meaning or universal cultural value. If White masculinity can be deconstructed and culturally decentred, it could theoretically be reconstructed and silently recentred in pastiche hegemonic manners. How is this possible? Three simple words: neo-liberalism and libertarianism.

We have tackled the concept of *neo-liberalism* in previous chapters, but *libertarianism* is a new one in this book. Ultimately, libertarianism is a movement emphasizing the *cult of the individual*. Because individuals are moral agents, they have a right to be secure in their life, liberty, and perhaps most importantly, should have access to *private property*. Across social time and space, libertarians as a group tend toward several common values. Libertarian thought emphasizes the dignity of each individual, which entails both intense personal rights and responsibility. Notwithstanding the diversity in libertarian views, they share a common history and set of interrelated beliefs. The key defining features of libertarianism and its ideological boundaries have developed over many centuries. The first inklings of libertarianism can be found in ancient China, Greece, and Israel and were developed into something resembling modern libertarian philosophy in the work of seventeenth- and eighteenth-century American thinkers such as John Locke, David Hume, Adam Smith, Thomas Jefferson, and Thomas Paine. Libertarianism as a globally relevant social philosophy is actually several centuries old.

Given the libertarian emphasis on the individual and each person's civic responsibilities, social order emanates from the actions of thousands or millions of individuals who coordinate their actions to achieve their self-interested goals. *Civil society* (the complex network of associations and connections among people) is an example of spontaneous order. Libertarians argue simultaneously that any society must be both bound by rules of law and that those laws must only be administered by limited government. Finally, and most important, libertarians believe individuals need to engage in unfettered economic activity. Libertarians believe that people will be both freer and more prosperous if government intervention in people's economic choices is minimized. Modern libertarians defend the right of so-called productive people to keep what they earn (sounds like a very White, middle-class idea to me!), and believe there is a natural harmony of interests among peaceful, productive people in a just society.

From Libertarianism to Transhumanism

Here is where things get a bit more interesting. *Libertarian transhumanists* are a sub-faction of transhumanists and believe the principles of *self-ownership and personal development* are the most fundamental ideas governing late-modern life. In particular, they embrace the prospect of using emerging biomedical technologies to enhance human capacities—capacities they believe stem from the self-interested application of reason and will in the context of the individual freedom to achieve a human state of complete physical, mental, and social well-being. They extend this rational and ethical egoism to advocate *bio-libertarianism*, or the ability of the individual to do whatever one wishes with one's body in order to ensure its integrity over the long, long, long term. Libertarian transhumanists like Ronald Bailey (2005) define social or cultural attempts to limit or suppress the asserted right to human enhancement as a violation of basic civil rights and liberties.

Okay, so let's recap just a bit before proceeding further. Whiteness is increasingly critiqued by post-colonialists and others in late-modern, neo-liberal spaces, and at the same time a sub-group of predominantly White middle-class men called libertarians offer a solution to crisis. The rise of economic, biological, and political libertarianism is a potential source of physical cultural solutions to a perceived masculinity crisis; as the reconstruction of 'White' masculinity through transhuman technological means. Hold onto your hats because this is where the theoretical ride gets a bit bumpy.

Transhumanism itself has been called the 'world's most dangerous idea' by its skeptics (Fukuyama, 2002), and transhumanist philosophy and associated ethical debates remain relatively novel in the study of gender, race, and other forms of identity in Canada and elsewhere (Atkinson, 2008c, 2010). Transhumanism is a mix of both ideas and physical cultural practices dealing primarily with libertarian-inspired *biological enhancement technologies*. Transhumanists favour the radical technological enhancement of human cognitive and physical capacities in order to free the body from its limited biological, or dare we say 'natural' abilities. To transhumanists, the body is simply an organic computer, which can and should be upgraded to a more technologically capable and potential-expanding entity. The tools transhumanists would use to achieve their ends include genetic manipulation, nanotechnology, cybernetics, pharmacological enhancement, and body-computer integration. Among the most ambitious and controversial transhumanist visions involves is the process of *mind uploading*. According to proponents of mind uploading, advances in computing and neurotechnologies will, within several decades, enable individuals to completely read the synaptic connections of the human brain, enabling an exact replica of the brain to exist inside a computer, and thus extending life without limit.

The history of transhumanism as a social philosophy and practice is as old as human consciousness itself, and indeed, proponents argue that the very moment humans started to produce the means of our own subsistence, we became transhumanists—literally humans *in transition* to becoming a more-than-human sentient being. Explicit transhumanist philosophy can be traced to the eighteenth-century philosophy of French theorists Julien Offray de La Mettrie and the Marquis de Condorcet, while the word *transhumanism* first appears in Huxley's *Religion Without Revelation* (1927, p.19):

Photo 7.1 To a transhumanist, it is not that we will be able to touch God's hand one day; it is that, one day, God will be able to touch ours.

The human species can, if it wishes, transcend itself—not just sporadically, an individual here in one way, an individual there in another way—but in its entirety, as humanity. We need a name for this new belief. Perhaps *transhumanism* will serve: man remaining man, but transcending himself, by realizing new possibilities of and for his human nature.

Radical transhumanists including Nick Bostrom and David Pearce argue that with the advent of late twentieth century medical and scientific technology (i.e., such as those discoveries and advances made by the Human Genome Project) the human species is already receiving a self-made evolutionary, transhuman turbo-boost. Instead of unplanned biological evolution—a slow process of survival, reproduction, and adaptation over time—human futures are now powered via deliberately employed technologies that will increasingly work their way inward, radically transforming our bodies and minds (Bostrom, 2005, 2008). Transhumanist projects of the future will strengthen or transcend basic human characteristics such as youth, creativity, and intelligence by using medical technology to develop, repair, activate, or eliminate certain defective, weak, or limiting genes; or, the use of other scientific innovations such as robotics to enhance movement. Such humans, as the transhuman credo promotes (WTA, 2002), will be capable of achievements of which present generations only dream about in science fiction.

Transhumanists point to many potential human futures through corporeal manipulation, such as the development of superintelligence via cerebral interface with computers; lifelong emotional well-being via the recalibration of the brain's pleasure-centres; the use of personality pills and complementary gene therapy to correct 'pathological conditions' like shyness; the development of biological nanotechnology to increase the lifespan; the uploading of thoughts and consciousness into virtual reality via neuroprostheses; and cryogenic freezing and then reanimation of 'dying' bodies or body parts. Transhumans will reap the bio-capital benefits of altered DNA, selective reproduction, prosthetic limbs, nanorobotics, synthetic organs, sensory magnification, anti-aging regimens, and drug therapy (Miah, 2008). Model transhumans are engineered X-Men who receive injections of anti-aging serum that replenishes cells. They are embodied with telecommunication systems transmitting text, voice, video, and large knowledge/data files to other machines, and whose eyes are rigged with an artificial oculus that measures colour, depth, heat, and distance. Their DNA has been genetically altered so they are virtually immune to disease, and their emotions are regulated by receptors implanted deep in their brains to render them free from stress, fear, doubt, paranoia, or depression. Skeptics including Dublin (1992) and Fukuyama (2002) argue that transhumanism is more or less a misnomer for *post-humanism,* or the complete transcendence of the natural human body.

In the end, transhumanists believe that people can and should use technology to become *more than human,* or pursue a state of being *beyond contemporary socio-cultural understandings of corporeal wellness.* A posthuman would transcend basic modes of human existence and reality, becoming a postmodern Gilgamesh or Nietzsche's *Overman*; two-thirds engineered god, one-third natural human. Groups including the World Transhumanist Association (now called *Humanity+*), Cryonics Institute, Transhumanist Arts, Alcor Life Extension Foundation, the Future of Humanity Institute, the Extropy Institute, and The Foresight Institute have, for the better part of the last 40 years promulgated transhuman visions and futures.

Key transhuman texts in this growing social movement include Ettinger's *Man into Superman* (1979), Esfandiary's *Are You Transhuman?* (1989), Regis's *Great Mambo Chicken and the Transhuman Condition* (1990), Drexler's *Nanosystems* (1992), Newman's *Promethean Ambitions: Alchemy and the Quest to Perfect Nature* (2004), and the World Transhumanist Association's (WTA) *Transhumanist Declaration* (2002). These texts theorize a society that transcends modernist notions of the human and human identity; this includes, though it is rarely acknowledged in post/trans-human debates, the implications of transhumanism on the dismantling or eradication of gender, race, ethnicity, and other socially ascribed identity markers (Fukuyama, 2002).

Now, among the many fascinating aspects of the *Humanity+* or transhumanist global movement is that it is, by and large, an incredibly White, middle- and upper-class movement despite its presentation by members as open, global, libertarian, and populist. The inherent essentialism of the movement's ideologies and their focus on the material over the socially constructed body would appear to legitimate its claims to universalism and post-identity freedom, but even a rudimentary inspection of transhumanist history, ideologies, and

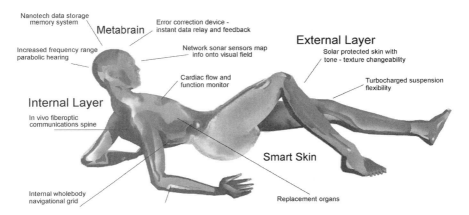

Nanotech data storage memory system

Metabrain

Error correction device - instant data relay and feedback

Increased frequency range parabolic hearing

Network sonar sensors map info onto visual field

External Layer
Solar protected skin with tone - texture changeability

Cardiac flow and function monitor

Turbocharged suspension flexibility

Internal Layer
In vivo fiberoptic communications spine

Smart Skin

Internal wholebody navigational grid

Replacement organs

FIGURE 7.1 The posthuman will look less like an organic being and more like a manufactured machine.

practices indicate otherwise. Transhuman concerns are popular among those with the social, cultural, and economic capital required to access cutting-edge technology. Likewise, transhumanism is popular among those who possess dispositions or habituses (remember, a habitus is a socially learned personality structure that directs a person's tastes) sensitive to the idea of pursuing scientifically designed physical perfection; and among those whose embodied, racialized identities are neither a source of outright social power nor stigma.

In locating the above ideas even further within the socio-cultural literature, transhumanism is rather representative of what Melucci (1997) and others call *new social movements* (NSMs). A new social movement is a voluntary and oftentimes globally connected consortium that primarily pursue identity-based rights or civic rights rather than changes to the distribution of opportunity and wealth in a society. The identity-rights battle waged by transhumanists is launched on a platform whose features include post-identity, body-as-private property; and intersections with technology. Many new social movements tend to emphasize social changes in identity, ideology, lifestyle, and culture, rather than pushing for specific changes in public policy or for economic change first. NSMs like transhumanism are thus *post-material* social movements. As a new social movement, transhumanism gathered steam in the 1980s, following the avant-garde writings of a futurist known as FM-2030. FM-2030 advocated the term *transhuman* as shorthand for *transitional human* (Bostrom, 1999, 2005). Transhumans were described as 'the earliest manifestation of new evolutionary beings, on their way to becoming posthumans'. By the 1990s, a series of groups emerged and embraced FM-2030's transhumanist ideology, including the Extropians, the Transtopians, and the Singularitarians.

I started reading about transhumanism as a new social movement roughly two years ago and feel somewhat foolish to have overlooked transhumanist leanings in White, middle-class enclaves of society during my research on men's physical cultural practices in Canada. The silent but prolific rise of transhumanism as a new social movement in Canada and elsewhere maps almost directly onto the evolution of (mass) identity crises in Canada, the rise of political, economic, and cultural neo-liberalism and libertarianism, post-colonial practice, and the social germination of particular physical cultural practices of men who feel in crisis. In short, the impact on transhumanist ideology and physical cultural practices in Canada is perhaps more relevant to the masculinity crisis than first appreciated.

Transhumanist physical culture (still a futuristic vision) may be especially appealing to White men in crisis who seek to transcend the cultural landmine field of racial politics in Canada by returning to a brand of scientific essentialism about the body (and identity). Transhumanist practices, in theory, are neither inherently race conscious nor culturally progressive in a multicultural sense, but rather silently promote 'scientifically improved' brands of personhood (at this stage almost exclusively White personhood) that possess their own unique social power. Transhumanists rarely if ever speak of racial politics because theirs is a movement that eschews the concept of race itself. For men struggling with being racialized in problematic manners (i.e., those who view whiteness as a stigmatizing and victimized identity), essentializing the body and perfecting scientifically without reference to race is liberating and an act of ostensible racial transcendence. Still, the relatively exclusive ownership amongst Whites to transhumanist medical and scientific ventures is an unspoken and unwritten form of cultural capital. While whiteness is ever deconstructed in institutional and popular cultural spaces, transhumanist White men in Canada may already be moving to 'whiter' pastures in a pastiche hegemonic manner. After all, wasn't the Terminator the baddest-ass White transhuman of all time? If we dig a bit deeper, weren't all the robots in the landmark artificial intelligence films *A.I.* (2001) and posthumans in *I, Robot* (2004) White? Why were the human replicants in *Blade Runner* (1982) White? Even the legendary cinematic villain Darth Vader is (despite being 'voiced' by James Earl Jones), White underneath his transhuman suit.

The Triumph of the Object-Body

The appeal of transhumanism for White men in their new social movement may rest in the ways scientific essentialism dismantles, on the surface, racial and all Other differences through embodied acts. The erasure of identity along these lines might be called, in Baudrillard's (2002) terms, an identity *catastrophe*. For Baudrillard, catastrophe is a commodity-based excess, acceleration, and precipitation typified by contemporary society in its pursuit to level differences between people rather than to celebrate those differences. Its potency resides in the unmaking of the identity-based subject through self-commodification, and the eventual triumph of the object over the subject. In different terms, catastrophe happens when physical objects (or the biological body) reign supreme over identities. It is a weird, and ironic, outcome of a supposedly libertarian and neo-liberal society of individuals! By rendering all differences obsolete in a society, catastrophic practices threaten the politics of identity, which are dependent on self/Other relations. Elsewhere, Baudrillard (1996) refers to the process as *aphanisis* (*creatio ex nihilo*), or the death of the subject behind the public screen of blank objects and signifiers. Transhuman body projects, from Baudrillard's (2002) perspective, are scientifically engineered and socially employed catastrophes because they venture beyond the politics of identity (at least on the surface). For White men in crisis, if being both White and masculine in a traditional sense is self-perceived as problematic in late-modern society, then projects that 'better' the body *object-ively* and extend it in powerful ways (i.e., strength, health, longevity, mental prowess, emotional control, and psychological stability) without appearing either masculinist or White may be especially attractive. Another term describing the potential interest in transhumanist body projects for White men in crisis is *extropianism*. Also referred to as extropism or extropy, extropianism is an evolving framework of values and standards for continuously improving the human body in 'objective' (read rationally *scientific*) ways. Extropianism is a descendant of Enlightenment ways of seeing the body and the mind. It describes a pragmatic unification of transhumanist thought guided by a proactive approach to human evolution and progress, and one devoid of the messy politics of identity. Simply put, *race does not matter to machines*. The Terminator was White and male in James Cameron's cinematic vision, but neither his whiteness nor his masculinity mattered to his functioning. Originated by a set of principles developed by Dr Max More (2006) in *The Principles of Extropy*, extropian thinking places strong emphasis on rational thinking and a practical optimism that in the future ascribed identity concerns will polarize history. *Extropy* is defined by More as the extent of a living or organizational system's intelligence, functional order, vitality, energy, life, experience, and capacity and drive for improvement and growth.

Each of these is universal, rather than identity-dependent. Still, critics point out that extropians like More tend to be White, male, and middle class. Theirs is a proposed future of personal evolution based on the perfection of the body through science: a process to which few rather than many have current access. Consider some of the 'goals' of extropian body projects, such as those espoused by the *Humanity*+ group and other transhumanist organizations. Ask whether or not their goals sound familiar to White eugenicist ideas embedded in scientific thought during the 1800s and early 1900s:

1. *Perpetual progress:* Extropians seek more intelligence, wisdom, and effectiveness, an indefinite lifespan, and the removal of political, cultural, biological, and psychological limits to self-actualization and self-realization.

Photo 7.2 To some, a transhuman future is one where we become 'singular'. We will be able to upload our minds and personalities to robotic shells with infinite lifespans.

2. *Self-transformation:* Extropians affirm moral, intellectual, and physical self-improvement through critical and creative thinking, personal responsibility, and experimentation.
3. *Practical optimism:* Extropians adopt rational, action-based optimism in place of blind faith, cultural belief, and stagnant pessimism.
4. *Intelligent technology:* Extropians apply science and technology creatively to transcend natural limits imposed by biological heritage, culture, and environment.
5. *Open society:* Extropians support social orders that foster freedom of speech, freedom of action, and experimentation. Extropians oppose authoritarian social control and favoring the rule of law, and the decentralization of power, and they prefer bargaining over battling.
6. *Self-direction:* Extropians seek independent thinking, individual freedom, personal responsibility, self-direction, and self-esteem.
7. *Rational thinking:* Extropians favour reason over faith and scientific questioning over dogma.

Historians of whiteness in North America and elsewhere identify how each of the above ostensibly neutral and democratic human goals, are tied to White, masculine ideologies of the nineteenth and twentieth centuries (Kincheloe, 2000). As White men have been the architects of the transhuman movement for nearly a century, it makes sense that men in 'whiteness' crisis may find future power in cultivating post-White bodies through science. Transhumanism is potentially only a thinly veiled eugenics or social engineering for a new millennium. Transhumanists aspire to invent a new social category of human as one beyond the trappings of everyday identity (attractive for someone who has access to transhuman technology and is in crisis, no?). It is a post-race, post-gender new social movement with deeply-seated race and gender implications nevertheless—as White men's near exclusive access to, and interest in, them may serve to create a new breed of hegemonic supermen. When I contemplate transhumanism and White guys in crisis, I remember the now clichéd line from the American classic baseball movie, *Field of Dreams:* 'If you build it, they will come'.

No More Mr White Guy: *Humanity+* in Popular Culture

Crisis almost always strikes fear in the heart of the vulnerable, or at least in the hearts of those who see themselves as vulnerable. Criminologist Ted Gurr (1973) believes individuals will (back)lash out in aggressive, anti-social, or even criminal manners when they feel 'relatively deprived' in comparison to others. Gurr's (1973) concept of relative deprivation is an important one for coming to terms with both the idea of White men in crisis and their physical cultural responses to crisis because, as existentialists argue, perception is the better part of lived reality. Cultural, social, and institutional twists and turns in Canadian society documented throughout this book doctor the social and political fields of gender, race, and social class. Whether it is a popular, politically correct, or accepted academic sentiment, identity-based shifts in Canadian power have produced a zeitgeist of relative deprivation among clusters of White men in the middle class who feel besieged, besmirched, singled-out, and unjustly punished for historical White male patriarchy in Canada. My reading of men's responses to the masculinity crisis across Canada returns to a repeated conclusion: the very concept of hegemonic masculinity is an ideological house of cards fraught with internal vulnerability. The social tectonics of the new millennium exposes its fragile nature, and legions of men have jumped off the sinking ship of dominant masculinity in pursuit of local recalibrated (pastiche) masculine power. Other new social movements captained by White men in the middle class—such as the transhumanist movement—welcome identity-based implosions in late modernity, and silently recover *uberwhite* masculinity through objective, scientific means.

While the realization of fully transhuman or posthuman (White) men may be decades away, the impact of extropian ideology on popular culture is, as Hebdige (1987) might argue, already 'hiding in the light'. Transhumanism and the desire to escape the culturally problematic (and not just biologically problematic) body are prevalent in contemporary physical cultures. Consider if you will a brief reanalysis of several physical cultural processes in this book. The most obvious connection to transhumanism doctrine and practice among men in crisis is cosmetic surgery. Even though cosmetic surgery is not owned by a particular race or gender, the manners by which men in crisis are reshaping their bodies into late-modern *man-nequins,* which resonate with transhuman philosophy. With each intervention on the body, cosmetic surgery patients come to resemble one another in an almost cookie-cutter, android/extropian way. As their faces are similarly smoothed, bodies streamlined, hairlines precisely implanted, and skin sandblasted, White men in the middle- and upper-classes are forging de-differentiated masculine bodies. These bodies are based less on esoteric difference and more on techno-medical theory, design, and application. Cosmetic surgery is already standardizing the corporeal signification of White middle-class masculinity, and granting it the universally lauded attributes of health, youth, vibrancy, and immunity from time and space.

Sports supplementation among men in crisis could be similarly re-examined as an offshoot of transhumanism in popular culture. In transhumanist discourse, the pharmacologically modified body in gym-based cultures is cutting edge. Attempts to subvert the natural human ability to produce muscle, red blood cells, oxygen-carrying capacity, and tissue repair through the consumption of over-the-counter ergogenic aids are more than innovative dietary regimes. They are as much techno-scientific attempts among White men to 'have' the bodies of Black men, whom they consider to be genetically advantaged. As images of the ripped, muscular, dominant Black male athlete, model, or entertainer crop up as desirable within popular culture, more White men have pursued physical intervention through ergogenics. The growth of the sports supplement industry over the past two decades is predominantly attributable to middle-class White men's desire to gain a transhuman advantage in the gym through scientific means (Atkinson, 2007). There is little reason to believe the range of sports supplement products will dwindle in future, or reason to witness shifts in the marketing strategies of supplement producers to reach anyone other than predominantly White men—review any edition of *Muscle & Fitness, Flex, Men's Health,* or *Men's Journal* to test the voracity of my marketing claim.

On the subject of sport and leisure physical cultural practices, forms of sport-related violence show definitive links to the transhuman movement. Technology theorist Bruno Latour (2005) might point to the ways in which safety equipment in sports like ice hockey operate as agents or *actants* to fuel the aggressively mimetic nature of the sport, thus ensuring, in some ways, violence will exist therein. High-tech helmets, shoulder pads, shin guards, chest protectors, and other devices that often make players feel invincible, are developed so that rough-and-tumble forms of play may continue, and convey a false impression to audiences that players are overprotected from serious injury.

Hockey players, who are predominantly White men from the upper-working- and middle classes, could be interpreted as technologically protected cyborgs

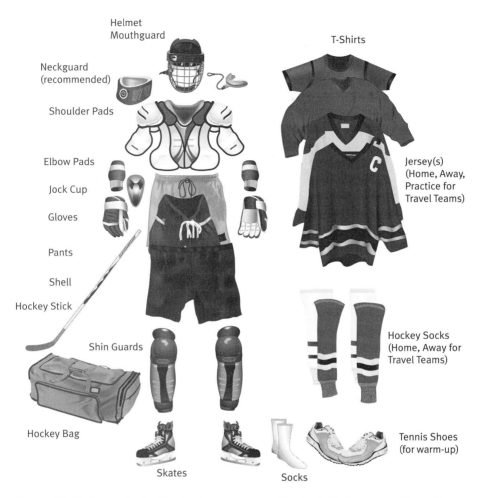

Helmet
Mouthguard

T-Shirts

Neckguard
(recommended)

Shoulder Pads

Elbow Pads

Jock Cup

Gloves

Pants

Shell

Hockey Stick

Shin Guards

Hockey Bag

Jersey(s)
(Home, Away,
Practice for
Travel Teams)

Hockey Socks
(Home, Away for
Travel Teams)

Tennis Shoes
(for warm-up)

Skates

Socks

Photo 7.3 Underneath all of the hockey gear, you will actually find a person. If sport is supposed to be about human potential and human movement, why do we use more and more high-tech equipment every year?

on the ice. This, coupled with enduring hyper-masculinist creeds and ethics in the sport, actually place the players at great risk of victimization. While ice hockey receives virtually no consideration as an extropian sport, the technological gear athletes wear from head to toe is unparalleled (along with, perhaps, triathlon and giant slalom skiing) in either amateur or professional North American sports cultures.

White men and boys, who due to social class or other conditions of inequality have little access to transhuman technologies, reject the commodity-based social movement or resist it aggressively as another source of their alienation.

They attribute little race or ethnic meaning to transhumanism, but interpret it as another form of cultural oppression. Straightedge is thus a form of contemporary *luddism*, or anti-technology, anti-science, and anti-consumerism in many ways. Straightedge luddism equates technologies and their consumption with the surrounding power relations that produce those technologies. Straightegers may see their luddism as a form of resistance to transhumanism as a clever form of self-purification. If commodities and technologies are rejected because they are products and symbols of capitalism adopted by society, then every intoxicating form of technology must be rejected. Straightedge is therefore the physical cultural foil to extropian social currents. Laddism and bugchasing can be regarded as similar forms of resistance to transhumanism because they are both intensely and excessively non-technological in their essence. Each physical cultural practice flamboyantly embraces and champions intense and, some might say, hedonistic, visceral experiences with the de-scientized body.

Summary

Race and ethnicity clearly matter in Canada and elsewhere, and whiteness certainly weighs heavy within discussions of identity crisis among men. While gay men, racial minority men, men of non-mainstream religions, and others who are at times pushed to the social margins experience structural, cultural, and existential crises in everyday life, the much ballyhooed masculinity crisis of the 1990s and early 2000s has been largely coloured in White ways and by White perceptions. In truth, part of the feminist and profeminist rejection of the very idea of crisis rests on these aforementioned identity grounds. Among the main analytic points I persistently return to in this book is the idea that we must neither reject the notion of crisis nor accept it outright; and instead, researchers must mine new theoretical ways of understanding why groups of White men in the Canadian middle class perceive crisis and measure appropriate responses to such perceptions. As potentially farfetched as the movement toward transhumanism may seem upon first glance, I am reminded how Baudrillard consistently encouraged radical 'theoretical violence' against extant ways of thinking in order to push the boundaries of knowledge. Hopefully, this chapter is convincing with regard to the ways trends like transhumanism may be embedded with forms of (post)identity politics, and how they may potentially interlace with perceptions of crisis across the masculinity landscape.

Discussion Questions

1. Discuss what you see as the significance of transhumanism on race relations in Canada.

2. Explore a post-colonial theorist of your choice and examine if and how their thoughts might be relevant in assessing why some White men in Canada experience identity crisis.

3. Whiteness scholars consistently argue that science has never been gender or race neutral, and that both masculinist and White ways of seeing the body underpin science. Do you agree or disagree?

4. Conduct some online research and discover a transhuman body project that is already available for public consumption. Discuss whether or not you feel as if the project is an 'open access' one; that is, available to all people.

5. An argument I have presented in this chapter suggests that whiteness is indeed front and center in transhumanist body projects all over the world. In fact, future bodies may look more overtly White than anything else! Can you think of any empirical examples that would back up, or contradict, my claim?

Key Readings

Bostrom, N. (2005). 'In Defence of Posthuman Dignity'. *Bioethics* 9: 202–214. Nick Bostrom is a prolific author and advocate of transhuman politics. The above is a brief paper critiquing a host of bio-conservative naysayers and so-called luddites who believe that enhancing human capacities and extending human health span undermines human dignity. Bostrom presents an argument outlining how the shift to trans- and posthuman ways of thinking and living might actually lead to the ethical and moral betterment of society.

Fukuyama, F. (2002). *Our Posthuman Future: Consequences of the Biotechnology Revolution.* New York: Farrar, Straus & Giroux. Fukuyama is among the most outspoken critics of posthumanism and in this book he reveals his deep concerns regarding the cultural turn to techno-bodies. Ultimately, he argues for strong international regulation of human biotechnology and thoughtfully disposes of the most compelling counter-arguments. While readers might not agree that we are at risk of creating the sort of cyborg society Fukuyama predicts, it is hard to ignore his warnings of the potential consequences of a posthuman society.

Hewitt, R. (2005). *White Backlash and the Politics of Multiculturalism.* New York: Cambridge University Press. Drawing on extensive amounts of Hewitt's own ethnographic research into the resistance of White communities to multiculturalism, this book relates these phenomena to the 'backlash' to multiculturalism in the 1990s in the US, Australia, Canada, the UK, and other European countries. It examines White backlash within the unfolding social and political responses to race inequalities in the UK and the US from the 1960s to the present in the context of changes in social class and national political agendas. This book is unique in linking a detailed study of a community at a time of its critical importance to national debates over racism and multiculturalism, to historically wider international economic and social trends.

Said, E. (1978). *Orientalism.* New York: Pantheon Books. This book is normally singled out by post-colonial scholars as the pioneering text in the field. In the book, Said describes and critiques 'Orientalism' (which he perceived as a constellation of false assumptions underlying Western attitudes toward the East) and outlines its legacy on global power relations. Said claims that a subtle and persistent Eurocentric prejudice against Arabo-Islamic peoples and their culture is still alive and well in society. He further argues that a long tradition of false and romanticized images of Asia and the Middle East in Western culture had served as an implicit justification for Europe's and the United States' ongoing colonial and imperial ambitions.

Wise, T. (2007). *White Like Me: Reflections on Race from a Privileged Son*. New York: Soft Skull Press. Wise offers a highly personal examination of the ways in which racial privilege shapes the lives of most White Americans, overtly racist or not, to the detriment of people of colour, themselves, and society. The book shows the breadth and depth of the phenomenon within institutions such as education, employment, housing, criminal justice, and health care. What I especially like about the book is how Wise provides a rich memoir that will inspire activists, educators, or anyone interested in understanding the way that race continues to shape the experiences of people in America and elsewhere.

World Transhumanist Association. (2002). *The Transhumanist Declaration*. http:// transhumanism.org/index.php/WTA/declaration/. The WTA's declaration is widely regarded as a key public definition on the promises and prospects of a transhuman future. This is a straightforward and relatively jargon-free introduction to the spirit and ethos of the transhumanist new social movement.

Web Links

Anders transhuman web page (www.aleph.se/Trans). This web resource provides perhaps the most comprehensive analysis and cataloguing of key transhumanist ideas and concepts. Contained on its pages is a veritable treasure trove of information on the social and political implications of transhumanism, and a dictionary of transhumanist terms.

Center for the Study of White American Culture (www.euroamerican.org). This page is an academic resource site linking to key publications related to the ways in which whiteness in America affects the lives of racialized Others.

Humanity+ (http://humanityplus.org). Perhaps the flagship website of the transhumanist new social movement. The *Humanity+* website is not only an information beacon for anyone interested in the subject of transhumanism, it is an organizing tool for conferences, workshops, and speaker series at universities and other social institutions.

Nick Bostrom (www.nickbostrom.com). Nick Bostrom is the Director of the Future of Humanity Institute and the most outspoken advocate of transhumanism. Bostrom's page contains a wealth of information and reading resources for people interested in either introductory or advanced understandings of transhumanism.

Stelarc (www.stelarc.va.com.au). Stelarc is a transhuman performance artist whose works focus heavily on extending the capabilities of the human body; usually involving robotics or other relatively modern technology integrated with his body. He is currently a Professor in the School of Arts at Brunel University (UK).

Key Terms

Backlash: The concept of backlash typically refers to a negative reaction from a majority group directed against those minorities or underprivileged following an advance or progress in the latter's civic or legal rights. A backlash is, in many ways, a political, material, and popular cultural 'push back' by the majority against an upstart minority. Critics of the masculinity crisis often view its advocates as a pedantic backlash movement against feminism, gay and lesbian movements, and multiculturalism movements.

Extropian: A person who views the physical body as merely a prosthesis of the mind, and who embraces advanced technology as a means of saving the mind from the trappings and faults of the organic body. An extropian believes individuals must be allowed to pursue self-modification without limit, and believes one should constantly strive to extend the human life-course by integrating the body with life-enhancing computer and nanotechnological equipment. This person is roughly equivalent to a transhuman, or perhaps even a posthuman.

Libertarianism: A term with multiple meanings, but generally refers to an ideology or a political philosophy maintaining that all persons are the absolute owners of their own lives and as such should be free to do whatever they wish with their persons or property, provided they grant others the same liberty. Libertarianism is an old political belief in North America with roots in capitalist conceptions of free market relationships between producers and consumers.

New social movement: A new social movement is a voluntary and oftentimes globally connected consortium of actors primarily pursuing identity-based rights or civic rights rather than seeking outright material changes to the distribution of opportunity and wealth in a society. Many new social movements (women's rights, gay rights, or the environmentalist movement, for example) tend to emphasize social changes in identity, ideology, lifestyle, and culture, rather than pushing for specific changes in public or economic policy.

Physical cultural studies (PCS): A disciplinary perspective or socio-cultural sub-field of studies that pays particular attention to how bodies, their experiences, and their representations are articulated as meaningful within particular socio-cultural and historical contexts. In other words, PCS researchers pay attention to, and critique, the manners by which bodies are organized and shaped through social relationships, how they are influenced by relations of social power, and how physical styles of life common among a group signify their collective identities.

Post-colonial studies: A sub-field within the social sciences drawing together researchers and theorists from disciplines such as literary studies, political science, art history, human geography, sociology, women's studies, media and communications, and philosophy to name a few. Post-colonial studies examines the impacts of Western colonialism on developing nations and their cultural practices, and how contemporary relations of power across the globe tend to be framed by dominant Western ways of thinking, knowing, and acting.

Posthuman: A person who has transcended the limitations and needs of the organic body through interfacing with machines and technology. A posthuman is neither pure person nor pure machine but an amalgamation of both. Posthumans could be a symbiosis of human and artificial intelligence, uploaded consciousnesses, or the result of making many smaller but cumulatively profound technological augmentations to a biological human. Some examples of the latter are redesigning the human organism using advanced nanotechnology or radical enhancement using some combination of technologies such as genetic engineering, psychopharmacology, life extension therapies, neural interfaces, advanced information management tools, memory enhancing drugs, wearable or implanted computers, and cognitive techniques.

Transhuman: A person in *transition* between human and posthuman. The difference between the posthuman and other hypothetical sophisticated non-humans is that a posthuman *was once* a relatively pure human, either in its lifetime or in the lifetimes of some or all of its direct ancestors. A prerequisite for a posthuman is a transhuman, the point at which the human being begins surpassing his or her own limitations, but is still recognizable as a human person. In this sense, the transition between human and posthuman may be viewed as a continuum rather than an all-or-nothing event.

Epilogue

A short while ago my friend Chris came to visit from his home in England. He was a reminder of what I loved about living in England, and I enjoyed reminiscing with him about my time there in the few days he lodged with us. But frustratingly, almost every conversation with Chris involves a lengthy account of his recent dating exploits and mishaps. Chris has spent the better part of the last five years as a member of an online dating community. Dozens of dates, liaisons, and online hook-ups during the period have not led him to a soulmate. While he excels at work and has a dense social network in the UK, the fear of never settling down and having a family is written across Chris's face. His athletic abilities wane with every passing year, the physical accoutrements he surrounds himself with progressively lose their lustre, and he struggles to understand the masculine teleology of his life. He could very well be a man in crisis because a part of him remains committed to the lifestyles, life paths, and life choices of our modernist fathers. In many ways, Chris is a carbon copy of me with a few important distinctions. Legions of men in Canada are the same; the pages of this book provide whispers of such testimony. They cling to past ideals about men and being male, but also explore the merits of new masculinities.

Writing the final words in this book compel me to confront the failing and frail masculine image of my brother. At 47 years old, he is divorced for the fifth time. He is the father of four children whom he never sees, and probably never will for the majority of his life. Spartacus was diagnosed with epilepsy in the past year, and his condition worsens on a monthly basis. He is a caricature of his former self, an aging playboy with a bleak future. His jokes and his charm are no longer alluring, his body is broken, and any semblance of hegemony in his life has evaporated. The once sexual satyr and respected businessman is an overweight and distraught recluse. I cry on a regular basis when I remember the summer days from our youth when the world sat at his feet and he was a god. I recall driving around in his gleaming, sex-on-wheels 1979 Trans-Am listening to Foreigner or Loverboy while everyone in the neighbourhood waved. What happened? Was Spartacus a part of the last generation of macho men for whom our society no longer has patience? If a case could be made for crisis masculinity, surely it is my brother. Or even now, in his mid-life, do his trials and tribulations only represent an extreme case of the folly of chasing, embodying, and reproducing a bastardized idea of hegemonic masculinity? My brother certainly identified and embodied the standards of traditional hegemonic masculinity, but did not ever access the structural or political economic basis of being truly hegemonic. This is a common tale in North America—hegemony in hyper-real form or image with no material substance. Perhaps the greatest difference between my brother's generation and mine, as I believe stories contained in this book attest, is that men have learned how to buy and live and represent small-scale, pastiche hegemony in very clever ways.

At the end of a lecture when a student is challenging me about crisis masculinities, or I force myself to render an analytic conclusion on the subject, I cannot say that Chris or I or the men of our generation face any quantitatively greater or more existentially dire crisis than generations of boys and men preceding us. But the kinds of crisis we face are qualitatively different. Most men of my age never worried about conscription and going to war, we faced no major economic implosion (perhaps until now), we encountered unparalleled access to education and leisure time, and we have matured with girls and women who support rather than subvert or challenge our social ambitions. But boys in my age cohort were medicalized, scientized, policed, counselled, secularized, silenced, blamed, culturally dissected, and oftentimes derided as perpetrators of discrimination, more so than any generation of boys before us in Canadian history. This level of cultural and social governmentality creates crisis. Like others in our complex socio-cultural milieu in Canada, we were also moulded to consume, objectify ourselves, feel fear and doubt about our futures, and evolve in hyper-reflexive and obsessed ways. Even more crisis is created in such a nexus. The result is that men like Chris, me, and those whom I have introduced in this book are at times perplexed about what constitutes gender, race, class, nationality, and other aspects of our identities. We wonder if masculinity is a socially good or a bad thing, and whether the identity category should figure into our habituses or inform our life choices.

My own research on men and masculinities over the last decade and a half further teaches me that while many men rarely reflect on masculinity or view it as anything other than a cultural given, growing numbers of boys and men have adopted a chameleon-like, omnivore masculinity. The men I have studied frequently describe how, in order to secure power, one needs to dramaturgically present oneself as a flexible, liquid male across social settings. Hegemonic masculinities now strive to incorporate rather than negate or dissolve other masculinities. When it serves a purpose, the powerful adopt feminine, classed, sexed, religious, ethnically or racially different, or transnational masculinities to appear as anything ranging from cool, hip, indifferent, cultured, tough, worldly, emotional, austere, or down-to-earth. A man can be hegemonic, powerful, and authoritarian in any context if he simply knows the codes and rules dictating wanted versus unwanted (gender) performances in that setting. The global male chameleon David Beckham is a prime example. Beckham has success-fully embodied hard, soft, gay, raced, and classed masculinities to be 'the man' in the widest range of settings possible. Beckham teaches us how there can be no singular hegemonic masculinity in late-modern, liquid society because what constitutes the 'ideal' male in one setting can be completely dissimilar to the gender rules in another. Furthermore, by firmly and finally dislodging the political–economic basis of hegemonic masculinity from theoretical under-standings of it, sociologists grasp hegemony as part of the micro-politics of power. Contemporary hegemonic males shift wardrobes, languages, assertive-ness, demeanours, and gestures to order the space in which they exist. At any given time these men are not simply the directors but are the lead characters in the power play of their everyday lives. Men in crisis do not understand this social script and attempt to force a singular, rigid construction of maleness in every situation. They nearly always fail. The former are men who find local hegemony in many places, the latter perhaps one, two, or even none.

Upon further reflection of what 'men in (and out) of crisis' have taught me, mainstay academic accounts of men's gender anxiety and doubt appear largely exaggerated and dismissive of the recuperative and co-opting powers of dominant and hegemonic masculinities. Men are not dupes, I have learned, and may reframe crisis in power-producing manners. Notwithstanding diffuse cultural confusion about the stability of modernist identities and practices within Canada (which is palpable in any Canadian urban environment), the proliferation of new and alternative masculinities in Canada, as an offshoot of a supposed breakdown in the gendered vertical mosaic, has not been part of a new era of gender equality. What startles is the lack of empirically informed sociological accounts of how at least two generations of white, middle-class, urban boys and men 'in crisis' continue to wield situated dominance and power in a majority of social institutions. Crisis advocates and naysayers might do well to theorize masculinities in the middle; in that, while attacks to traditional masculine identities have been waged in North America for well over four decades and have created gender crisis, such a crisis partly spawned the rein-vention of dominant masculinities. As I stated earlier in the book, hegemonic masculinity had to die so that a legion of everyday hegemonic masculinities could be born. My friend Chris will forever exist in gender purgatory until he realizes the power of multiple masculinities.

Two huge watercolour portraits hang over my workspace at home, one of my father and the other of my Grandfather Atkinson. I stare at them from time to time and reflect on the kind of power each embodied as matured men. My father was a quasi-dominant figure in the house who laboured with his mind for endless hours and distanced himself from his family. His power surfaced at the end of every month, summarized neatly by a few imprinted numbers on a pay stub. Grandfather led men into battle, supervised them at work, and held court at his social club on Friday nights. He died in agony in a small hospital bed in Halifax after years of struggling with illness, alienation from his family, and nightmares from the field of war. According to most sociological theory and discourse, these men were never members of a crisis generation. If they were not, how the hell could I think I was ever in crisis?

References

Acland, C. 1995. *Youth, Murder, Spectacle: The Cultural Politics of 'Youth in Crisis'*. Boulder: Westview Press.

Adkins, L. 2002. *Revisions: Gender and Sexuality in Late Modernity*. New York: McGraw-Hill.

Adorno, T., and M. Horkheimer. 1944. *The Dialetic of Enlightenment*. London: Verso.

Agliata, D., and S. Tantleff-Dunn. 2004. 'The Impact of Media Exposure on Males' Body Image', *Journal of Social and Clinical Psychology*, 23: 7–22.

Agnew, R. 1992. 'Foundation for a General Strain Theory of Crime and Delinquency', *Criminology*, 30: 47–87.

Alba, J. 2000. 'Dimensions of Consumer Expertise . . . or Lack Thereof. *Advances in Consumer Research*, 27: 1–9.

Allen, J. 2002. 'Men Interminably in Crisis? Historians on Masculinity, Sexual Boundaries, and Manhood', *Radical History Review*, 82: 191–207.

Allen, T. 1994. *The Invention of the White Race*. London: Verso.

Althusser, L. 1971. *Lenin and Philosophy and Other Essays*. London: Monthly Review Press.

American Society of Plastic Surgeons. 2007. '2006 Quick Gender Facts Cosmetic Plastic Surgery', Arlington Heights, IL: Department of Public Relations, www.plasticsurgery.org.

Anderson, B. 1991. *Imagined Communities*. London: Verso.

Andrews, D. 2002. 'Coming to Terms with Cultural Studies', *Journal of Sport & Social Issues*, 26: 110–17.

———. 2004. *Manchester United: A Thematic Study*. London: Routledge.

———. 2006. *Sport-Commerce-Culture*. New York: Peter Lang.

———. 2008. 'Kinesiology's Inconvenient Truth and the Physical Cultural Studies Imperative', *Quest*, 60: 45–62.

Anderson, E. 2004. *In the Game: Gay Athletes and the Cult of Masculinity*. Albany: SUNY Press.

Appadurai, A. 1997. *Modernity at Large: Cultural Dimensions of Globalization*. Minneapolis: University of Minnesota Press.

Ashe, F. 2007. *The New Politics of Masculinity*. London: Routledge.

Associated Press. 2009. 'Players, NHL: League Should Handle It'. *Calgary Herald*, 8 March.

Atkinson, M. 2003a. *Tattooed: The Sociogenesis of a Body Art*. Toronto: University of Toronto Press.

———. 2003b. 'The Civilizing of Resistance: Straightedge Tattooing', *Deviant Behavior*, 24: 197–220.

———. 2004. 'Tattooing and Civilizing Processes: Body Modification as Self-Control', *Canadian Review of Sociology and Anthropology*, 42: 1–31.

———. 2006. 'Masks of Masculinity: Cosmetic Surgery and (Sur)passing Strategies', pp. 247–61, in *Body/Embodiment: Symbolic Interaction and the Sociology of the Body*, P. Vanni and D. Waskul, eds. London: Ashgate.

———. 2007. 'Playing with Fire: Masculinity and Exercise Supplements', *Sociology of Sport Journal*, 24: 166–86.

———. 2008a. 'Exploring Male Femininity in the Crisis: Men and Cosmetic Surgery', *Body & Society*, 14: 67–87.

———. 2008b. 'Triathlon, Suffering, and Exciting Significance', *Leisure Studies*, 27: 165–80.

———. 2008c. Battleground: Sports. Boulder: Greenwood.

———. 2010. 'Tattoos and Transhumanism: On the Bioethics of Popular Culture', Unpublished paper presented at Lehigh Humanities Center, Lehigh University, January 28.

Atkinson, M., and K. Young. 2003. 'Terror Games: Media Treatment of Security Issues at the 2002 Winter Olympic Games', *Olympika: An International Journal of Olympic Studies*, 11: 53–78.

———. 2008. *Sport, Deviance and Social Control*. Champaign: Human Kinetics.

Attwood, F. 2005. '"Tits and Ass and Porn and Fighting": Male Heterosexuality in Magazines for Men', *International Journal of Cultural Studies*, 8: 83–100.

Awkward, M. 2002. 'Black Male Trouble: The Challenges for Rethinking Masculine Differences', pp. 290–304 in J. Gardiner, ed. *Masculinity Studies and Feminist Theory: New Directions*. New York: Columbia University Press.

Baglia, J. 2005. *The Viagra Ad Venture: Masculinity, Media, and the Performance of Sexual Health*. New York: Peter Lang Publishing.

Bagramyan I. 2008. *Changing Masculinities: Discourse Analysis of Masculinity*. Saarbrucken: VDM Verlag.

Bailey, R. 2005. *Liberation Biology: The Scientific and Moral Case For the Biotech Revolution*. New York: Prometheus Books.

Bargh, J. 2002. 'Losing Consciousness: Automatic Influences on Consumer Judgment, Behavior, and Motivation', *The Journal of Consumer Research*, 29: 280–5.

Barnes, J. 1988. *Sport and the Law in Canada*. Toronto: Butterworths.

Baudrillard, J. 1983. *Simulations*. New York: Semiotext(e).

———. 1986. *America*. Paris: Grasset.

———. 1990. *Fatal Strategies*. New York: Semiotext(e).

———. 1994. *Figures de L'alterite*. Paris: Descartes & Cie.

———. 1995. *Simulation and Simulacra*. Ann Arbor: University of Michigan Press.

———. 1996. *The Perfect Crime*. New York: Verso.

———. 2001. 'The Spirit of Terrorism', *Le Monde*, November 2, p. 32.

———. 2002. *Screened Out*. London: Verso.

———. 2003. *Cool Memories IV*. London: Verso.

Bauman, Z. 2000. *Liquid Modernity*. Cambridge: Basil Blackwell.

Baurneister, R. 2002. 'Yielding to Temptation: Self-Control Failure, Impulsive Purchasing, and Consumer Behavior', *Journal of Consumer Research*, 28: 670–6.

Beal, B. 1995. 'Disqualifying the Official: An Exploration of Social Resistance through the Subculture of Skateboarding', *Sociology of Sport Journal*, 12: 252–67.

Beasley, C. 2008. 'Re-Thinking Hegemonic Masculinity in a Globalising World', pp. 108–21 in M. González and V. Seidler, eds., *Gender Identities in a Globalized World*. New York: Prometheus books.

Beck, U. 1991. *Ecological Enlightenment: Essays on the Politics of the Risk Society*. Amherst: Prometheus.

———. 1992. *Risk Society: Towards a New Modernity*. London: Sage.

———. 1999. *World Risk Society*. Cambridge: Polity Press.

Belknap, J. 2006. *The Invisible Woman: Gender, Crime, and Justice*. Florence: Wadsworth.

Benedict, J. 1997. *Athletes and Acquaintance Rape*. Thousand Oaks: Sage.

———. 2004. *Out of Bounds: Inside the NBA's Culture of Rape*. New York: Harper Collins.

Benwell, B. 2003. *Masculinity and Men's Lifestyle Magazines*. Oxford: Blackwell.

———. 2004. 'Ironic Discourse: Evasive Masculinity in British Men's Lifestyle Magazines', *Men and Masculinities*, 7: 3–21.

Berger, M. 1999. *White Lies: Race and the Myths of Whiteness*. New York: Farrar, Straus & Giroux.

Bhabha, H. 1994. *The Location of Culture*. London: Routledge.

Biederman, J., E. Mick, S. Faraone, E. Braaten, A. Doyle, T. Spencer, T. Wilens, E. Frazier, and M. Johnson. 2002. 'Influence of Gender on Attention Deficit Hyperactivity Disorder in Children Referred to a Psychiatric Clinic', *American Journal of Psychiatry*, 159: 36–42.

Blechner, M. 2002. 'Intimacy, Pleasure, Risk, and Safety', *Journal of Gay and Lesbian Psychotherapy*, 6: 27–33.

Bonnett, A. 2000. *White Identities: Historical and International Perspectives*. Harlow: Prentice-Hall.

Bordo, S. 1995. 'Reading the Slender Body', pp. 467–90 in N. Tuana and R. Tong, eds., *Feminism and Philosophy*. Boulder: Westview Press.

———. 1999. 'Reading the Male Body', pp. 265–306 in *The Male Body*, L. Goldstein, ed. Ann Arbor: Michigan University Press.

————. 2000. *The Male Body: A New Look at Men in Public and in Private*. New York: Farrar, Straus & Giroux.

Borgmann, T. 1993. *Crossing the Postmodern Divide*. Chicago: University of Chicago Press.

Bostrom, N. 1999. 'The Doomsday Argument is Alive and Kicking', *Mind*, 108: 539–50.

————. 2005. 'In Defence of Posthuman Dignity', *Bioethics*, 9: 202–14.

————. 2008. 'Why I Want to be Posthuman When I Grow Up', pp. 107–37 in B. Gordijn and R. Chadwick, eds., *Medical Enhancement and Posthumanity*. New York: Springer.

Bourdieu, P. 1984. *Distinction: A Social Critique of the Judgement of Taste*. Cambridge: Harvard University Press.

————. 2005. *Masculine Domination*. Stanford: Stanford University Press.

Brackenridge, C. 1997. *Child Protection in Sport: Politics, Procedures, and Systems. Report on a Sport Council Seminar for National Governing Bodies*. Cheltenham: C&GCHE.

————. 2001. *Spoilsports: Understanding and Preventing Sexual Exploitation in Sport*. London: Routledge.

Brake, M. 1995. *Comparative Youth Culture*. London: Routledge.

Braun, D., S. Sunday, A. Huang, and K. Halmi. 1999. 'More Males Seek Treatment for Eating Disorders', *International Journal of Eating Disorders*, 25: 415–24.

Brinkgreve, C. 2004. 'Elias in Gender Relations: The Changing Balance of Power Between the Sexes', pp. 67–88 in S. Loyal and S. Quilley, eds., *The Sociology of Norbert Elias*. Cambridge: Cambridge University Press.

Burstyn, V. 1999. *The Rites of Men: Manhood, Politics, and the Culture of Sport*. Toronto: University of Toronto Press.

Butler, J. 1990. *Gender Trouble: Feminism and the Subversion of Identity*. New York: Routledge.

Butryn, T. 2003. 'Posthuman Podiums: Cyborg Narratives of Elite Track and Field Athletes', *Sociology of Sport Journal*, 20: 17–39.

Byron, R. 2003. *Retrenchment and Regeneration in Rural Newfoundland*. Toronto: University of Toronto Press.

Campos, P. 2004. *The Obesity Epidemic*. New York: Penguin.

CANSIM. 2007. Data retrieved from http://www4.hrsdc.gc.ca/.3ndic.1t.4r@-eng.jsp?iid=57.

Castells, M. 2000 [1996]. *The Rise of the Network Society*. Oxford: Blackwell.

CBC News. 2003. 'Alberta Hockey Coaches suspended for Ending Violent Games', www.cbc.ca, 16 January.

Chaney, D. 1994. *The Cultural Turn*. London: Routledge.

Chapman. R., and J. Rutherford. 1988. *Male Order: Unwrapping Masculinity*. London: Lawrence and Wishart.

Clare, A. 2000. *On Men: Masculinity in Crisis*. London: Chatto and Windus.

Coakley, J., and P. Donnelly. 2005. *Sports in Society: Issues and Controversies*. Toronto: McGraw-Hill Ryerson.

Cohen, A. 1955. *Delinquent Boys: The Culture of the Gang*. New York: Free Press.

Cohen, J., and P. Harvey. 2006. 'Misconceptions of Gender: Sex, Masculinity, and the Measurement of Crime', *The Journal of Men's Studies*, 14: 223–33.

Cohen, L., and M. Felson. 1979. 'Social Change and Crime Rate Trends: A Routine Activity Approach', *American Sociological Review*, 44: 588–608.

Cohen, P. 1972. 'Subcultural Conflict and Working Class Communities', *Working Papers in Cultural Studies, 2*. Birmingham: Centre for Contemporary Cultural Studies.

Cohen, S. 1972. *Folk Devils and Moral Panics: The Creation of the Mods and Rockers*. London: MacGibbon and Kee.

Colburn, K. 1985. 'Honour, Ritual, and Violence in Ice Hockey', *Canadian Journal of Sociology*, 10: 153–70.

Collier, R. 1998. *Masculinities, Crime and Criminology*. London: Sage.

Connell, R. 1983. *Which Way Is Up?* London/Boston: Allen & Unwin.

———. 1987. *Gender and Power: Society, the Person and Sexual Politics*. California: Stanford University Press.

———. 1990. 'A Whole New World: Remaking Masculinity in the Context of the Environmental Movement', *Gender & Society*, 4: 452–478.

———. 1993. 'The Big Picture: Masculinities in Recent World History', *Theory and Society*, 22: 597–623.

———. 2005. *Masculinities*. Berkeley: University of California Press.

Connell, R., and J. Messerschmidt. 2005. 'Hegemonic Masculinity: Rethinking the Concept', *Gender & Society*, 19: 829–59.

Connell, R., and J. Wood. 2005. 'Globalisation and Business Masculinities', *Men and Masculinities*, 7: 347–64.

Copenhaver, M., S. Lash, and R. Eisler. 2000. 'Masculine Gender-Role Stress, Anger, and Male Intimate Abusiveness: Implications for Men's Relationships', *Sex Roles*, 5/6: 405–14.

Coupland, D. 1991. *Generation X: Tales for an Accelerated Culture*. New York: St. Martin's Press.

Cregan, K. 2006. *The Sociology of the Body*. London: Sage.

Crewe, B. 2003. *Representing Men: Cultural Production and Producers in the Men's Magazine Market*. Oxford: Berg.

Critser, G. 2002. *Fat Land: How Americans Became the Fattest People in the World*. New York: Houghton Mifflin.

Culbertson, L. 2007. 'Human-ness, Dehumanisation, and Performance Enhancement', *Sport, Ethics and Philosophy*, 1: 195–214.

Daly M., and M. Wilson. 2005. 'Human Behavior as Animal Behavior', pp. 393–408 in J. Bolhuis and L. Giraldeau, eds., *Behavior of Animals: Mechanisms, Function, and Evolution*. Oxford: Blackwell Publishing.

Davidson, J., and N. Moore. 2005. *Speaking Of Sexuality: Interdisciplinary Readings*. Los Angeles: Roxbury.

Davis, A. 1983. *Women, Race and Class*. New York: Vintage.

Davis, K. 2002. *Dubious Equalities and Embodied Differences: Cultural Studies and Cosmetic Surgery*. New York: Rowman and Littlefield.

Dawkins, R. 1976. *The Selfish Gene*. Oxford: Oxford University Press.

de Certeau, M. 1984. *The Practice of Everyday Life*. Berkeley: University of California Press.

Debord, G. 1967. *Society of the Spectacle*. Detroit: Black & Red.

DeKeseredy, W., D. Ellis, and S. Alvi. 2005. *Deviance and Crime: Theory, Research and Policy*. Cincinnati: Anderson Publishing.

DeKeseredy, W., and M. Schwartz. 2005. 'Masculinities and Interpersonal Violence in North America', pp. 353–66 in R. Connell, J. Hearn, and M. Kimmel, eds., *The Handbook of Studies on Men and Masculinities*. Thousand Oaks: Sage.

Delaplace, J.-M. 2005. *George Hébert: Sculpter du corps*. Paris: Vuibert.

Deleuze, G., and F. Guattari. 1987. *A Thousand Plateaus*. Minneapolis: University of Minnesota Press.

Deleuze, G., and C. Parnet. 1987. *Dialogues*. New York: Columbia University Press.

Denzin, N. 1989. *Interpretive Interactionism*. Newbury Park: Sage.

Derrida, J. 1978. *Writing and Difference*. London: Routledge.

Digby, T. 1998. *Men Doing Feminism*. New York: Routledge.

Dipiero, T. 2001. *White Men Aren't*. Durham: Duke University Press.

Donaldson, M. 1993. 'What Is Hegemonic Masculinity?' *Theory and Society*, 22: 643–57.

Drexler, K. 1992. *Nanosystems: Molecular Machinery, Manufacturing, and Computation*. New York: John Wiley & Sons.

Dublin, M. 1992. *Futurehype: The Tyranny of Prophecy*. New York: Penguin Books.

Duneier, M. 2000. *Sidewalk*. New York: Farrar, Straus & Giroux.

Dunn, R. 1998. *Identity Crises: A Social Critique of Postmodernity*. Minneapolis: University of Minnesota Press.

Dunning, E. 1999. *Sport Matters: Sociological Studies of Sport, Violence, and Civilisation*. London: Routledge.

Durkheim, E. 1956. *The Division of Labor in Society*. New York: The Free Press.

Dutton, D. 2006. *Rethinking Domestic Violence*. Vancouver: University of British Columbia Press.

Dyer, R. 1997. *White*. New York: Routledge.

Edwards, T. 2006. *Cultures of Masculinity*. London: Routledge.

———. 2007. *Men in the Mirror*. London: Cassell.

Ehrenreich, B. 1997. *Blood Rites: Origins and History of the Passions of War*. New York: Henry Holt and Company.

Elias, N. 1978. *What is Sociology?* London: Hutchinson.

———. 1983. *The Court Society.* Oxford: Basil Blackwell.

———. 1996. *The Germans: Studies of Power Struggles and the Development of Habitus in the Nineteenth and Twentieth Centuries.* Oxford: Polity Press.

———. 2002. *The Society of Individuals.* Oxford: Basil Blackwell.

———. 2004. *The Civilizing Process.* Oxford: Basil Blackwell.

Elias, N., and E. Dunning. 1986. *Quest for Excitement: Sport and Leisure in the Civilizing Process.* New York: Basil Blackwell.

Elias, N., and J. Scotson. 1965. *The Established and the Outsiders.* London: Sage.

Esfandiary, F. 1970. *Optimism One: The Emerging Radicalism.* New York: Norton.

Ettinger, R. 1979. *Man into Superman: The Startling Potential of Human Evolution.* New York: St. Martin's Press.

Evans, J., and E. Rich. 2006. 'Fat Ethics—the Obesity Discourse and Body Politics', *Social Theory and Health*, 3: 341–58.

Faludi, S. 1999. *Stiffed: The Betrayal of the American Man.* New York: William Morrow & Company.

———. 2007. *The Terror Dream: Fear and Fantasy in Post-9/11 America.* New York: Metropolitan Books.

Farr, K. 1988. 'Dominance Bonding Through the Good Old Boys Sociability Group', *Sex Roles*, 18: 259–77.

Farrell, W. 2001. *The Myth of Male Power: Why Men are the Disposable Sex.* London: Finch.

———. 2007. *Does Feminism Discriminate Against Men?* New York: Oxford University Press.

Faulkner, R. 1973. 'On Respect and Retribution: Toward an Ethnography of Violence', *Sociological Symposium*, 9: 17–36.

Featherstone, M. 1991. 'The Body in Consumer Culture', pp. 170–96 in M. Featherstone, M. Hepworth, and B. Turner, eds, *The Body: Social Process and Cultural Theory.* London: Routledge.

———. 2000. *Body Modification.* London: Sage.

Feirstein, B. 1982. *Real Men Don't Eat Quiche.* London: New English Library.

———. 1986. *Nice Guys Sleep Alone: Dating in the Difficult Eighties.* New York: Dell.

———. 1992. *Real Men Don't Bond: How to Be a Real Man in an Age of Whiners.* New York: Grand Central Publishing.

Ferree, M., J. Lorber, and B. Hess. 1999. *Revisioning Gender.* London: Sage.

Fiske, J. 1989. *Understanding Popular Culture.* Boston: Unwin Hyman.

Flocker, M. 2002. *The Metrosexual Guide to Style: A Handbook for the Modern Man.* New York: Perseus Books.

Flood, M., 1998. 'Men's Movements', *Community Quarterly*, 46: 62–71.

Flowers, R. 2003. *Male Crime and Deviance.* Springfield: Charles C. Thomas Publishers.

Fornäs, J. 1995. *Cultural Theory and Late Modernity.* London: Sage.

Foucault, M. 1967. 'Of other Spaces', Reprinted in *Diacritics*, 16 (1986): 22–7.

———. 1977. *Discipline and Punish: The Birth of the Prison*. London: Penguin Books.

———. 1978. 'Politics and the Study of Discourse'. *Ideology and Consciousness*, 3: 7–26.

———. 1980 [1979]. *Power/Knowledge: Selected Interviews and Other Writings 1972–1977*. New York: Pantheon.

———. 1981. *The History of Sexuality, volume 1: An introduction*. London: Allen Lane/Penguin Books.

———. 1983. *This is Not a Pipe*. Berkeley: University of California Press.

———. 1987. *The Use of Pleasure: The History of Sexuality, volume 2*. Harmondsworth: Penguin Books.

———. 1988. *Politics, Philosophy, Culture: Interviews and Other Writings*. London: Routledge.

Fox, J., and J. Levin. 2004. *The Will to Kill: Making Sense of Senseless Murder*. Needham Heights: Allyn & Bacon.

Francis, B. 1999. 'Lads, Lasses and New Labour: 14–16 Year Old Students' Responses to the Laddish Behaviour and Boys Underachievement Debate', *British Journal of Sociology of Education*, 20: 355–71.

Frank, A. 1991. *At the Will of the Body: Reflections on Illness*. Boston: Houghton.

———. 1995. *The Wounded Storyteller: Body, Illness and Ethics*. Chicago: University of Chicago Press.

———. 2004a. 'Emily's Scars: Surgical Shapings, Technoluxe, and Bioethics', *Hastings Center Report*, 34: 18–29.

———. 2004b. *The Renewal of Generosity: Illness, Hospitality, and Dialogue*. Chicago: University of Chicago Press.

Freud, S. 1962. *Civilization and its Discontents*. London: W.W. Norton.

Fromm, E. 1941. *The Anatomy of Human Destructiveness*. New York: Holt, Rinehart & Winston.

Fukuyama, F. 2002. *Our Posthuman Future: Consequences of the Biotechnology Revolution*. London: Farrar, Straus & Giroux.

Garcia, G. 2008. *The Decline of Men: How the American Male is Turning Out, Flipping Off, and Giving Up His Future*. New York: Harper.

Garlick, S. 2004. 'What is a Man? Heterosexuality and the Technology of Masculinity', *Men and Masculinities*, 6: 156–72.

Garovich-Szabo, L., and M. Lueptow. 2001. 'Social Change and the Persistence of Sex Typing: 1974–1997', *Social Forces*, 80: 1–36.

Garrison, E. 2000. 'US Feminism—Grrrl Style! Youth Subculture and the Technologics of the Third Wave', *Feminist Studies*, 6: 141–70.

Gauthier, D., and C. Forsyth. 1999. 'Bareback Sex, Bug Chasing, and the Gift of Death'. *Deviant Behavior*, 20: 85–100.

Giddens, A. 1991. *Modernity and Self-Identity: Self and Society in the Late Modern Age*. Cambridge: Polity.

———. 1998. *The Third Way: The Renewal of Social Democracy*. Cambridge: Polity.

———. 2001. *The Global Third Way Debate*. Cambridge: Polity.

Gill, R. 2004. 'Power and the Production of Subjects: A Genealogy of the New Man and the New Lad', pp. 79–210 in B. Benwell, ed., *Masculinity and Men's Lifestyle Magazine*. Oxford: Blackwell.

———. 2005. *Gender and the Media*. Cambridge: Polity.

Gill, R., K. Henwood, and C. McLean. 2005. 'Body Projects and the Regulation of Normative Masculinity', *Body and Society*, 11: 37–62.

Gill, R., and C. McLean. 2002. 'Knowing Your Place: Gender and Reflexivity in Two Ethnographies', *Sociological Research Online*, 7, www.socresonline.org.uk/7/2/gill.html.

Gillespie, R. 1996. 'Women, the Body, and Brand Extension in Medicine: Cosmetic Surgery and the Paradox of Choice', *Women and Health*, 24: 69–85.

Gillett, J., P. White, and K. Young. 1999. 'The Prime Minister of Saturday Night: Don Cherry, the CBC and the Cultural Production of Intolerance', pp. 59–72 in H. Holmes and D. Taras, eds., *Seeing Ourselves: Media, Power and Policy in Canada*. Toronto: Harcourt, Brace & Jovanovich.

Gilman, C. 1951. *Herland*. New York: Pantheon.

Gilroy, P. 2006. 'Post-Colonialism and Multiculturalism', pp. 656–76 in J. Dryzek, B. Honig and A. Phillips, eds., *The Oxford Handbook of Political Theory*. Oxford: Oxford University Press.

Gilroy, P., L. Grossberg, and A. McRobbie. 2000. *Without Guarantees: In Honour of Stuart Hall*. London: Verso.

Godenzi, A. 1999. 'Style or Substance: Men's Response to Feminist Challenge', *Men and Masculinities*, 1: 385–92.

Goffman, E. 1959. *The Presentation of Self in Everyday life*. Garden City: Doubleday-Anchor.

———. 1961. *Asylums*. Chicago: Aldine.

———. 1963. *Stigma*. Garden City: Doubleday-Anchor.

Goldberg, S. 1977. *The Inevitability of Patriarchy*. New York: Maurice Temple Smith.

Gomme, I. 2006. *The Shadow Line: Deviance and Crime in Canada*. Toronto: Nelson Thomson.

Gottfredson, M., and T. Hirschi. 1990. *A General Theory of Crime*. San Jose: Stanford University Press.

Gramsci, A. 1971. *Selections from the Prison Notebooks*. London: Lawrence & Wishart.

Grogan, S., and H. Richards. 2002. 'Body Image: Focus Groups with Boys and Men', *Men and Masculinities*, 4: 219–32.

Grossberg, L. 1997. *Bringing it All Back Home: Essays on Cultural Studies*. Durham: Duke University Press.

Grov, C., and J. Parsons. 2006. 'Bugchasing and Giftgiving: The Potential for HIV Transmission Among Barebackers on the Internet', AIDS *Education and Prevention*, 18: 490–503.

Gruneau, R., and D. Whitson. 1993. *Hockey Night in Canada: Sport, Identities, and Cultural Practices*. Toronto: Garamond.

Gubrium, J., and J. Holstein. 1997. *The New Language of Qualitative Method*. New York: Oxford University Press.

Gurian, M. 1997. *The Wonder of Boys: What Parents, Mentors and Educators Can Do to Shape Boys Into Exceptional Men*. Los Angeles: Harcher.

Gurr, T. 1973. *Why Men Rebel*. Princeton: Princeton University Press.

Gurr, T., and J. Ross. 2003. *Violence in Canada: Sociopolitical Perspectives*. New Brunswick: Transaction.

Hall, S. 1980. 'Encoding/decoding', pp. 128–38 in *Culture, Media, Language: Working Papers in Cultural Studies, 1972–79*, Centre for Contemporary Cultural Studies. London: Hutchinson.

Hall, S., and T. Jefferson. 1976. *Resistance Through Rituals: Youth Subcultures in Post-war Britain*. London: Hutchinson.

Hamilton, R. 1996. *Gendering the Vertical Mosaic: Feminist Perspectives on Canadian Society*. Toronto: Pearson Prentice Hall.

Hannerz, U. 1990. 'Cosmopolitans and Locals in World Culture', *Theory, Culture & Society*, 7: 237–51.

———. 1996. *Transnational Connections*. London: Routledge.

Hardt, M., and A. Negri. 2004. *Multitude*. London: Routledge.

Harpham, G. 1987. *The Ascetic Imperative in Culture and Criticism*. Chicago: University of Chicago Press.

Hathaway, A., and M. Atkinson. 2003. 'Active Interview Tactics in Research on Public Deviance: Exploring the Two Cop Personas', *Field Methods*, 15: 161–85.

Hatty, S. 2000. *Masculinities, Violence, and Culture*. London: Sage.

Hearn, J. 1998. *The Violence of Men: How Men Talk About and How Agencies Respond to Men's Violence to Women*. London: Sage.

———. 1999. 'Policy Development and Changing Men Inside and Outside Agencies', *International Association for Studies on Men Newsletter*, 6: 61–64.

Heartfield, J. 2002. 'There is No Masculinity Crisis', *Gender Online Journal*, 35, www.genders.org/g35/g35_heartfield.html.

Hebdige, D. 1979. *Subculture: The Meaning of Style*. New York: Methuen and Company.

———. 1987. *Hiding in the Light: On Images and Things*. London: Routledge.

Heidegger, M. 1977 [1954]. 'On the Question Concerning Technology', pp. 283–317, in D. Krell, ed., *Martin Heidegger: Basic Writings*. New York: Harper and Row.

Helmes-Hayes, R., and J. Curtis. 1998. *The Vertical Mosaic Revisited*. Toronto: University of Toronto Press.

Hewitt, R. 2005. *White Backlash and the Politics of Multiculturalism*. New York: Cambridge University Press.

Hill, M. 2004. *After Whiteness: Unmaking an American Majority.* New York: New York University Press.

Hise, R. 2004. *The War Against Men*. Oakland: Elderberry Press.

Hoff-Sommers, C. 2000. *The War Against Boys: How Misguided Feminism Is Harming Our Young Men*. New York: Simon & Schuster.

hooks, b. 1984. *Feminist Theory from Margin to Center*. Boston: South End Press.

———. 2003. *We Real Cool: Black Men And Masculinity*. New York: Routledge.

Horrocks, R. 1994. *Masculinity in Crisis: Myths, Fantasies, and Realities*. Basingstoke: St Martin's Press.

Huggins, C. 2002. 'Baby's Injury Points to Danger of Kids Imitating TV', *Toronto Star*, June 26, B4.

Hughes, R., and J. Coakley. 1991. 'Positive Deviance Among Athletes: The Implications of Overconformity to the Sport Ethic', *Sociology of Sport Journal*, 8: 307–25.

Huxley, J. 1927. *Religion Without Revelation*. London: E. Benn.

Ingham, A. 1997. 'Toward a Department of Physical Cultural Studies and an End to Tribal Warfare', pp. 157–82 in J. Fernandez-Balboa, ed., *Critical Postmodernism in Human Movement, Physical Education, and Sport*. Albany: State University of New York Press.

Irwin, D. 1999. 'The Straight Edge Subculture: Examining the Youths' Drug-free Way', *Journal of Drug Issues*, 29: 365–80.

Jackson, P., N. Stevenson, and K. Brooks. 2001. *Making Sense of Men's Magazines*. Cambridge: Polity.

Jacoby, J., G. Johar, and M. Morrin. 1999. 'Consumer Behavior: A Quadrennium', *Annual Review of Psychology*, 49: 319–44.

Jameson, F. 1991. *Postmodernism or the Logic of Late Capitalism*. London: Verso.

Jefferson, T. 2002. 'Subordinating Hegemonic Masculinity', *Theoretical Criminology*, 6: 63–88.

Jeffords, S. 1989. *The Remasculinization of Gender and the Vietnam War*. Bloomington: Indiana University Press.

———. 1993. *Hard Bodies: Hollywood Masculinity in the Reagan Era*. New Brunswick: Rutgers University Press.

Jensen, R. 2005. *The Heart of Whiteness: Confronting Race, Racism and White Privilege*. New York: City Lights Publishers.

Johnson, J., and K. Holman. 2004. *Making the Team: Inside the World of Sport Initiations and Hazing*. Toronto: Canadian Scholars' Press.

Johnson, M. 2001. 'Exploring Masculinity with Male Medical Students', *Sexual & Relationship Therapy*, 16: 165–71.

Jones, P. 2009. 'Hundreds Honour Hero Who Died After Hockey Fight'. *Calgary Herald*, January 6, D1.

Jillson, J. 1982. *Real Women Don't Pump Gas*. New York: Pocket Books.

Katz, J. 1988. *Seductions of Crime*. New York: Basic Books.

Kessler, S., D. Ashenden, R. Connell, and G. Dowsett. 1982. *Ockers and Disco-Maniacs*. Sydney: Inner City Education Center.

Keyes, C. 2002. *Rap Music and Street Consciousness*. Chicago: University of Illinois Press.

Kimbrell, A. 1995. *The Masculine Mystique: The Politics of Masculinity*. New York: Ballantine.

Kimmel, M. 1987. *Changing Men: New Directions in Research on Men and Masculinity*. Newbury Park: Sage.

———. 2000. *The Gendered Society*. London: Oxford University Press.

———. 2008. *Guyland*. New York: Harper Collins.

Kimmel, M., and M. Messner. 1999. *Men's Lives*. New York: Macmillan.

Kincheloe, J. 2000. *White Reign: Deploying Whiteness in America*. New York: Palgrave Macmillan.

Kindlon, D., and M. Thompson. 2000. *Raising Cain: Protecting the Emotional Life of Boys*. New York: Ballantine.

Krims, A. 2004. *Rap Music and the Poetics of Identity*. Cambridge: Cambridge University Press.

Labre, M. 2002. 'Adolescent Boys and the Muscular Male Body Ideal', *Journal of Adolescent Health*, 30: 233–42.

Lacan, J. 1977. *Écrits: A Selection*. New York: Sheridan.

Landsman, J. 2008. *Growing Up White*. Minneapolis: Rowman & Littlefield.

Lash, S. 2007. 'Power After Hegemony', *Theory, Culture & Society*, 24: 55–78.

Lash, U. 1999. *Another Modernity: A Different Rationality*. Oxford: Blackwell.

Latour, B. 2005. *Reassembling the Social: An Introduction to Actor–Network Theory*. Oxford: Oxford University Press.

Leblanc, B. 2007. 'An Exploratory Study of "Bug Chasers"', *Sociological Imagination*, 43: 13–20.

Leblanc, L. 1999. *Pretty in Punk: Girls' Gender Resistance in a Boys' Subculture*. New Brunswick: Rutgers University Press.

LeBreton, D. 2000. 'Playing Symbolically with Death in Extreme Sports', *Body & Society*, 6: 1–11.

Lefebvre, H. 1991. *The Production of Space*. Cambridge: Wiley Blackwell.

Lehman, P. 2007. *Running Scared: Masculinity and the Representation of the Male Body*. Detroit: Wayne State University.

Leit, R., J. Gray, and H. Pope. 2002. 'The Media's Representation of the Ideal Male Body: A Cause For Muscle Dysmorphia?', *International Journal of Eating Disorders*, 31: 334–8.

Lipsitz, G. 2006. *The Possessive Investment in Whiteness: How White People Profit from Identity Politics*. Philadelphia: Temple University Press.

Luciano, L. 2001. *Looking Good: Male Body Image in Modern America*. New York: Hill and Wang.

Lull, J. 2001. *Culture in the Communication Age*. London: Routledge.

Lupton, D. 1999. *Risk and Socio-Cultural Theory: New Directions and Perspectives.* Cambridge: Cambridge University Press.

Lusane, C. 1993. 'Rap, Race and Politics', *Race and Class,* 35: 41–56.

Lyng, S. 2008. 'Risk-taking in Sport: Edgework and Reflexive Community', pp. 83–109 in *Tribal Play: Subcultural Journeys through Sport,* K. Young and M. Atkinson, eds. London: Emerald.

Lyotard, J-F. 1979. *The Postmodern Condition: A Report on Knowledge.* Paris: Bourgois.

———. 1983. *The Differend: Phrases in Dispute.* Minneapolis: University of Minnesota Press.

———. 1985 [1979]. *Just Gaming.* Minneapolis: University of Minnesota Press.

———. 1989. 'Scapeland', pp. 212–19 in The Lyotard Reader, A. Benjamin, ed. Oxford: Basil Blackwell.

MacKinnon, C. 1989. *Toward a Feminist Theory of the State.* Cambridge: Harvard University Press.

———. 2005. *Women's Lives, Men's Laws.* Cambridge: Harvard University Press.

Maffesoli, M. 1988. *Le Temps des Tribus.* Paris: Klincksieck.

Maguire, J. 1993. 'Bodies, Sport Cultures and Societies: A Critical Review of Some Theories in the Sociology of the Body', *International Review for the Sociology of Sport,* 28: 33–50.

———. 1999. *Sport Worlds.* Champaign: Human Kinetics.

———. 2005. *Power and Global Sport: Zones of Prestige, Emulation, and Resistance.* London: Routledge.

Males, M. 1996. *The Scapegoat Generation: America's War on Adolescents.* Monroe: Common Courage Press.

Malin, B. 2005. *American Masculinity Under Clinton: Popular Media and the Nineties Crisis of Masculinity.* New York: Peter Lang.

Malossi, G. 2001. *Material Man: Masculinity, Sexuality, Style.* New York: Abrams.

Marcuse, H. 1964. *One Dimensional Man.* London: Routledge.

Martinez, T. 1997. 'Popular Culture as Oppositional Culture: Rap as Resistance', *Sociological Perspectives,* 40: 265–86.

Mason, L. 2002. 'The Newfoundland Stock Collapse: A Review and Analysis of Factors', *Electronic Green Journal,* 17, http://escholarship.org/uc/item/19p7z78s.

Mauss, M., and H. Hubert. 1966. *Sacrifice: Its Nature and Function.* Chicago: University of Chicago Press.

McKay, J., M. Messner, and D. Sabo. 2000. *Men, Masculinities, and Sport.* Thousand Oaks: Sage.

McKinney, K. 2004. *Being White: Stories of Race and Racism.* London: Routledge.

McRobbie, A. 2008. *The Aftermath of Feminism.* London: Sage.

Medicard. 2006. *Report on Cosmetic Surgery in Canada*. Toronto.

Melucci, A. 1997. *Challenging Codes: Collective Action in the Information Age*. Cambridge: Cambridge University Press.

Messner, M. 1990. 'When Bodies are Weapons: Masculinity and Violence in Sport', *International Review for the Sociology of Sport*, 25: 203–21.

Messner, M., D. Hunt, and M. Dunbar. 1999. *Boys to Men: Sports Media Messages About Masculinity*. Oakland: Children Now.

Messner, M., and D. Sabo. 1994. *Sex, Violence, and Power in Sports: Rethinking Masculinity*. Champaign: Human Kinetics.

Miah, A. 2008. 'Engineering Greater Resilience or Radical Transhuman Enhancement', *Studies in Ethics, Law and Technology*, 2: 1–18.

Miracle, A., and R. Rees. 1994. *Lessons of the Locker Room: The Myth of School Sports*. Amherst: Prometheus Books.

Moore, S. 1998. *'Here's Looking at You Kid!' The Female Gaze — Women as Viewers of Popular Culture*. London: The Women's Press.

More, M. 2006. 'How to Live Forever', *Hustler*, March, 43–6.

Moskowitz, D., and M. Roloff. 2007. 'The Existence of a Bug Chasing Subculture', *Culture, Health & Sexuality*, 9: 347–35.

Mosse, G. 1996. *The Image of Man: The Creation of Modern Masculinity*. Oxford: Oxford University Press.

Muggleton, D. 2000. *Inside Subculture: The Postmodern Meaning of Style*. Oxford: Berg.

Nathanson, P., and K. Young. 2001. *Spreading Misandry: The Teaching of Contempt for Men in Popular Culture*. Montreal: McGill-Queen's University Press.

———. 2006. *Legalizing Misandry: From Public Shame to Systemic Discrimination Against Men*. Montreal: McGill-Queen's University Press.

Neal, A. 2005. *New Black Man*. New York: Routledge.

Newkirk, T. 2003. *Misreading Masculinity: Boys, Literacy, and Popular Culture*. Portsmouth: Heinemann.

Newman, W. 2004. *Promethean Ambitions: Alchemy and the Quest to Perfect Nature*. Chicago: University of Chicago Press.

Niedzviecki, H. 2004. *Hello, I'm Special: How Individuality Became the New Conformity*. New York: Penguin.

Niva, S. 1998. 'Tough and Tender: New World Order Masculinity and the Gulf War', pp. 109–28 in M. Salewski and J. Parpart, eds., *The 'Man' Question in International Relations*. Boulder: Westview Press.

Nixon, S. 2001. 'Re-Signifying Masculinity: From New Man to New Lad', pp. 373–85 in D. Morley and K. Robins, eds., *British Cultural Studies*. Oxford: Oxford University Press.

Nuwer, H. 2002. *Wrongs of Passage: Fraternities, Sororities, Hazing, and Binge-Drinking*. Bloomington: Indiana University Press.

———. 2004. *The Hazing Reader*. Bloomington: Indiana University Press.

Ommer, R. 2002. *The Resilient Outport: Ecology, Economy, and Society in Rural Newfoundland*. St John's: Institute of Social and Economic Research.

Pascall, B., and S. White. 2000. *Violence in Hockey*. Commissioned by the Honourable Ian Waddell, Minister Responsible for Sport, British Columbia, Canada.

Pease, B. 2000. *Recreating Men: Postmodern Masculinity Politics*. London: Sage.

Pease, B., and K. Pringle. 2002. *A Man's World?* New York: Palgrave Macmillan.

Petersen, A. 1998. *Unmasking the Masculine: 'Men' and 'Identity' in a Sceptical Age*. Thousand Oaks: Sage.

Pinar, W. 2001. *The Gender of Racial Politics and Violence in America: Lynching, Prison Rape, and the Crisis of Masculinity*. New York: Peter Lang.

Pollack, W. 1999. *Real Boys: Rescuing our Sons from the Myths of Boyhood*. New York: Owl Books.

Pope H., K. Phillips, and R. Olivardia. 2000. *The Adonis Complex: The Secret Crisis of Male Body Obsession*. New York: The Free Press.

Porter, J. 1965. *The Vertical Mosaic*. Toronto: University of Toronto Press.

Potts, A. 2002. 'The Essence of the Hard-on: Hegemonic Masculinity and the Cultural Construction of Erectile Dysfunction', *Men and Masculinities*, 3: 85–103.

Pringle, K. 2005. *Men, Masculinities, and Welfare*. London: UCL Press.

Pronger, B. 2002. *Body Fascism: Salvation in the Technology of Physical Fitness*. Toronto: University of Toronto Press.

Purdy, C. 2008. 'Fights Club Investigated', *Regina Leader-Post*, January 29, A1.

Putnam, R. 1995. *Bowling Alone: America's Declining Social Capital*. New York: Simon & Schuster.

Regis, E. 1990. *Great Mambo Chicken and the Transhuman Condition: Science Slightly Over the Edge*. Reading: Addison-Wesley.

Rivel, P. 2002. *Uprooting Racism: How White People Can Work for Racial Justice*. Gabriola Island: New Society Publishers.

Robidoux, M. 2001. *Men at Play: A Working Understanding of Professional Hockey*. Montreal: McGill-Queen's University Press.

Robinson, L. 1998. *Crossing the Line: Violence and Sexual Assault in Canada's National Sport*. Toronto: McClelland & Stewart.

Robinson, S. 2000. *Marked Men: White Masculinity in Crisis*. New York: Columbia University Press.

Roediger, D. 1991. *The Wages of Whiteness: Race and the Making of the American Working Class*. New York: Verso.

Rowe, D. 2002. *Biology and Crime*. Los Angeles: Roxbury.

Said, E. 1978. *Orientalism*. New York: Pantheon Books.

Sargent, P. 2000. 'Real Men or Real Teachers? Contradictions in the Lives of Men Elementary Teachers', *Men and Masculinities*, 2: 410–33.

Sarwer, D., and C. Crerand. 2004. 'Body Image and Cosmetic Medical Treatments', *Body Image: An International Journal of Research*, 1: 99–111.

Schenk, R. 1996. *We've Been Had: Writings on Men's Issues*. Alachula: Bioenergetics Press.

Schinkel, W. 2008. 'Contexts of Anxiety: The Moral Panic over "Senseless Violence" in the Netherlands'. *Current Sociology*, 56: 735–56.

Schmitt, R. 2001. 'Proud to be a Man?', *Men and Masculinities*, 3: 393–404.

Schugart, H. 2008. 'Managing Masculinities: The Metrosexual Moment', *Communication in Critical/Cultural Studies*, 5: 280–300.

Schwalbe, M. 1996. *Unlocking the Iron Cage: The Men's Movement, Gender Politics, and American Culture*. New York: Oxford University Press.

Sefa Dei, G. 2005. *Critical Issues in Anti-racist Research Methodologies*. New York: Peter Lang.

Seidler, V. 1991. *The Achilles Heel Reader: Men, Sexual Politics and Socialism*. London: Routledge.

———. 1994. *Unreasonable Men: Masculinity and Social Theory*. London: Routledge.

———. 2006. *Young Men and Masculinities: Global Cultures and Intimate Lives*. London: Zed Books.

Shepherd, N. 2002. 'Anarcho-Environmentalists: Ascetics of Late Modernity', *Journal of Contemporary Ethnography*, 31: 135–57.

Shilling, C. 1993. *The Body and Social Theory*. London: Sage.

———. 2008. *Changing Bodies: Habit, Crisis, and Creativity*. London: Sage.

Sicile-Kira, C., and T. Grandin. 2003. *Autism Spectrum Disorders: The Complete Guide*. London: Vermilion.

Simpson, M. 1999. *Male Impersonators: Men Performing Masculinity*. London: Cassell.

Smith, D. 1987. *The Everyday World as Problematic: Toward a Feminist Sociology*. Toronto: University of Toronto Press.

Smith, M. 1983. *Violence and Sport*. Toronto: Butterworths.

Smith-Maguire, J. 2007. *Fit for Consumption*. London: Routledge.

Solanas, V. 1968. *SCUM Manifesto*. New York: AK Press.

Sparkes, A. 2005. 'Narrative Analysis: Exploring the *Whats* and the *Hows* of Personal Stories', pp. 191–209 in M. Holloway, ed., *Qualitative Research in Health Care*. Milton Keynes: Open University Press.

Spivak, G. 1994. 'Can the Subaltern Speak?', pp. 66–111 in P. Williams and L. Chrisman, eds., *Colonial Discourse and Post-Colonial Theory: A Reader*. New York: Harvester Wheatsheaf.

———. 1999. *A Critique of Postcolonial Reason*. Cambridge: Harvard University Press.

Stebbins, R. 1992. 'Concatenated Exploration', *Journal of Contemporary Ethnography*, 35: 483–94.

Stern, B. 2003. 'Masculinism(s) and the Male Image: What does it mean to be a Man?', in T. Reichert and J. Lambiase, eds., *Sex in Advertising:*

Perspectives on the Erotic Appeal (electronic version). Mahwah: Lawrence Erlbaum Associates.

Stoltenberg, J. 1993. *The End of Manhood: A Book for Men of Conscience*. New York: Dutton.

Stoudt, B. 2006. 'You're Either In or You're Out: School Violence, Peer Discipline, and the (Re)Production of Hegemonic Masculinity', *Men and Masculinities*, 8: 273–87.

Straw, W. 1991. 'Systems of Articulation, Logics of Change: Communities and Scenes in Popular Music', *Cultural Studies*, 35: 368–88.

Sutherland, E. 1947. *The Professional Thief*. Chicago: University of Chicago Press.

Suzuki, D. 2002. *The Sacred Balance: Rediscovering Our Place in Nature*. Vancouver: Greystone Books.

Sykes, G., and D. Matza. 1956. 'Techniques of Neutralization', *American Sociological Review*, 22: 664–70.

Tait, G. 1999. 'Rethinking Youth Subcultures: The Case of Gothics', *Social Alternatives*, 18: 15–20.

Tanner, J. 2001. *Teenage Troubles: Youth and Deviance in Canada*. Toronto: Nelson.

Tewksbury, R. 2004. 'Bareback Sex and the Quest for HIV: Assessing the Relationship in Internet Personal Advertisements of Men Who Have Sex with Men', *Deviant Behavior*, 25: 467–84.

Tittle, C. 1995. *Control Balance: Toward a General Theory of Deviance*. Boulder: Westview.

———. 2000. 'Refining Control Balance Theory', *Theoretical Criminology*, 8: 395–428.

Thiele, D. 2005. 'The Problem With Sociology: Morality, Anti-Biology and Perspectivism', *Quadrant*, 10: 210–24.

Thornton, S. 2005. 'The Social Logic of Subcultural Capital', pp. 184–192 in K. Gelder and S. Thornton, eds., *The Subcultures Reader*. London: Routledge.

Tiger, L. 2000. *The Decline of Males: The First Look at an Unexpected New World for Men and Women*. New York: Griffin Trade Paperback.

Turner, V. 1969. *The Ritual Process: Structure and Anti-Structure*. New York: Aldine Publishers.

Vallières, P. 1971. *White Niggers of America: The Precocious Autobiography of a Quebec Terrorist*. New York: Monthly Review Press.

Virilio, P. 1986. *Speed & Politics*. New York: Semiotext(e).

Vitellone, N. 2003. 'The Syringe as a Prosthetic', *Body & Society*, 9: 37–52.

Walklate, H. 2004. *Gender, Crime, and Criminal Justice*. Devon: Willan Publishing.

Wallerstein, I. 1978. 'World-System Analysis: Theoretical and Interpretive Issues', pp. 219–35 in B. Kaplan, ed., *Social Change in the Capitalist World Economy*. Beverly Hills: Sage.

Weber, M. 1958. *The Protestant Ethic and the Spirit of Capitalism*. New York: Scribner's Sons.

———. 1968. *Economy and Society: An Outline of Interpretive Sociology*. New York: Bedminster.

Weed P., D. Brooks, and C. Blanaru. 2003. 'Group of Three Oppose Body-Checking', *Hockey Talk*, February 27: 29.

Weinstein, M., M. Smith, and D. Wiesenthal. 1995. 'Masculinity and Hockey Violence', *Sex Roles*, 33: 831–47.

Welch, M., E. Price, and N. Yankey. 2002. 'Moral Panic over Youth Violence: Wilding and the Manufacture of Menace in the Media', *Youth & Society*, 34: 3–30.

Wells, M. 1994. 'Slimmer Dooner Revs Up McCann'. *Advertising Age*, October 10: 9–15.

Weltzien, F. 2005. 'Masque-ulinities: Changing Dress as a Display of Masculinity in the Superhero Genre', *Fashion Theory: The Journal of Dress, Body & Culture*, 9: 229–50.

West, P. 2000. 'From Tarzan to the Terminator: Boys, Men and Body Image', Paper presented at the Institute of Family Studies Conference, Sydney, 24 July.

Whannel, G. 2002. *Media Sport Stars: Masculinities and Moralities*. London: Routledge.

Wheaton, B. 2004. *Understanding Lifestyle Sport: Consumption, Identity, and Difference*. London: Routledge.

Whelehan, I. 2000. *Overloaded: Popular Culture and the Future of Feminism*. London: Women's Press.

White, P., and J. Gillett. 1997. 'Reading the Muscular Body: A Critical Decoding of Advertisements in Flex Magazine', *Sociology of Sport Journal*, 11: 18–39.

White, P., and K. Young. 1997. 'Masculinity, Sport, and the Injury Process: A Review of Canadian and International Evidence', *Avante*, 3: 1–30.

———. 1999. 'Is Sport Injury Gendered?', pp. 145–69 in *Sport and Gender in Canada*, P. White and K. Young, eds. Toronto: Oxford University Press.

White, P., K. Young, and J. Gillett. 1995. 'Bodywork as a Moral Imperative: Some Critical Notes on Health and Fitness', *Loisir et Société*, 18: 159–82.

White, P., K. Young, and W. McTeer. 1994. 'Body Talk: Male Athletes Reflect on Sport, Injury, and Pain', *Sociology of Sport Journal*, 11: 175–95.

Whitehead, S. 2002. *Men and Masculinities: Key Themes and New Directions*. Cambridge: Polity.

———. 2006. *Men and Masculinities: Critical Concepts in Sociology*. New York: Routledge.

Williams, R. 1977. *Marxism and Literature*. Oxford: Oxford University Press.

Willis, P. 1978. *Profane Culture*. London: Routledge and Kegan Paul.

Wilson, B. 2002a. 'The Canadian Rave Scene and Five Theses on Youth Resistance', *Canadian Journal of Sociology*, 27: 373–412.

————. 2002b. 'The Anti-Jock Movement: Reconsidering Youth Resistance, Masculinity, and Sport Culture in the Age of the Internet', *Sociology of Sport Journal,* 19: 207–34.

————. 2006. *Fight, Flight, or Chill: Subcultures, Youth, and Rave into the 21st Century.* Montreal: McGill-Queen's University Press.

Wilson, B., and M. Atkinson. 2005. 'Rave and Straightedge, the Virtual and the Real: Exploring On-Line and Off-Line Experiences in Canadian Youth Subcultures', *Youth & Society,* 36: 276–311.

Wilson, E. 1975. *Sociobiology: The New Synthesis.* Cambridge: Belknap Press.

Wise, T. 2007. *White Like Me: Reflections on Race from a Privileged Son.* New York: Soft Skull Press.

Wood, R. 1999. 'Nailed to the X: A Lyrical History of the Straightedge Youth Subculture', *Journal of Youth Studies,* 2: 133–51.

————. 2001. 'Straightedge Youth: Subculture Genesis, Permutation, and Identity Formation', Unpublished doctoral dissertation, University of Alberta, Edmonton, Alberta.

————. 2006. *Straightedge Youth: Complexity And Contradictions of a Subculture.* Syracuse: Syracuse University Press.

World Transhumanist Association. 2002. *The Transhumanist Declaration,* http://transhumanism.org/index.php/WTA/declaration/.

Wykes, M. 2004. *The Media and Body Image: If Looks Could Kill.* London: Sage.

Yeung, K-T. 2006. 'Challenging the Heterosexual Model of Brotherhood: The Gay Fraternity's Dilemma', pp. 184–209 in C. Torbenson and G. Park, eds, *Brothers and Sisters: Diversity in College Fraternities and Sororities.* Madison, NJ: Fairleigh Dickinson University Press.

Young, J. 2007. *The Vertigo of Late Modernity.* Thousand Oaks: Sage.

Young, K. 1991. 'Violence in the Workplace of Professional Sport from Victimological and Cultural Studies Perspectives', *International Review for the Sociology of Sport,* 26: 3–14.

————. 1993. 'Violence, Risk, and Liability in Male Sports Culture', *Sociology of Sport Journal,* 10: 373–396.

————. 2000. 'Sport and Violence', pp. 382–408 in J. Coakley and E. Dunning, eds., *Handbook of Sport and Society.* Thousand Oaks: Sage.

————. 2002. 'From Sports Violence to Sports Crime: Aspects of Violence, Law, and Gender in the Sports Process', pp. 207–24 in M. Gatz, M. Messner, and S. Ball-Rokeach, eds., *Paradoxes of Youth and Sport.* New York: SUNY Press.

————. 2003. *Sporting Bodies, Damaged Selves: Sociological Studies of Sports Related Injury.* London: Elsevier.

Young, K., and L. Craig. 1995. 'Beyond White Pride: Contradiction in the Canadian Skinhead Subculture', *Canadian Review of Sociology and Anthropology,* 34: 175–206.

Young, K., and C. Reasons. 1989. 'Victimology and Organizational Crime: Workplace Violence and the Professional Athlete', *Sociological Viewpoints*, 5: 24–34.

Young, K., and P. White. 1995. 'Sport, Physical Danger, and Injury: The Experiences of Elite Women Athletes'. *Journal of Sport and Social Issues*, 19: 45–61.

Young, R. 1990. *White Mythologies: Writing History and the West*. London: Routledge.

Credits

Grateful acknowledgement is made for permission to reprint the following:

Index

patriarchy, 5, 7, 31, 47; meta-narrative of, 38, 49; residual, 17, 20, 24, 44, 140, 141–53; spectacle and, 61; vertical mosaic and, 167
Pearce, David, 193
Pease, B.: *Recreating Men*, 27
Peterson, A.: *Unmasking the Masculine*, 4
petits récits, 49
Phillips, Lawrence, 144
physical culture studies (PCS), 28–30, 188–9, 205
Pollack, W.: *Real Boys*, 81
Pope, H., et al, 160
popular culture: misandry in, 162–3, 163–5
popular music, 14
Porter, John, 166, 167; *The Vertical Mosaic*, 166
post-colonial studies, 205; whiteness studies and, 189–91
posthuman, 205–6
post-humanism, 194
post-material social movements, 195
power: essentialism and, 27–8; gender and, 115; social, 25–30
predestination, 86
Pringle, L., 32
private property, 191
Pronger, B., 119

quality of life data: gender and, 23–4

Race Across America, 73
rap and hip-hop pioneers, 110–11
Ravers, 36, 83
Real Men Don't Eat Quiche (Feirstein), 102, 103, 104
Real Women Don't Pump Gas (Jillson), 103
reflexive individualism, 37, 63, 73
reflexive society, 107
Regis, E., *Great Mambo Chicken and the Transhuman Condition*, 194
relative deprivation, 199
representation, 157, 183
residual patriarchy, 17, 20, 24, 44; in sport, 140, 141–53
'reverse discrimination', 190
Ricky (fic.), 176, 177, 178
risk societies, 105, 128; crisis and, 107
Robidoux, M., 137
Robinson, Laura, 143
Rocky IV, 109
Rose, Nikolas, 167
routine activities theory, 142–3
Roy, Patrick, 144
Royal, Andre, 152

Sacks, Glenn, 162
Said, Edward: *Orientalism*, 190
Sanderson, Don, 133–4, 138
Sarwer, D. and C. Crerand, 125–6
Saskatchewan: gangs in, 56
scapeland, 40
Schenk, R., 6
Schinkel, W., 57
schooling: boys and, 80–1
school shootings, 55
Schugart, H., 28
Scragg, Rick, 134
SCTV, Bob and Doug McKenzie in, 170
SCUM (Society for Cutting Up Men), 163; *SCUM Manifesto*, 163–4, 179
Sefa Dei, George, 185
Seidler, V., 58, 106
self: techniques of the 69, 112; technology of the, 124–5
self-bullying, 66; pastiche hegemony and, 63; spectacle and, 50, 62
self-care, 109; ethic of, 62
self-ownership and personal development, 191
sex ratio: in Canada, 23
sexual abuse, 142; athletes and coaches, 142–3, 146
sexual assault, 54–5; in sport, 141–7
sexuality: Straightedge and, 95–6
sexual objectification, 160
Shepherd, N., 83, 93, 97
shopping culture, 109
signs, 159, 183
Simpson, M., 104, 120
simulacrum, 113
Singularitarians, 195; *see also* transhumanism
situationalists, 77–8
Skaters, 83
slam dancing, 95
Smith, D., 47; *The Everyday World as Problematic*, 29–30
Smith, Doug, 144
Smith, M., 138
Smith, Mike (actor), 176, 178
Snake (fic.), 175
social bads, 105, 106, 107, 119
social crisis, 3–4
social disorganization theories, 51
social goods, 107
social roles: gendered, 5, 13
sociobiology, 52–3, 77
Solanas, Valerie, 163–4
Sparkes, A., 28
Spectacle/spectacle, 50, 61; self-destruction and, 63
Spivak, Gayatri, 10, 37, 190

Straightedgers and, 85; against women, 51

Virilio, P., *Speed and Politics*, 9

Volpe, Michael, 177

voter turnout: drop in, 106

Wall Street, 108

Wamsley, Kevin, 149

Ward, Christopher, 173, 174

Warhol, Andy, 163

wars: of position/wars of manoeuvre, 31; on terror, 58

Wayne's World, 170

Weber, Max, 86, 93

Weinstein, M., M. Smith, and D. Weisenthal, 136

Wells, Rob, 176, 177

Whannel, G., 137

What Women Want, 26–7

Wheels (fic.), 174, 175, 176

Whitehead, S., 5

White masculinity: backlash movements, 190; physical culture studies and, 189; supplementation and, 200; accounts of importance of, 186–7

whiteness, 187, 185, 191; in masculinity crisis, 202; physical culture studies and, 188–9; post-colonialism and, 189–91; studies, 185–8; transhumanism and, 198–9

White, P. and K. Young, 137

White, P., K. Young, and J. Gilbert, 119–20

Willert, Kent, 131, 133

Williams, Harvey, 144

Williams, Michael, 173–4

Wilson, E.: *Sociobiology*, 52

Wilson, B. and M. Atkinson, 36

Windsor Spitfires: hazing incident, 150–2

Wise, Tim: *White Like Me*, 186

women: as competitors in gyms and athletics, 124; power, status, and quality of life in Canada, 23–4; in vertical mosaic, 167

World Transhumanist Association (WTA), *Transhumanist Declaration*, 194

wrestling federations: backyard wrestling and, 65

www.badjocks.com, 146

Yeung, K-T., 28

Young, Jock, *The Vertigo of Late Modernity*, 40

Young, K., 138